'Bernie Krause will make you rethink much of what you know about music. A man whose first job was recording the sound of corn growing in a Kansas field, he has spent forty years listening with professional intent to things the rest of us never hear. He has studied the way ants sing and whales roar. He can track the sound a virus makes as it moves from one surface to another. Krause is David Attenborough without the pictures and accompanying orchestra. He takes us close to the roots of the music and reminds us to stop and listen, not just lose our bearings in noise. It's such an unusual book—and, in its quiet way, so important. Remarkable.' Norman Lebrecht

'This fascinating book awakens our ancient ears to the source of all music. Read it, and you'll yearn to muffle our din—and hear anew.' Alan Weisman, author of *The World Without Us* and *Countdown*

'A *vade mecum* of ordered tranquillity—a gift that came with the harmony of the spheres, allowing even the smallest livings things to sing love songs in many diverse ways while bragging that they are the fittest and will survive above the cacophony of war. A fascinating book of natural history, worthy to be read in the silence of your own library, please listen to what it warns about all our futures.' David Bellamy

'Krause always reveals wondrous stories of the meaning of music and sounds of our natural environment. Bernie's research into the subtleties of animal and insect sounds is unparalleled, but it is his description of the radical changes that are taking place on this planet that really makes one stop and wonder … listen carefully, for the sounds you hear may never be the same again.' Sir George Martin

'Discover how each species has its own vocal niche in the intricate soundscape of a stable ecosystem.' Temple Grandin, author of *Animals in Translation*

'*The Great Animal Orchestra* speaks to us of an ancient music to which so many of us are deaf. Bernie Krause is, above all, an artist. I have watched him recording the calls of chimpanzees, the singing of the insects and birds, and seen his deep love for the harmonies of nature. In this book he helps us to hear and appreciate the often hidden musicians in a new way. But he warns that these songs, an intrinsic part of the natural world and essential to human well being, are vanishing, one by one, snuffed out by human actions.' Jane Goodall, PhD, DBE, Founder, The Jane Goodall Institute & UN Messenger of Peace

'Bernie Krause, one of the lions of soundscape recording, shares his tales of jaguars, wind, and waterfalls, and how hard it is to capture their sounds. Who knew that the most emotional animal sound he would ever hear was the wail of a beaver after seeing his dam destroyed? Krause has spent decades hunting for those few sonic oases untrammelled by human noise, and at last he brings us his life philosophy. This expansive tale of living amidst wild and beautiful sounds has been well worth waiting for.' David Rothenberg, author of *Why Birds Sing*, *Thousand Mile Song* and *Survival of the Beautiful*

The
GREAT ANIMAL
ORCHESTRA

BERNIE KRAUSE is both a musician and a naturalist. During the 1950s and '60s, he devoted himself to music and replaced Pete Seeger as the guitarist for the Weavers. For more than forty years, Krause has traveled the world, recording and archiving the sounds of creatures and environments large and small. He has recorded more than fifteen thousand species and four thousand hours of wild soundscapes, over half of which no longer exist in nature, due to encroaching noise and human activity. Krause and his wife, Katherine, live in California.

The
GREAT ANIMAL
ORCHESTRA

FINDING THE ORIGINS OF MUSIC
IN THE WORLD'S WILD PLACES

Bernie Krause

P

PROFILE BOOKS

First published in Great Britain in 2012 by
PROFILE BOOKS LTD
3A Exmouth House
Pine Street
London EC1R 0JH
www.profilebooks.com

First published in the United States of America in 2012 by
Little, Brown and Company, a division of the Hatchette Book Group, Inc.

1 3 5 7 9 10 8 6 4 2

Printed and bound in Great Britain by
Clays, Bungay, Suffolk

A CIP catalogue record for this book is available from the British Library.

ISBN 978 1 78125 000 6
eISBN 978 1 84765 853 1

The paper this book is printed on is certified by the © 1996 Forest Stewardship
Council A.C. (FSC). It is ancient-forest friendly. The printer holds FSC chain of
custody SGS-COC-2061

FSC
Mixed Sources
Product group from well-managed
forests and other controlled sources
Cert no. SGS-COC-2061
www.fsc.org
© 1996 Forest Stewardship Council

To Kat, to R. Murray Schafer, and to the memory of
Paul Shepard and Joe Axelrod

Sonnet VIII

William Shakespeare

Music to hear, why hear'st thou music sadly?
Sweets with sweets war not, joy delights in joy.
Why lovest thou that which thou receivest not gladly,
Or else receivest with pleasure thine annoy?
If the true concord of well-tuned sounds,
By unions married, do offend thine ear,
They do but sweetly chide thee, who confounds
In singleness the parts that thou shouldst bear.
Mark how one string, sweet husband to another,
Strikes each in each by mutual ordering,
Resembling sire and child and happy mother
Who all in one, one pleasing note do sing:
    Whose speechless song, being many, seeming one,
    Sings this to thee: "thou single wilt prove none."

Contents

Echoes of the Past

It is sixteen thousand years ago, and the plains teem with life. With the presence of the giant armadillo, American chee-tahs, saber-toothed tigers, giant beavers, mastodons, camels, caribou, dire wolves, and ground sloths that stand as high as fourteen feet on their hind legs, wildlife is everywhere. Humans haven't made their appearance in North America yet, but birds in great numbers — including pied-billed grebes, storks, Canada geese, ducks, teals, common crows, turkeys, bobwhites, and dowitchers — fill the air with flight and song, while tree frogs, peepers, insects, and reptiles saturate the sound field with the intricate tapestry of their voices.

It is the end of an ice age, and the leading edge of the massive Wisconsin glacier slowly recedes to the Arctic Circle. With the earth's warming, the floral world thrives. Pine, oak, and spruce trees, along with larch, aspen, balsam, and poplar, have advanced far to the north along with low-lying shrubs and grasses. The first signs of the boreal forest have taken root in the Western Hemisphere — it thrives through the cold winters and the warm summers, and it is jam-packed with nonhuman life, whose individual voices coalesce into an intense and collective symphony.

In the heart of the young forest, an area surrounding a small stream is luxuriant and green, set under a deep-blue sky with a few tufted clouds; it is infused with the gentle warmth of a summer breeze. This habitat is densely populated with creature life; in fact, at this time, animal life — both numbers of species and individual creatures — is at a numerical peak in our planet's history. In this one verdant spot thousands of creatures sing in choruses at all times of the day and night. The visual spectacle is impressive, but the sound is absolutely glorious.

This place conveys a complex sonic narrative loaded with significant messages for any sentient being within earshot. The sounds expand to their greatest volumes at dawn and dusk — a loud-soft-loud progression that would be familiar to modern listeners of many styles of music.

Animals are hooting, bleating, growling, chirping, warbling, cooing. They are tweeting, clucking, humming, clicking, moaning, howling, screaming, peeping, sighing, whistling, mewing, croaking, gurgling, panting, barking, purring, squawking, buzzing, shrieking, stridulating, cawing, hissing, scratching, belching, cackling, singing melodies, stomping feet, leaping in and through the air, and beating wings — and doing it in a way that each voice can be heard distinctly, so that the animals seem able to hear and to distinguish one voice from another. The only sound louder than their collective chorusing is the howling wind of a great storm, a clap of thunder, an erupting volcano. The sound of water — a nearby stream — is the one constant nonbiological acoustic signature of the surroundings.

4

Then the ground shifts unexpectedly; a low, ominous rumble causes leaves in the upper stories of the trees to rustle for a moment like hundreds of muted castanets. Groups of insects and frogs suddenly become very quiet. But birds cry out, abandoning their well-ordered choral hierarchy and scattering in every direction; the air above explodes with the rush of staccato-like wing beats and cries of alarm. Throughout every fiber of each animal courses a sense of unfamiliar danger. Roaming predators steal into view, magnifying the tension of the moment.

Each organism is enveloped in more waves of sonic energy—great vibrations that come from everywhere—above, around, and below the ground itself. Predators take advantage of the moment to pursue those that are less agile and stunned by the earth's motion. The dominant opportunists—the lions, bears, raptors, and teratorns (with a wingspan of sixteen feet)—generate thundering footfalls and powerful edge-tones from fluttering wings as they propel themselves into the air and crash through the vegetation after their doubly terrified prey. Then come the final cries of the vanquished, a new message that punctuates the moment.

The world's waters—its oceans, lakes, rivers, estuaries, and coastal mangrove swamps—are packed full with fish, amphibians, reptiles, mollusks, mammals, and crustaceans, along with anemones and calcium carbonate coral structures that nurture and shelter many communities of smaller organisms. The ecosystems that rely on the contributions of marine organisms mark every shore. Like the habitats on land, these, too, are bursting with sound.

The Gulf of St. Lawrence, where that river and the Atlantic join, is home to thousands of species. The typical cod measures six or seven feet in length and weighs more than two hundred pounds. But it can hardly swim any distance without careening into another body, the waters are so vividly heaving with fish. Some bluefin tuna outstrip the cod, with adults measuring more than twelve feet long and weighing over fifteen hundred pounds. Plentiful, too, are the smaller herring and haddock, capelin, salmon, halibut, mackerel, shad, sea turtles, and even tiny smelt. Upriver are the striped bass, sturgeon—individuals can weigh as much as a thousand pounds—and trout. The ocean-dwelling fish supply food sources for the seals, dolphins, and larger toothed whales, while their baleen counterparts rely on krill, copepods, euphausiids, and cyprids.

Abundant sound is complete across the breadth of this marine environment. Some of the fish create acoustic signals with their swim bladders. Others signify their presence by gnashing their teeth. But each fish species generates a unique pressure wave through the oscillation of its tail fin—a signature sound recognized by others in the gulf, especially predators. With water limiting vision, sound is crucial to these animals' survival and reproduction, just as it is on land. From animals as small as protozoa, copepods, and phytoplankton to large whales, each species creates an acoustic sound-mark. The world's waters are saturated with living chatter, sighs, drumming, glissandos, cries, groans, grunts, and clicks.

Closer to the equator, coral reefs abound and make up a significant living mass. And they, too, pulsate with sound. Anemones, damselfish, three-spot dascyllus, and clown fish; parrot fish, wrasses, puffers, cardinalfish, grunts, triggerfish, fusiliers, goatfish, butterfly fish, red drum fish, many kinds of surgeonfish, jacks, sharks, snapping shrimp, and black drum fish—each leaves a distinct acoustic impression that, when combined with the others, forms part of a chorus that is set in the subtle acoustic background ambience generated by waves at the surface. Out in the open ocean, the songs of humpback, blue, and right whales are so loud that if unimpeded by landmasses—and when weather and ocean-current conditions conspire to moments of perfection—their voices could circle the earth in just under seven hours. The only sound louder than this combined contingent of mammals, fish, and crustaceans is the raging effect of a hurricane, typhoon, or tsunami.

The ready food supply in this marine environment supports an abundance of shorebird populations and, in the process, the attendant racket. There is the great auk—also called a spearbill—a stately flightless creature that has long since abandoned the air, given that it is a great swimmer. Nearby ocean-based food is so plentiful that it need not waste valuable energy flying to distant places. Then there's the raucous *ow-ow-ow* of the shearwaters mixed with the unique voices of puffins, gulls, terns, gannets, petrels, skuas, kittiwakes, fulmers, murres, and cormorants, creating a din that seems to make each vocalist indistinguishable from another. But it's a curious deception: these are the sounds of survival, reproduction, and communication, and each species has evolved so that it is heard distinctly among the others—and so that it projects over the thunderous, turbulent sounds of the ocean waves.

Mangrove swamps—saline woodlands that hug the subtropical and tropical coastal waters of every continent except the Antarctic—pulsate with curious mixes of insects, mammals, birds, and crustaceans. As the tides recede in these Mesoamerican biomes, crabs lose their grip on the branches and trunks of trees, falling with the distinctive *plop* of a large, flat, round stone into the exposed muddy sediment below. The crabs will return to the trunks and branches when they become submerged again, on the next incoming tide. When night falls, frog choruses swell and bats *ping* their echolocation signals in order to find edible insects in the dark. Barnacles clinging to the exposed rocks and mangrove roots twist noisily in their shells, causing tiny high popping sounds that resonate throughout the habitat above and below the waterline. Even at night, when the creatures are enveloped in darkness, many voices persist, competing for recognition.

Glacial ice still covers much of the planet north of the Arctic Circle, even as the planet warms. It's a cold and desolate place, five to ten degrees colder than it will be some sixteen millennia from now. The receding layers of ice carry with them spores and seeds from the recovered landscape. While these will impregnate the moraine once it becomes fertile enough to spawn the boreal forests of the Arctic's future, there is not much acoustic life on the surface. But even this environment is not quiet: explosive sounds occur when crevasses—deep elongated cracks—form in the glacial span. The ice mass shatters as it is compressed under great pressure and undergoes periods of melting and snow accumulation, and in addition to the startling popping and groaning of the ice and the ever-present wind and frequent storms, calving glaciers release huge walls of frozen water into the shorelines of rivers, fjords, and seacoasts with a volatile, thunderous burst of sound, the fallen accumulation generating huge waves in the water below. Then there is the sound of the glacier's own movement: a slight, ominous oscillation caused by its relentless progression overland — a slow, creeping sensation more felt than heard.

Just about halfway to the opposite pole, far from the receding edge of the ice and located within a few degrees of the equator, the tropical rain forests are the most densely populated biological provinces on the planet. Here, too, the vegetation and animal life are adapting to the warming earth, some species being replaced by others better suited to the new climate — but animal and plant life flourish here to an extent that it is difficult to imagine having room for one more species of anything. Rain forests cover nearly 15 percent of the earth's surface and contain an estimated fifteen to twenty million species of plants and animals. The sound there is riotous.

Mammals, reptiles, and amphibians — from jaguars and spectacled bears to crocodiles and even some frogs — vocalize in relatively low ranges, while other frogs and some birds warble and thrum in the lower-mid range. Still others — insects, along with more frogs, birds, and mammals — have established their voices in the high-mid and upper ranges. So many creature voices scream for attention at such a high volume, it seems miraculous that any one animal can hear another of the same clan, let alone make out the sound of another species, whether friend or foe.

The planet itself teems with a vigorous resonance that is as complete and expansive as it is delicately balanced. Every place, with its vast populations of plants and animals, becomes a concert hall, and everywhere a unique orchestra performs an unmatched symphony, with each species' sound fitting into a specific part of the score. It is a highly evolved, naturally wrought masterpiece.

Humans, too, are making their sound heard. They are dispersing now, spreading across the planet, leaving behind tangible, visible, and acoustic symbols of their presence wherever they go—detailed pictographs and petroglyphs, bone instruments, hunting and skinning tools, and evidence of larders to store excess grain, which they've managed to harvest from early seed plantings. They're pulling together in larger and larger groups, but basically they're still hunters. The forest is whispering to them, luring them in and revealing where the objects of their hunt can be found. At this stage of their development, sound-rich habitats are humans' most significant acoustic influences. The sounds of animal life—organisms from microscopic to huge—and those from the nonbiological landscape dominate the rather modest noises humans generate. They have limited language skills to express what they feel, but they borrow some from what they hear all around them to convey emotion. Perhaps, through their body movement and vocal responses—so evocative of the successful life heard everywhere—these modern humans will convince the other creatures that they are all just an extension of one sonorant family.

This is the tuning of the great animal orchestra, a revelation of the acoustic harmony of the wild, the planet's deeply connected expression of natural sounds and rhythm. It is the baseline for what we hear in today's remaining wild places, and it is likely that the origins of every piece of music we enjoy and word we speak come, at some point, from this collective voice. At one time there was no other acoustic inspiration.

CHAPTER ONE

Sound as
My Mentor

Recording late one night deep in the Amazon jungle, my colleague Ruth Happel and I were alone in the forest several kilometers from camp with no light apart from the beams of our flashlights. Hoping to record the night ambience at several locations, we walked the trail quite aware of the tapestry of sounds around us. Along the way, we also picked up the unmistakable marking scent of a nearby jaguar. We never saw or heard the animal, but we knew it was close, perhaps even just a few feet away; it was frequently scent-marking as it followed us.

The musky feline odor was a constant presence. Our senses were heightened, but neither of us was afraid or perceived any immediate danger. Sitting quietly about fifty meters apart, we recorded the acoustic texture of the nighttime rain forest—the delicate admixture of raindrops on leaves, and insects, birds, frogs, and mammals performing their unified chorus as they have each day and night since the beginning.

After about an hour, we packed our gear and hiked deeper into the forest, listening for recording sites with more varied combinations. Then, around midnight, we decided to split up in order to gather the even greater variety of night sounds we hoped to encounter in this wonderfully rich environment. Ruth went down the path in one direction, and I went off in another.

After trekking for about fifteen minutes, I sat down beside the trail and began to record the intense tropical choruses of frogs, insects, and reptiles. Only then did I hear the cat's low growl in my headphones. It must have singled me out and followed me. Because I had the headphones' volume turned up to catch the fragile acoustic composition and detail of the forest, I wasn't attuned to my unlikely visitor—or aware that it had come that close. The sudden register of the jaguar's growls in my headset indicated that the cat was not more than an arm's length from the mics I had set up about thirty feet down the trail.

Fully alert in an instant, a rush of adrenaline catching me off guard, I felt my chest convulse. Trying to think of an exit strategy—there was none—I made some effort to calm down. In the moment, I thought that the sound of my heart was so audible, it would startle the animal. But I kept absolutely still, holding my breath in the darkness.

The incident lasted no more than a minute, but it seemed like a couple of hours as I sat mesmerized by the power of the animal's voice, its breathing, and the sounds of rumbles in its stomach. Then, as suddenly as it appeared, the jaguar moved silently off into the forest, leaving behind rhythmic waves of frog and whirring insect choruses, and what remained of my pounding heart.

• • •

It was by a happy accident that I was drawn to natural sound. My first career was as a studio guitarist, playing sessions of all kinds in Boston and New York. Then, in the mid-1960s, when musicians began experimenting with synthesizers, I moved to California to audit electronic music sessions at Mills College, where I met Paul Beaver, a Los Angeles studio musician and concert pipe organist who had made a career out of creating weird sound effects for feature films such as *Creature from the Black Lagoon* and *War of the Worlds.*

The wondrous-sounding tools of Paul's special trade were early synthesizer-like instruments such as the Ondes Martenot, the Hammond Novachord, and the Theremin, which produced an eerie, wavering soprano-like voice, and his own inventions, including an archetypal two-octave keyboard synthesizer that generated high-pitched sci-fi effects—he called it the "Canary." We immediately found creative synergy and formed the duo Beaver and Krause, and together introduced the synthesizer to pop music and film in California and the United Kingdom, produced five albums of our own, and performed music and effects for many features—including *Rosemary's Baby, Apocalypse Now, Invasion of the Body Snatchers,* and *Performance*—and on TV shows such as *Mission: Impossible, The Twilight Zone,* and *Bewitched.* We were so busy working one session after the other—sometimes as many as eighty hours a week—that the only recording date I clearly remember is one with the Doors on *Strange Days.* Early in the session the music was tight and energetic. As time passed over the course of a very long evening, the tracks became more fragmented and seemed to fall apart. When

I finally realized that the deterioration wasn't the result of fatigue, I vowed never to touch another drug. The year: 1967.

Paul and I were commissioned to do a series of albums for Warner Brothers in 1968. The first, titled *In a Wild Sanctuary,* would be the earliest musical piece to use long segments of wild sound as components of orchestration, and also the first to feature ecology as its theme. But being first meant that we had to collect the sounds ourselves. Wary of shedding his blue serge double-breasted suit and wing tips — his daily costume even in the most stifling L.A. weather — Paul refused to head into the field, leaving the task to me.

The writer Thomas Hardy spoke of chance encounters that alter the course of our lives. A chance meeting with another person. A missed or unread letter. The vivid colors in a sunset. A musical performance. This first venture was bursting with the possibility of such a Hardyesque chance, and I set off, with a compact portable recorder and a pair of mics, to record in and around San Francisco, my home at the time.

In October there was not much birdsong in the area — most birds had fledged, had migrated, or were silent. Nevertheless, the instant I switched on my recorder in resplendent Muir Woods one lovely fall day in 1968, my acoustic sensibilities were transformed by the ambient space that enveloped me. The summer fog was at long last gone, and shafts of dappled fall sunlight perforated the canopy of the old-growth coastal redwoods. Except for a few small aircraft and an occasional distant automobile, the muted ambience heard throughout the woods — a constant reassuring whisper — came from a soft breeze in the upper reaches of the forest. Though I was at first quite afraid of being alone — even in a managed forest like Muir Woods — stillness overcame and calmed me.

Like a pair of binoculars, my mics and earphones brought the sound within a close and intimate range, exposing a range of vivid detail that was entirely new to me. A few birds flew overhead through the stereo space — right to left — the slow cadenced edge-tones of their undulating wings a diaphanous mix of whirr and shush. With my portable recording system, I didn't feel like I was listening as a distant observer; rather, I had been sucked into a new space — becoming an integral part of the experience itself. It was one of those moments you run toward and fully embrace with an open spirit, afraid it might not last and knowing you've experienced something you will always crave.

Sitting alone on the ground with my recorder, trying to appear small and unobtrusive, I was startled by each new sound. Many of the subtle acoustic textures around me were made larger than life through my stereo headphones, on which I cranked the monitor levels so that I wouldn't miss anything. The impact was immediate and forceful. Impressions of lightness and space were alluring and lustrous. The ambience was transformed into minute detail that I would have never caught with my ears alone — the sounds of my breathing; the slight movement of a foot adjusted into a more comfortable position; a sniffle; a bird landing nearby on the ground, stirring up leaves and then pushing air with its wing beats in short, quick puffs as it took off, alarmed.

I realized, even then, that wild sound might contain huge stores of valuable information just waiting to be unraveled. But to that point in my life, I'd had no way of understanding that the natural world was filled with so much wondrous chatter. How was anyone to know? Many of us don't distinguish between the acts of listening and hearing. It's one thing to hear passively, but quite another to be able to listen, fully and actively engaged.

My ears indifferently *heard* sound, but they weren't trained to distinguish the many subtleties of untamed natural environments. I had always used my ears as filters—for shutting noise out—rather than as portals allowing large amounts of information in. A fine microphone system lets me differentiate between what to listen *to* and what to listen *for*. Through headphones, I hear pieces of the aural fabric in such gloriously clear detail that I am still surprised by how much I was previously missing. A pair of stereo microphones transforms the acoustic space—when I turn up the volume slightly above what I can hear unaided, I get an "out of this world" impression that I imagine astronomers might feel when they receive Hubble telescope images of exploding supernovas from the far reaches of the universe.

Dorothea Lange, the Depression-era American photojournalist, used to say that a camera is a tool for learning to see without a camera. Well, a recorder is a tool for learning to listen without a recorder. The instant I first heard a spring dawn chorus, finally limning the visual setting with a proper sound track amplified through headphones, I immediately realized that with my unfocused ears I had been missing an exquisite part of real-world experience. Amplified sound gave me a way to decipher the language of the wild in ways my musically trained, "cultured" listening couldn't otherwise grasp. Sitting there recording, I often felt a sudden urge to join the performance. And a feeling of incompleteness nagged at me as I left the forest that day. It was a combination of important secrets left unspoken or unheard and a sense of having lucked into a path of discovery that was nothing short of a divine revelation.

While working on our fifth title, an updated version of an earlier hit for Nonesuch Records, Paul collapsed onstage during a concert in Los Angeles in January 1975. He died a day later from a brain aneurysm. Heartbroken by the loss of my good friend and music partner, I completed the album (*Citadels of Mystery*) with a group of musicians that featured Andy Narell and other studio friends. And at that point I began to rethink my career choices. In my mind, the last truly productive period in the record industry had passed. Ever more tired of the vagaries and egos of Hollywood — I had been fired and rehired more than half a dozen times during the making of *Apocalypse Now* alone — I decided to make a change. At forty years old, I quit the music world that I had always known and enrolled in a graduate studies program, earning a doctorate in creative arts with an internship in marine bioacoustics.

You might think I left the world of music behind for that of natural sound. Instead, that is where I truly found it.

Without water, life as we know it wouldn't exist. Giving off the most ancient of sounds, it is extremely hard to capture acoustically and replicate. Its burbling, hissing, lapping, roaring, crashing, multi-rhythmic periodicity has served as a setting for human themes since the first music was sung and the first words spoken.

It took the full course of musical history for a composer to produce an orchestral composition that approximated a sense of the sea — Debussy got close in *La Mer,* which was first performed in 1905. However, his piece still required that programmatic visual quality and verbal association in order to be reasonably successful. Here's an interesting exercise: play excerpts from the piece for a few people who've never heard the work and don't know the title, and ask them what they think it is trying to convey. The one time in the late '90s that I tried this test — playing the six-minute second movement ("Jeux de vagues") for a class of seventh graders—the answers ranged from "traveling in space," "music for a film about the country," "a scene about a family of dinosaurs," and "a Western movie" to "just plain boring." Not one student guessed that the music represented an impression of the sea or even water.

At first glance, the task of recording water looks simple: set up a microphone by the shore and hit the "record" button. But no matter how hard I tried, my early attempts at capturing the sound of water never seemed quite right. We're so sight-oriented that most of us who have reasonable vision tend to hear what we are looking at. When we're focusing our eyes on breakers far offshore, our ears and brains usually filter out all but the boom and crash of waves that suggest distance and incredible force. When we're staring at the leading edge of the waves as they wash up the rake of the beach, we hear the tiny bubbles crackling and snapping as they rupture in the sand at our feet, while the sounds of the distant breakers fade into the background.

Microphones, however, don't have eyes or brains. They indiscriminately pick up everything within the scope of their design. So, I discovered, if I want to portray the sound of an ocean shore, I need to record a variety of samples from different distances: a couple of hundred feet from the water's edge, mid-distance from the high dune grasses to the water's edge, and right at the waterline. By using sound-editing software to combine all the samples at various levels when I get back home, I am able to capture audio that sounds very much like the magic of waves at the ocean. But in its most granular form, what exactly is it that I'm recording? What is sound?

Sound is a medium that's hard to describe beyond its physical properties—frequency, amplitude, timbre, and duration. Yet it plays a key role in the ways societies express themselves; it is fundamental to the collective voice of the natural world, to music, and to acoustic noises of all kinds.

The basic elements of sound are just outside our linguistic grasp, and to most of us sound has always been an enigma. Once, when asked to describe it, the composer, naturalist, and philosopher R. Murray Schafer responded: "How should I know? I have never seen a sound." Schafer put his finger on the problem: how many times have you heard the expression "I *see* what you're saying"? Our language is so sight-oriented that when Paul and I were asked to score films, directors often described the music they wanted in visual terms: dark, light, bright, really brown and murky in color.

Although we receive sound physically, the recognition that sound cannot be seen, touched, or smelled led the Academy Award–winning sound designer Walter Murch to speak of it as the "shadow sense"—one that exists all by itself in an ethereal, amorphous realm. In their craft as film sound designers, Murch and his colleagues tie the shadow of sound—whether as dialogue, effects, or music—to the much more concrete visual reality of the picture, adding context and thereby transforming both elements.

Only very recently have we attempted to deconstruct the mysteries of sound. Because sound is not easy to conceptualize, discoveries did not materialize quickly. Pythagoras, in about 500 BCE, first described the harmonic structure of the vibrating string, thus laying the groundwork for the principle of acoustics. Centuries later, Aristotle proved that air was essential as a conductor of sound. Scientists, including Greek and Roman amphitheater designers, and then Galileo and Newton, have been uncovering different aspects of sound for the past two millennia. But it wasn't until Hermann Helmholtz's book *On the Sensations of Tone* was first published in the mid-nineteenth century that sound was summarized in a consequential way. Helmholtz dissected every known aspect of his subject—from music to physics—and compiled the history into one volume. In frail health as a child of the 1820s, and coming from a relatively poor family that could not afford a highly prized science and math education for their son, Helmholtz was encouraged by his parents to study medicine in order to gain access to the institutions that would provide the education he desired. After earning his medical degree, he worked for a short time as a surgeon for the Prussian Army, and in addition to acoustics, his young career was marked by significant writings and discoveries across a wide range of fields, including physics, chemistry, optics, electricity, meteorology, and theoretical mechanics. One of his most important findings was in the field of physiology, where he identified the precise measurement of nerve impulses through the electrical stimulation of frog legs. The legs, although not attached to the body, moved when a small current was applied. Helmholtz was able to compute the exact time that elapsed between stimulus and movement, thereby calculating the exact rate of the nerve responses. But as an influential teacher—one of his pupils was Heinrich Hertz, after whom the unit measurement of sound frequency is named—he spent a large part of his academic life outside medicine, addressing the mysteries of music.

What strikes me in particular are his writings on acoustics—especially his descriptions of the famous "Helmholtz resonator" that, like a prism that partitions the light spectrum, could separate and identify individual frequencies of sound from within a complex acoustic structure. Also astonishing—though almost an afterthought, given the resonator's significance—is his appendix of orchestral reference tunings collected from various towns and villages across Europe at the time of publication of his book. Even though the tuning fork — an early-eighteenth-century two-pronged metal instrument that when struck produces a steady pure tone — was widely used as a reference, Helmholtz discovered that the middle, or "concert," A ranged anywhere from 373.1 hertz (Hz) in Paris to over 505 Hz in Saxony. Imagine a soprano soloist trying to hit the high E-flat she hit last night with a concert A500 tuning as a reference — the equivalent of almost reaching a high F-sharp in current tuning: nearly impossible. Today, many orchestras tune to an A440, although when I first came to Hollywood in the mid-1960s, the L.A. Philharmonic had a reputation for tuning to an A442, while some European orchestras were still using the darker-sounding A438.

One explanation for the curious musical anomaly of the differing concert As is the variable hardness of the European woods used to make frames and soundboards for the plucked or bowed stringed instruments, including harpsichords, of the time. A harder and denser type of wood would have enabled the strings to accommodate more tension, and thus the instruments could endure a higher tuning — and a "brighter" sound.

Given the growing amount of time I was spending in the wild, Helmholtz's writings gave me much to consider. Instruments were man-made to complement one another, and from my work with animal sound, I began wondering why particular species would, in the same way, settle on a particular range — higher or lower than another. Do animals, as part of the complex chorus in a given habitat, use one or more certain pitches as some sort of crude reference? How and why did their respective vocal ranges develop? What roles did physiology and environment play?

• • •

Thanks in part to Helmholtz's historical review of sound as well as his own contributions to the science of acoustics, we know that sound is transmitted as waves of pressure coursing through air, solids, or liquids, and we know that the attributes of many sounds include frequency (sometimes referred to as *pitch,* but that tends to be a more relative term), timbre, amplitude, and envelope. But even though I had played and composed music through two-thirds of my life, it wasn't until I began working with synthesizers that I started to understand its components and how they all came together. To generate sounds that would fit in a musical composition, I needed to know precisely how all four sound characteristics interacted with one another. If sound—which by itself is very abstract—was to mean anything, then it was control over those four parameters and the placement of the results within a recognizable milieu that gave it form.

Humans with perfect reception can hear frequencies between 20 wave cycles per second, or 20 Hz, at the low end to 20,000 Hz at the high end. The lowest note on a typical piano is 27.5 Hz, and the highest is about 4,186 Hz. Nonhuman animals have evolved different ranges of hearing, the widest of which can be found in whales. We think whales generate and hear vocalizations from below 10 Hz (the blue whale) to a reported 200 kHz (the blind Ganges dolphin)—nearly four octaves beyond the highest pitch we can hear. Other animals typically fall somewhere in between— a large percentage within the range of human hearing.

Pitch is closely related to frequency, but the two are not the same thing. *Pitch* is mostly used in the comparative framework of sounds or tones that make up a musical scale. So while frequency is a physical property of sound—it's a measurement of the number of cycles per second of a sound wave—pitch refers to what we hear. The chromatic scale, for example, is made up of twelve equally spaced pitches. As we go up the scale, we hear each note as going up in pitch by an equal amount—a semitone, or half step. However, the change in frequency from note to note is not equal—each successive increment of semitone requires a greater jump in frequency than the last. For example, going from a C pitch to a C-sharp on a piano (261.626 Hz to 277.183 Hz—a difference of about 15.56 cycles) requires less of a jump in frequency than going from that same C-sharp to a D (277.183 Hz to 293.665 Hz—a difference of about 16.48 Hz). The wider spread between C-sharp and D is the result of how the auditory cortex of our brains processes and perceives the sounds that reach our ears. Our brains trick us into hearing the same half-step interval between notes while the spread in actual units of frequency increases as the scale gets higher.

Timbre is the emblematic tone, or voice, generated by each type of instrument or biological sound source. Not only do musical instruments have singular voice characteristics but so does every living organism and most man-made machines. The difference between the sound of a violin and that of a trumpet is as distinctive as that between a cicada and an American robin, or a cat and a dog—or between a Rolls-Royce and a Formula 1 automobile.

When Paul Beaver and I first began to reproduce sounds on an analog synthesizer, we needed to understand how each instrumental voice was produced. At first we had no idea how complicated this would be. Part of our problem lay in trying to define the sound, or timbre, of each instrument. In the nonelectronic, purely physical world, instruments are made of metal or wood, or a combination of both. Some involve strings and/or skins, and many are played by blowing, striking, plucking, or creating friction. These different instruments have different shapes, and each manages to resonate, or "sound," in a different way.

Most instruments produce tones that are quite complex, each generating a series of overtones that contribute to our perception of their timbre and that exist in each note played on the instrument, defining its unique, haunting sound. A clarinet, for instance, produces a series of overtones in which some of the harmonics—the overtones that are a whole-number multiple of the note played on the instrument—drop out. A violin, on the other hand, produces an entirely different series of overtones. As the rosined bow is drawn downward across a string from the frog to the tip—a *down-bow,* in musical terms—exciting it into motion, the string produces a set of overtones in which every harmonic is heard in a descending order of loudness, thus producing the violin's particular tonal color. Because of a combination of its unique physical structure and the techniques required to generate sound, each sound-producing entity—whether animal or constructed of nonliving material components—yields a distinctive resonance.

Loudness, or amplitude, is measured in decibels. One decibel, or dB, is the smallest discernible unit by which humans can detect a change. If you can hear the sound of a mosquito flying by you at ten feet, then you've got a set of ears that can pick up the quietest sound humans can hear—around 5 dBA. (The *A* appended to the symbol *dB* signifies that the measurement is calibrated to the ways in which a "normal" human ear processes acoustic signals over the entire frequency range.) Hearing damage will occur for many of us at around 115 dBA—the loudness of a pneumatic drill—and, if sustained, will cause the hair cells in your cochleas to fail; this can result in deafness. A few of us, however, experience pain and damage at much lower levels. For me, sounds much louder than 90 dBA begin to cause discomfort, if not actual pain. I just happen to be extremely sensitive to sounds, particularly loud ones.

Some animals, such as toothed whales, can generate sound levels that, if produced in the air, would be equivalent to a large-bore firearm being discharged a few inches from your ear. But, pound for pound, one of the loudest organisms in the animal kingdom is, oddly enough, the inch-and-a-half-long snapping shrimp. Many snorkelers and scuba divers are familiar with this marine sound, since the crustacean appears along most ocean shorelines and reefs, and in estuaries. It has a staticlike sound that permeates the entire underwater region, and it generates a signal with its large claw that can meet or exceed 200 dB underwater—a sound-pressure level equivalent to around 165 dB in air. With every 6 dB change representing a doubling or halving of intensity, we can compare the shrimp output to a symphony orchestra, which may generate loud moments peaking around 110 dBA. Indeed, the lowly, unsophisticated shrimp will not be outdone even by the Grateful Dead, a rock group whose concerts have been measured at levels exceeding 130 dB. Get this, Deadheads: the shrimp is louder by close to a factor of five—all that without a huge stack of stage speakers!

The loudest human sound I've ever tested came from a female's scream. It measured 117 dBA at ten feet—a bit greater than the volume of an average, painfully loud rock concert. But with the exception of a volcanic eruption on the order of Krakatoa, or a very loud crack of thunder, there are very few other natural sounds generated in air that could cause hearing damage.

The fourth major sound property, acoustic envelope, determines the shape and texture of a sound through time, from the moment it is first heard to the time it fades out. No matter where you live or what you hear—no matter if it is an entire wild habitat, such as a rain forest, or a single bird; whether it is a note played on a piano or guitar, or a chord played by an entire orchestra—every sound or series of sounds has a beginning and end point, and between those two points can get softer or louder. The entire sounding period, including the whole transformation of the character of a sound, is the acoustic envelope.

Impact sounds such as gunshots or rim shots on a snare drum have a very fast rise time—they go from nothing to really loud in microseconds—and they also have a very fast decay, depending on whether the environment in which they are generated is reverberant or not. The onset of other sounds, such as a crescendo played on a violin or articulated by cicadas in a tropical rain forest, is marked by a slow rise from their softest to their loudest point. These types of sounds may sustain for a period before becoming quieter over time until they are no longer heard. The envelope can, simultaneously, define the shape of an instrumental sound's tonal color, taking the very smooth and delicate tone of a steel-string guitar, for instance, to a raunchy fuzz tone, or enabling a trumpet to produce a blurt, growl, or muted sound over an articulated phrase.

While the elements of sound are part of every acoustic signal—whether generated by animals, humans, musical instruments, or machines—they make up only one part of what collective sounds amount to in a given location. The word *soundscape* first appeared in our language toward the end of the last century; it refers to all of the sound that reaches our ears in a given moment. The term is credited to R. Murray Schafer, who embraced and studied the sounds of various habitats. Schafer was searching for ways to frame the experience of sound in new, nonvisual contexts. At the same time, his goal was to encourage us to pay more attention to the sonic fabric of our environments, wherever we happen to live.

Schafer and his colleagues at Simon Fraser University in Vancouver showed that each soundscape uniquely represents a place and time through the combination of its special blend of voices, whether urban, rural, or natural. The geological and architectural features of Vancouver's Stanley Park, where Schafer and his friends worked and recorded during the 1970s, generated a soundscape on Sundays at dawn with a particular blend of park animal life and minimal traffic — one that sounded very different from that of the same location during the week at afternoon or morning rush hour. The combination of seasonal birds, amphibians, and insects, together with road and air traffic — all enhanced by the passive acoustic features of the landscape and the vegetation — generated an acoustic signature distinct to that location whenever times and conditions were comparable.

Natural soundscapes, in particular, are the voices of whole ecological systems. Every living organism — from the tiniest to the largest — and every site on earth has its own acoustic signature. Soundscapes acquire their individuality through a combination of factors: In hilly habitats, sound tends to be more contained. But when the area is flat, open, and dry, sound disperses more quickly and seems to get lost. The acoustics of a single location can vary greatly over the course of each season, too, depending on the density and type of dominant vegetation (e.g., the needle-like leaves of conifers versus the broad leaves of deciduous plants) and the area's basic geological features (i.e., rocky, hilly, mountainous, or flat). Sound reflects off saturated or uniquely shaped leaves that certain bats use as lures for pollination; the bark of forest vegetation; and ground that is wet with rain or early-morning dew, causing reverberation throughout a habitat. When dry, a forest will usually be hushed and quiet, with sounds tending not to travel as far or to last as long.

In the mid-1990s, just before a horrifying outbreak of social and political upheaval in Zimbabwe, I recorded a spectacular old-growth morning soundscape there. It was a site that had remained intact for a very long period of time—according to our guide, Derek Solomon, a knowledgeable landscape ecologist and naturalist, large areas of the environment and its voice probably hadn't changed much over tens of thousands of years. The experience gave me a rough idea of what this type of dry, mostly deciduous forest must have been like when our early human ancestors first appeared in Africa millions of years ago.

The dawn chorus was infused with a tightly orchestrated ensemble of barred owlets, sounding much like lazy California gulls; a Scops owl, with its low, slow series of short burbling sounds; Natal francolins, their quickly repeated kiss-squeaks augmenting the sense of rhythm; freckled nightjars, with quick up-and-down medium-frequency whistles—three to five repetitions in succession; ground hornbills singing high-pitched repeated chirp sequences; bearded robins, their melodious three-note phrase followed by a high chirp; rattling cisticolas, repeating long, high-mid-range melodious sequences; a chinspot batis, with its slow, staccato quasi-half-step descending note songs; and thirty or so other bird species, along with baboons and dozens of species of insects. The acoustic moment was so rich with counterpoint and fugal elements that it immediately brought to mind some of the same intricate compositional techniques used by Johann Sebastian Bach (as in his Prelude and Fugue in A Minor).

But this wasn't an ordinary dawn chorus. I had noticed at our campsite in nearby Gonarezhou that, unlike in tropical rain forests, I wasn't sweating much even though it was quite warm. Everything sounded incredibly "dry," the low humidity making it seem as if I were in a sound-proofed recording studio with no reverberation—every sound being quickly absorbed. The birds and insects were vocalizing in a habitat that had seen no rainfall for several weeks, and there were no reflective surfaces in this environment and thus no echoes. But the baboons, always onstage, were not to be denied their moment: they had found a nearby kopje—a type of granite outcropping that can rise three hundred feet above the forest or plains floor seemingly out of nowhere—and used the partially concave surface of the structure to send their sharp vocal retorts reverberating throughout the forest, the acoustic decay lasting for six or seven seconds before fading into silence. It was a unique gathering of sounds specific to this singular place, and their voices created an eerie imbalance within the soundscape—the dry, nonreverberant sound of the many birds and insects set off against long-echoed voices of the few baboons.

The acoustic features of a landscape play an important role in the way vocal organisms eventually populate a habitat. Some insects, birds, and mammals like to vocalize when the habitat dries out—at midmorning, when the forest has given up its surface moisture and the soundscape becomes redefined by the acoustic properties of dryness. Others take advantage of when the water of a pond or lake is still, and sounds tend to travel farther, the creatures' voices repeatedly echoing everywhere in a magical, dreamlike effect. This is especially true for the early mornings and late nights of spring and summer: when the weather changes and the wind comes up, reverberation tends to disappear, and a hushed, extended breathlike atmosphere cloaks the landscape.

As a seasoned listener, I especially love the sounds produced by creatures that have evolved to vocalize at night, when dew settles on the ground or on the leaves and branches of trees. The nighttime imparts the sense of a resplendent echoey theater—a beneficial effect for nocturnal terrestrial creatures whose voices need to carry over great distances. Coyotes and wolves likely choose nighttime to vocalize because their sound signatures resonate and travel so well.

The pleasure of hearing our voices echo is one reason why many of us sing in the shower—reverberation is a sound quality that seems to be particularly alluring to many creatures. The elk that live in the American West rut in the fall and often use the more pronounced echo of the forest environment during that season to project their modulated bellows, extending the illusion of their territory and securing their harems. These calls can be heard everywhere elk live throughout the western United States—especially in the Tetons and Yellowstone National Park. Hyenas, baboons, many species of frogs, and a nightjar called the pauraque also often vocalize when climate and landscape conditions conspire to produce reverberation.

In marine habitats, water temperature, salinity, currents, and the diverse bottom contours of an environment affect the transmission of sound in both subtle and profound ways. The enclosed bottom contour of sections of Glacier Bay in Southeast Alaska causes sound to take on a reverberant and amplified quality. As a result, signals produced by both vessels and animals can appear much larger than life. Meanwhile, inland lakes and some other marine habitats, such as coral reefs, produce little reverberation. I once heard the biologist Roger Payne lecture about the songs of humpback whales that he and his then wife Katy discovered in the 1960s. During his talk he speculated that the vocal syntax learned by male humpback vocalists for a given season featured themes and structures commonly found in the most intricate forms of human music.

A while back, when I was cataloging my analog tape recordings and transferring them into digital formats, I had a dream about sound—actually, a nightmare. In the dream, I went out to my lab at dawn and found that all of my ambient recordings had been transferred to thousands of little CDs, each with only one short clip of a single animal voice removed from the context of the soundscape. The CDs were scattered ankle-deep all over the floor, and I couldn't figure out how in the world I'd put the parts back together again. It still frightens me to think about it.

A few years later, I happened across *Finding Beauty in a Broken World,* Terry Tempest Williams's book about mosaics—how they are whole structures of magnificence built from disparate broken pieces. The same can be said for graphics, words, and film sound design, but not for natural soundscapes. What reaches out to us from the wild is a deeply profound connection—a constantly evolving multidimensional weave of sonic fabric. Natural soundscapes are never expressed the same way from one day to another. Even with the best technologies, we can only partially capture these sonorous moments, the main reason being that the voices that make up these choruses are always adjusting slightly to accommodate for the most successful transmission and reception—a kind of perpetual self-editing mechanism. For that reason, it is extremely difficult to re-create those choral expressions from their separate abstract parts unless we are able to grasp the underlying infrastructure characterizing how each component voice fits within an ever-changing bioacoustic composition.

Except through written and performed music, there was no mechanism by which to capture and preserve sound until very recent history — the mid-nineteenth century. The earliest forms of musical notation that appeared in the Middle East around 2000 BCE made it possible to accurately reproduce a series or combination of notes, thus enabling repeat performances. We are able to enjoy Mozart's music today because it has been written down, performed, and performed again — not because we've heard him play it.

The first actual mechanical reproduction of recorded sound took place in 1860, when the Parisian printer Édouard-Léon Scott de Martinville invented the phonautograph. It was followed almost two decades later by an invention of Thomas Edison's. His phonograph system featured the addition of easy playback options absent in the earlier prototypes.

Manageable technology for reproducing sound from the wild surfaced a few years after the invention of the bias-calibrated analog tape recorder by Ampex in 1948. Based on a German invention developed a decade earlier, tape recorders of the Ampex era were the first electromechanical devices able to capture and replicate sound encompassing nearly the full range of human hearing — all on a thin quarter-inch strip of tape. The recording tape consisted of three elements: a Mylar (or plastic) backing, a very thin coating of oxide, and a type of adhesive that held the oxide to the backing. The oxide was made up of a layer of tiny magnetic elements, each about the size of a single particle of cigarette smoke. When the tape was drawn smoothly across the electromagnetically charged record head, the oxide particles, normally aligned in random patterns, were realigned such that they could be "read" by the playback head and would reproduce an analog, or continuous stream, of captured sound.

Audiotape in its different forms — reel-to-reel as well as standard and mini-audiocassettes — was the principal medium until the mid-1980s, when digital audiotape (DAT), a transitional format that combined elements of both analog and digital systems, took over. In a short time, the recording world became dominated by digital recording systems, moving from complex, heavy, and power-dependent technologies to extremely light, versatile, and high-quality handheld models. By 2005 field and audio delivery systems became digitally based — whether on hard drive, compact flash, or both — and have remained so to date. Each time I think I have a version of the ultimate system, I'm seduced by a new and better one.

But even with all the technology to record and reproduce dramatic audio performances, recordists interested in the natural world have not, for the most part, focused on soundscapes as whole structures. Except for limited use in film and television sound tracks, whole-habitat recordings were virtually unheard-of when I began in the late 1960s. Rather, sound fragmentation — acoustic snapshots of solo animals, like those in my nightmare — remained the dominant field-recording model from the onset of the craft. Throughout much of the twentieth century, those of us in the field were charged with carefully abstracting brief individual sound sources from within the whole acoustic fabric.

The inspiration for sound fragmentation came about because a couple of researchers simply figured out that they could do it. That, and the fact that they were on a mission. After discovering that they could isolate the sound of a single bird by using what ornithologists of the 1920s called a sound mirror — an early version of the parabolic dish—and recording the signal to the optical track of a Movietone sound recorder originally designed for film, Arthur Allen and Peter Paul Kellogg from the Cornell University Lab of Ornithology and a few other colleagues decided to chase down and record the rare ivory-billed woodpecker. In the spring of 1935 this team of birders, mounted on a mule-drawn wagon loaded with hundreds of pounds of recording gear, entered a gator-infested Georgia fen. After the bird and its nest were finally spotted, the researchers captured one clear recording of the likely now-extinct creature.

Meanwhile, across the Atlantic, Ludwig Koch was recording individual birds in Great Britain and on the Continent using a device more akin to a Vitaphone—a disk recorder in which the needle records and plays back tracking grooves on the disk from the inside out. The decontextualized single-species model these scientists established ushered in a narrow academic recording format still favored nearly eight decades later. Based on the idea of *life lists*—finding and identifying single species of birds and mammals and, more recently, frogs and insects—the approach of collecting animal sounds by the numbers became firmly entrenched.

Focusing on capturing single sound fragments initially forced me—and everyone else, from casual listeners to serious researchers—to confine my inquiries to the limits of each vocalization, whatever its origin. But for humans, the sound-fragment model distorts a sense of what is wild by giving us an incomplete perspective of the living landscape. And the result is that a necessary link between the human and nonhuman aural worlds is mostly ignored.

The soundscape's value as a window into ecological and musical literacy first became obvious to me while I was recording in the equatorial forests of Africa, Latin America, and Asia. Bored with chasing individual species and hearing single-channel monaural playbacks, I allowed the music-producer training in me to surface, and I set up a pair of stereo microphones and hunkered down. As night fell, I felt enchanted and blessed to be enveloped in that world of 3-D sound. It was a deliverance from the monotonous single-track recordings of older models, and the sound was more illuminating and evocative of a place than was any photograph. The captured ambiences — rich textures that infused the entire frequency spectrum with elegant structures, multiple tempi, and soloists — intensified my experience of the habitat through their luxurious and subtle nuances. They were generated as points of sound transported through the acoustic space. For me, listening with open ears enhanced a sense of extraordinary humility and imparted a sacred gift: a souvenir of living sound from a distinct place at a moment in time. Even now it brings me the greatest satisfaction I know.

Voices from the Land

Lake Wallowa in northeastern Oregon is sacred to the Nez
Percé. It was also the starting point for the 1877 flight led by
Chief Joseph and several other chiefs, who, after outrunning and
outfighting five American armies over the course of three months
and a passage of seventeen hundred miles—with their entire
tribes in tow, including children—were defeated at Bear Paw
Battlefield in Montana, just forty-four miles short of the Canadian border and freedom.

When I first saw this idyllic site in October 1971, nestled at the
foot of Chief Joseph Mountain in the Wallowa-Whitman National
Forest, the shore was covered in a frosty mantle glistening in the
early-morning sun. Guided there for a music lesson by Angus
Wilson, a Nez Percé elder whom a colleague and I had just met,
we were steered to his sacred learning ground and told exactly
where to sit. Then he moved some distance away while my friend
and I waited, our interest piqued the evening before when Wilson

alluded to the depths of our musical ignorance. Offering to reeducate us if we were at all curious, he cautioned that the tutorial might require a high degree of patience and a suspension of long-held beliefs. We were in.

Waiting by a feeder stream that flowed from a valley to the south, we squatted on our haunches, trembling—the temperature hovered in the midtwenties, and we lacked proper clothing to sit on the ground without cover. Anticipating an unnamed and unexpected event, we impatiently scanned the valley, where the woods were dense with lodgepole pine, Douglas fir, western larch, ponderosa, and low-lying scrub. Except for the sound of a few ravens, it was, at first, pretty quiet. Nothing moved. Wilson hadn't said much on the three-hour predawn journey from Lewiston, Idaho. When we got to our destination, he simply asked us to cool our heels and said that all would be exposed in time.

After about half an hour, the wind began to funnel down from the high southern pass, gaining more force with each passing moment. A Venturi effect caused the gusts passing upstream through the narrow gorge to compress into a vigorous breeze that swept past our crouched bodies, the combined temperature and windchill now making us decidedly uncomfortable. Then it happened. Sounds that seemed to come from a giant pipe organ suddenly engulfed us. The effect wasn't a chord exactly, but rather a combination of tones, sighs, and midrange groans that played off each other, sometimes setting strange beats into resonance as they nearly matched one another in pitch. At the same time they created complex harmonic overtones, augmented by reverberations coming off the lake and the surrounding mountains. At those moments the tone clusters, becoming quite loud, grew strangely dissonant and overwhelmed every other sensation.

While never unpleasant, the acoustic experience was disorienting.

The sound came out of nowhere and completely masked the natural soundscape; we couldn't connect the reverberation with anything we could see. With mixed emotions, my colleague and I looked at each other, puzzled and a bit apprehensive. Neither of us had ever heard of or experienced anything like this—nor had we thought to record in a way that caught the whole event.

Some time slipped by, and Angus slowly got to his feet, walking with arthritic stiffness over to us. He asked if we knew where the sound was coming from. Bordering on hypothermia, we both shook our heads. Placing himself between my friend and me, Angus motioned for us to stand up and walk with him to the stream bank. He asked again if we had any idea what was happening. Only then did we realize what he wanted us to hear and see. Before us stood a cluster of different-length reeds that had been broken off by the force of the wind and weather over the course of seasons. As the air flowed past the reeds, those with open holes at the top were excited into oscillation, which created a great sound—a cross between a church organ and a colossal pan flute. With that realization came the instantaneous release of all the tension in my hypothermic shoulders. If it hadn't been for this moment, we never would have given a collection of reeds growing in a remote area by an Oregon lake a second thought.

Seeing recognition in our faces, Angus then took a knife from the sheath at his belt and walked into the shallows, boots and all. He selected and cut a length of reed from the patch, bored some holes and a notch into it, and began to play. After performing a short melody—one that we did manage to capture on tape despite the freezing temperatures—he turned to us and, in a slow, measured voice, said: "Now you know where we got our music. And that's where you got yours, too." Humbled, I realized this was, beyond a doubt, my most memorable music lesson.

* * *

Even as animals' sounds will dominate a soundscape at different times, conscientious listening shows that the *geophony*—natural sounds springing from nonbiological subcategories such as wind, water, earth movement, and rain—has an effect not only on individual voice expression but also on the performance of all animals in a habitat taken together. The sounds of the geophony were the first sounds on earth—and this element of the soundscape is the context in which animal voices, and even important aspects of human sonic culture, evolved. Every acoustically sensitive organism had to accommodate the geophony; each had to establish a bandwidth in which its clicks, breaths, hisses, roars, songs, or calls could stand out in relation to nonbiological natural sounds. Humans, like others in the animal world, were drawn to geophonic voices because they contained fundamental messages: those of food, a sense of place, and spiritual connection.

By itself, the geophony is a source of beauty and complexity, and deserves to be explored on its own terms. I think it's likely that water would have been the first natural sound any sentient organism interacted with. If the fossil records of the first sea creatures—rangeomorphs—found in rock formations are any indication of the origins of life on earth, then the setting for this interaction was probably a marine ocean environment somewhere near where the coast of Newfoundland now lies, as far back as 550 to 600 million years ago. What we do know for sure is that organisms have always depended on water for life. Since water was life's first home, the sound produced by the medium would have been the first any evolving responsive organism would have heard.

While I was working in the Northwest along the Columbia

River, a local resident told me the story of a nearby Native American group whose communal life had completely revolved around a waterfall—a sound from their creation story. The waterfall animated their lives as a group and sustained them through every generation. When I told the local that I was curious to learn more, he introduced me to the tribal member Elizabeth Woody.

According to Woody, elders in the Wy-am tribe tell of a period spanning thousands of years when they fished all year long at Celilo Falls, just west of the Columbia River's midway point. (*Wy-am* means "echo of falling water.") So central were the falls to the tribe that the Celilo was considered a sacred voice through which divine messages were conveyed. Each season the wide, vital river at the cascade provided lots of fish—in the spring, chinook salmon; in the summer, chinook and bluebacks; in the fall, chinook, steelhead, and coho. When the catch was good, tribal members could harvest a ton of fish a day. For little more than the cost of a couple of balls of twine, tribesmen could quickly supply both close and extended family with fish for a year.

On the morning of March 10, 1957, the U.S. Army Corps of Engineers, hoping to improve navigation on the river, ordered the massive steel gates of the newly built Dalles Dam shut tight, strangling the natural downstream flow of the river. Six hours later, the sacred waterfall and fishing site of the Wy-am, eight miles upstream, was completely submerged. Although they had been forewarned, the Wy-am elders stood on the riverbank, astonished, watching as a way of life that had flourished for centuries disappeared in less than a day. There wasn't a dry eye on the banks near Celilo, the small namesake village on the river's edge. And yet the elders were not weeping for the loss of salmon. They wept because the river no longer lent its wise voice to the community. The submerged Celilo Falls were dead silent.

"It was a place revered as one's own mother," said Elizabeth Woody. "I [now] live with the...absence and silence of Celilo Falls much as an orphan lives hearing of the kindness and greatness of her mother."

The world is filled with ancient myths about water and its effect on our perceptions of the natural world, and stories of sounds created by and around water have many intricate variations. By far the favorites of mine draw connections to the human and nonhuman animal worlds, and the geophony. Where large rivers and human populations intersect, there tend to be flood myths—for example, the descriptions of the great floods in the Epic of Gilgamesh and, of course, the story of the flood in the Book of Genesis.

As humans have traveled more widely, many have noticed that it's not only the great natural events that have left an impression on our story. We may have arrived late in recognizing the wonders of the terrestrial orchestra, but we came even later to exploring the abundance of living sound in the streams, ponds, swamps, lakes, reefs, and oceans of the world. Although sailors in ancient times occasionally heard the voices of whales through the hulls of their wooden ships, today giant leaps in accessible technologies, combined with an inveterate curiosity, have led us to drop hydrophones (underwater mics) in the earth's waters, adding greatly to our sense of an element that covers more than two-thirds of the planet's surface.

Soundscape ecologists who have recorded shorelines on different continents and dozens of ocean beaches of the world frequently remark on the subtleties of sound that we've easily overlooked—and that are just beginning to be understood by those in the field. The water sounds at each beach have their own acoustic signatures as a result of the beaches' rakes, offshore and shoreline depths, currents, composite materials, weather patterns, salinity, water temperature, climate, season, surrounding terrestrial environment, geological features, and a range of other dynamic components. The offshore depth of the water changes from one section of beach to another, and it affects whether the waves begin breaking at a distance or closer to the shoreline. I am always struck by how the marine soundscape of the seashore at Coney Island in Brooklyn—over its entire dynamic range—is very different from that of the beaches in Dar es Salaam on the Indian Ocean in Tanzania, or Ocean Beach in San Francisco, or Praia Beach in the Azores, or the East Anglia coast of the United Kingdom, or the sandy shores of Martha's Vineyard, or Ipanema in Rio de Janeiro.

Until I heard side-by-side recordings made at the waterline of various beaches at slack-water high or low tide, it would never have occurred to me that ocean-shore ambiences could sound so different from one another. Wild terrestrial habitats, yes. But the sandy beaches at the shore? When my parents first took me to Coney Island, where the broad sandy beaches of the 1940s and '50s caused gentle waves to wash onshore with long periods in between, I was struck by the placidness of the sound. With the space so open and expansive, and with my parents venturing out only in the calmest of weather, I found that Coney Island became a signature acoustic experience to which I would eventually compare all others as I grew older.

In Dar es Salaam, when the weather is calm, small Indian Ocean waves come ashore from the east in quick, staccato-like patterns—sounding almost like the frequent successive lapping at a freshwater lake. The rake of the beach is at a steep angle, causing the waves to collapse just as they reach the shore. Of all my ocean-beach recordings, no others from a saltwater environment sound quite like this one. On the opposite side of the world, waves that wash up on the few sandy beaches in Big Sur—which is about midway between California's northern and southern borders—and those on Ocean Beach in San Francisco are far more robust and powerful. In even the calmest weather, their curl and booming crashes give me a contradictory sense of both a stark beauty and an awesome yet cryptic threat.

Praia Beach on the Island of Faial in the Azores is about a third of the distance to North America from Portugal in the Atlantic Ocean. Thrust up from eons of volcanic action, the shoreline is rocky. Sound bounces off the geological structure of the site, amplifying each hit with a sharp, percussive, slaplike crack. Located on the leeward side of the island, Praia is a more protected beach than the others. Most of the time the wave action is caused by swells rather than wind. The action is rhythmic and higher pitched, with slightly shorter periods between hits than the waves at Big Sur.

While Coney Island is calm, the waves along the shore at East Anglia in Great Britain near Aldeburgh, even on the brightest and most placid days, have an almost angry sound to them. The rake of the beach is steep as it drops off into the North Sea, and perhaps the sound results from a combination of the drop-off and the small rocks that line the shore jostling against one another as the waves break. Even small wave action has an agitated feel.

The soundscapes of Martha's Vineyard's beaches vary widely, from the protected, shallow water coves off Vineyard and Nantucket Sounds along the northern part of the island to the impressive constant roar and low rumble of the Atlantic-exposed shores to the south.

In calm weather, the waves at the beach of Ipanema in Rio de Janeiro come ashore at relatively short intervals as a result of a medium rake and periodic swells generated from the northeast. I always find the alluring, slow-rhythmic sound of these waves to be welcoming, beckoning me toward the tempting surf. In winter the wave action, enhanced by the wind coming off the South Atlantic, can stir Ipanema's waters into waves ten or twelve feet high.

Of course, water sounds can shift based on changes in the environment and on what kind of geography the water inhabits. A friend and fellow recordist Martyn Stewart, who had gone to the Louisiana shore along the Gulf of Mexico after the 2010 BP oil disaster, remarked on the surf's odd sound at the beaches affected by oil. He described it as having a slurpy, muddy, sluggish signature, almost as if the water were choking on itself or gasping for air. Aside from the initial absence of wildlife sounds, the muted slosh of the water-oil mixture at the beach was the most devastating impression he came away with—what he heard was far more powerful than what he saw. I had a similar chilling acoustic experience in Prince William Sound in the late spring and summer immediately following the 1989 Exxon Valdez oil spill. I had never before heard any part of Alaska so eerily quiet.

Freshwater inland lakes, no matter how big, create shore waves that tend to be smaller in size, higher in pitch, and more rapid in sequence than those at the ocean—the lapping wave action on a calm day occurs at a much faster rate than would be heard at an ocean beach. These variations are, in part, a result of the different densities of fresh water and salt water, the latter being more dense. Lake waves have their own distinct acoustic signature, and likewise each lake is as different from the others as snowflakes: their sound depends on surrounding habitat; the position of our ears relative to the source; the weather; the season; and a plethora of other conditions described earlier. Wave action, whether with salt or fresh water, affects the calls and songs of shorebirds such as gulls, killdeers, and waterfowl. Each species must develop a voice that can carry over the sounds of the marine environment, with its distinct and dynamic range of turbulence. Anyone who has grown up by a remote lake and listened carefully to the setting will recognize unique seasonal patterns of the soundscape.

Beach and lake soundscapes aren't the only examples of water-based natural sound. Streams still flowing through viable riparian habitats create a wide range of voicings, depending on terrain, vegetation, time of day, season, precipitation, and flow rates. While each stream has a unique voice, variations tend to be much more subtle than with ocean shorelines. Nonetheless, streams inspire the same creative vocal solutions in the animal world. The American dipper is a medium-size bird that often lives and breeds under waterfalls or near fast-flowing water. Its voice — high-trilled expressions — can easily be heard above the rush of falling water, reaching a level that few in the avian world are able to outdo.

Weather produces its own dynamic range of acoustic variants in the geophony. In the tropics, guides warned us that it wasn't the snakes or the jaguars or the small critters that would do us in while we worked in the rain forests. It was the trees. Rain causes the canopies to take on weight, and since the root systems of most rain-forest trees are shallow, with the fertile topsoil only inches deep, top-heavy trees will crash down at the most inopportune times. I know. One fell only a few feet from where I was sitting one afternoon. I had no idea what was happening until after it landed, inches from my mic stand, as I crouched, completely astonished, nearby.

Thunder can be dramatic and foreboding. When I was creating a series of commercial natural soundscape albums in the 1980s, I was told that the titles featuring thunder were taken off the shelves of Japanese stores because the clientele felt threatened by the sound; it reminded them of war. But the power of thunder can also be a harbinger of good things — such as the relief of a drought — as it booms and rumbles in the distance and rolls in ever closer. It can express itself as dry-sounding (as in an open desert environment), reverberant (as in many rain forests), or accompanied by rain or wind. I love the drama of weather sounds that are vivid and ominous but, when distant, can also be calming. I try to record thunder whenever it occurs. It's tricky to capture, however. The force of the thunder's loudest retort can almost never be anticipated correctly. When the level is set too high, the sound will easily overload the best recorders, but when the level is set too low, I'll miss the subtle after-rumbles.

Rain creates differing acoustic expressions depending on the force of the downpour and environment — urban, rural, or natural. Various weather dynamics over land and sea result in acoustic experiences that even acoustic ecologists sometimes miss but that are, nevertheless, extremely varied. Storm cells in tropical rain forests tend to pass by every afternoon, even in the "dry season." When they do, the dense wall of falling water sounds like a freight train approaching. It moves remarkably fast. In a matter of a minute or so from the time you first hear thunder, the deluge advances with a force so powerful that it is always breathtaking to be caught in it. Because the vegetation in the upper canopies is so thick, the roar comes first from above, where the downpour initially hits. The full might of the rainstorm often fails to strike the forest floor directly. What you hear are melodic drips on the leaves — the sound of which depends on drop size — and periodic drops of water hitting small pools that have formed on the ground. In the best of stereo or surround recordings, we are able to capture this illusion of both near and distant rain events all at once. Just as quickly, though, the surge passes, the whole episode not lasting more than three or four minutes.

If trees haven't toppled on you or your mics, you'll hear the rain forest's insects begin to stridulate as the storm cell recedes into the distance — first one creature, then dozens, then thousands. As if cued by an unseen hand, and building dynamically like a great performance of Gabriel Fauré's "Requiem," the birds will then start to fill the unoccupied acoustic slots until the forest is once again alive with a complex sonic texture that builds, climaxes, and shifts when the next cell forms or as time swings from late afternoon to dusk. The Sumatra and the mid-Amazon forests are my favorite places to witness moments like these — and the performance repeats in one form or another almost every day.

In urban centers, rain sounds very different. There's usually no forest canopy to divert and absorb the falling water, so the drops hit concrete or other hard, man-made surfaces directly. With all the structural facades in cities, rain often splashes and echoes off the sides of buildings or on metal roofs. If you listen closely, you can always tell the difference between rain recorded in a wild natural setting and rain recorded in a city — even without periods of telltale auto traffic and the sounds of tires splashing through puddles on wet pavement.

Snow, too, creates a distinct acoustic environment — one that is as capricious in range as are the conditions under which snow occurs. It is extremely hard to capture an acoustic impression of a falling snowflake. The sound of snow falling is, for recordists, a tranquil delicacy akin to a fine gourmet treat. As with the few molecules of air displaced by a descending feather or a mote of dust, it is possible, if you're very lucky, to catch that moment. A few have done it, although not in a way that the falling snow can be easily heard on a regular sound system. I record snow when it's cold and damp. The problem is that many kinds of microphones don't particularly like either situation. The best conditions to record the sounds of snow are when the temperature is near freezing—the snowflakes tend to be large, moisture-laden, and heavy. When the flakes have weight, and if I've managed to set up my mics properly—usually small ones pinned to the branches of low-lying bushes—I can catch the delicate vibrations of twigs as the snowflakes land on them. The impression is a soft, muffled tapping sound unique to snow.

In common English vocabulary, we have only one word: *snow.* Unless you're Barry Lopez describing snow in *Arctic Dreams,* one size fits all. More detailed descriptions are mostly visual—we almost never think of an attendant sound experience of snow other than remarking on the stillness that accompanies the moment. And while Western mythologies of the Inuit insist that their language has dozens of words that illuminate different snow-related experiences, a more careful look at Inuit vocabulary reveals a snow lexicon of about a half dozen or so words. Given the best terms in English, as Lopez shows us, we can discern fine or wet snow, frost, drifting or clinging fragments, snowbanks, blizzards, crusted snow, melting snow, candle ice, snow hitting standing water, and sleet, among other variations.

A few years ago, R. Murray Schafer created a sound-sculpture commission for a German radio station titled "Winter Diary," which poignantly captured the subtle elements of human interaction with the wintry soundscape as part of a larger piece. He recorded the various elements of the composition "live." The piece unfolds with the sound of footsteps over crusted snow moving across a rural sound field from one space to another. After a segment of snow shoveling, we're enveloped by stillness for a long period until the whistle of a train, far off in the distance, redirects our ear to a human sound that, to some of us, is a lovely resonance. The soundscape oscillates back and forth between a nonreverberant, all-absorbing calm and our engagement with percussion instruments, voices hollering, Native Americans performing, and melting ice dripping on metal—all set within an exterior snowbound scene, until the mind is wholly sated with a feeling of utter serenity.

During the 1990s, I led a series of natural-sound listening and recording trips throughout Latin and North America, Africa, and Indonesia. On a kayak trip in Southeast Alaska, we set up camp on the southern Russell Fjord shoreline, about half a mile across the channel from Hubbard Glacier. Throughout the three or four days we spent there, the leading edge of the glacier continually released 300-foot-high masses of ice that would thunderously crash into the fjord below. These calving ice masses displaced large amounts of water, generating great waves that after a minute or so—traveling some 2,700 feet—would crash on the rocky beach below, where we had pitched our tents and set up our outdoor kitchen. It was a formidable sound, and it reminded us to pull our kayaks way beyond the high-tide line if we didn't want to see them washed away.

After a couple of days, I became curious enough to see if there was perhaps some acoustic energy generated by the glacial mass as a whole as it moved over the ground, forming the moraine below. After conferring with our guide, we decided that it was safe to paddle over to the glacial mass and hike back a kilometer or so from the calving face to investigate if there was anything to be heard. The mass of a constantly moving glacier is a geophysical sound source—a category that also includes avalanches, earthquakes, and thermal mud pots. These sounds, like all others, depend on our perspective in relation to the source and on the characteristics of the physical environment in which they occur. After we crossed the fjord and hiked onto the glacier, I crawled down into a crevasse and set a hydrophone in a shallow melting pool. While the group stood at a safe distance, I managed to catch an ominous and continuous low rumble more felt than heard, the movement of the entire glacier as it advanced a few centimeters an hour, and the first time that signature had ever been recorded from that perspective. (A word of caution: crawling down glacier crevasses is not a recommended activity!)

Because it consists mostly of very low frequencies and sharp, loud spikes, ground movement itself is a difficult class of sound to capture. But if you can manage to record it, the sound is unforgettable. Mammoth Lakes is a very active seismic zone in the Sierra Nevada mountains, where periodic earthquake swarms frequently occur. In 1989 there were more than three hundred small quakes in a period of two days alone. This is not unusual. In the early 2000s, I managed to capture a nearly continuous swarm of invigorating jolts at Mammoth Lakes. Many of the rumblings, ranging between 3.5 and 5.5 on the Richter scale, were recorded for the first time with special types of microphones that—akin to a hydrophone—are referred to as *geophones,* or special *contact mics.* These microphones come in direct contact with a vibrating source, hence how I was now able to record the earth's movement as a reproducible geophony — a sound anyone could actually hear.

While capturing the sound of the ground moving was thrilling, among my favorite natural sounds is one that we cannot actually record: wind. That is, we cannot record the wind itself — we can only capture its effects. I am utterly transported when listening to the subtle differences as wind rustles through leaves or grasses, or the sound of pitched wind as it blows around snags or across the open ends of reeds by a lake or river, or as it courses through the needles or branches of conifers in a forest.

John Muir, the late-nineteenth- and early-twentieth-century naturalist who hiked the Sierra Nevada mountains and for whom Muir Woods is named, claimed that he could determine his location solely by the sound of wind that wafted through the spruce forests. He described such a moment when, in 1874, he rhapsodized:

> Even when the grand anthem had swelled to its highest pitch, I could distinctly hear the varying tones of individual trees, — Spruce, and Fir, and Pine, and leafless Oak, — and even the infinitely gentle rustle of the withered grasses at my feet. Each was expressing itself in its own way, — singing its own song, and making its own peculiar gestures, — manifesting a richness of variety to be found in no other forest I have yet seen.

Strong wind can cause branches of trees to rub together, making them groan and creak. Depending on its force, wind in a microphone can produce "pops" and rumbles by overloading the extremely fragile *capsule*—the main component that detects sound waves and transforms them into electrical energy or digital formats. Capsules can pick up the slightest change in air pressure—shifts that most human and many animal ears would not discern. When the sound of wind is hushed and subtle, it sometimes reminds me of the breath of living organisms; it becomes the crossover between animals and an alive-sounding earth. This *spiritus* ("breath," in Latin) is an intersection between all of the basic soundscape sources; many cultures recognize the wind's effect as a root of spirituality, whether its origins are trees in a forest or the sound of a creature's breathing.

Among the most ethereal of geophonic sounds, wind comes to us as a kind of mystical force that we experience as it changes from raging to light, from gusty to a gentle, constant breeze. Combined with other weather elements, it will have the might of a tornado or hurricane or the explosive force of a whale's breath. I was lucky to capture an expression of wind in the Southwest desert: Numerous storm cells were passing over our campsite in the New Mexican panhandle, interspersed with strong gusts that preceded each spectacular squall. I was recording the soundscapes of spring when, trying to get past a barbed-wire fence blocking my path, I happened to hear what I thought at first was a caricature of whistled wind just at the point where I was about to spread the wires and crawl through. The wind, howling in great surges, happened to flow by a pair of low-lying rusted strands that were perfectly wrapped to "sing" (i.e., vibrate in a tonal-producing way). Placing a couple of small mics in the grass to protect them from the elements, I managed to capture one of those rare moments recordists are always looking for—one that provides pure illusion and effect without other distractions.

When I play those recordings, even many years later, I am

always surprised by how "dry" and "hot" they sound. The thick, medium-pitched tones make my lips feel parched. I also have wind recordings that are suggestive of cold or menacing feelings—a bone-chilling sound that changes ominously, occurring when high-pitched howls alter frequency and signal a weather event about to occur. Recordings of wind are often used to establish moods in films. The sound effect created much of the feeling and emotion in *No Country for Old Men,* as well as in Robert Altman's *McCabe & Mrs. Miller.* One of the opening scenes in Altman's film is a long shot depicting a Western frontier town in winter, the wind employed at just the right pitch and level to set the stage for events to come with a foreboding chill.

Wind whipping around the globe; water in streams, lakes, and oceans; the movement of the earth; the violent eruptions of volcanoes; storms on land—these elements once combined to generate biotic-free soundscapes that infused a world on the brink of change.

Around six hundred million years ago, geophonies were the only sounds on the planet, and no living organism would have been around to hear them. But as life arrived, and as smaller organisms evolved over millions of years into more complex and vocal creatures, the soundscapes of the earth began to shift. Joining water, wind, and the rumblings of the planet, bacteria, viruses, insects, fish, reptiles, birds, amphibians, and mammals appeared, each establishing its place within a new sonic order, a world abounding with life.

CHAPTER THREE

The Organized Sound of Life Itself

It was my third day at the late Dian Fossey's camp in Karisoke, Rwanda — a remote place where one quickly acclimates to contact with the nonhuman animal world. At that time, a few years before the political turmoil that devastated the country in the 1990s, some protected biomes in the Virunga Mountains — despite occasional poaching and deforestation pressure — existed at a high level of viability, and still do today.

When I visited in 1987, the mountain gorillas had begun to slowly increase in numbers, and poaching in general had enjoyed a period of moderation, with the sometimes uneasy truce between government and outside agencies such as Fossey's Digit Fund. I was eager to be in that world, and a couple of hours into a short, half-day orientation, my ADHD kicked in and I convinced myself that I had absorbed all I needed to know about the rhythms of the forest creatures. Most notably, I thought, I had sufficiently learned to avoid the danger of contact with forest elephants and Cape buffalo, and how to behave around the gorillas.

Confidently secure in my new knowledge, I assured the other researchers and guides that I knew the field protocol and could be left alone with the study animals and my gear. They went off to do their own observations, and I sat quietly in one spot. Juvenile mountain gorillas played all around me as the adults tenderly groomed one another, resting between periods of daytime foraging while constantly reassessing the status of male hierarchies.

It was obvious by the look of the vegetation that there had been a fight. Torn up bamboo and scrub lay all around, and the general soundscape — filled with a combination of nearby shrikes, bulbuls, cuckoos, parrots, turacos, orioles, flycatchers, and multiple insect species — telegraphed a palpable tension, as did the pungent scent of the alpha male and the body language of the other apes. The richly defined soundscape of the Virungas had left an initial impression, but it soon became apparent that I had missed some subtle yet crucial signals provided by the location's fabric of animal voices. In a fraction of a second, the avian section of the chorus became tentative and quiet. Many of the insects abruptly stopped stridulating. A hush came over the forest, as if it were trying to avoid involvement with something that was about to happen. At the edge of my field of vision, almost behind me, I could just see the juvenile male Pablo as he crouched, skulking some distance from the others — partially hidden in a cluster of dense vegetation. Evidently he had been caught trying to mate with one of Ziz's favorite females, and Ziz, the alpha male of the group, had battered Pablo with the clear intention of reminding him who was in charge.

My stereo microphones were mounted on top of my San Francisco Giants baseball cap, and my recorder was running.

Unfamiliar with the individual characters, I had absentmindedly positioned myself between Pablo and Ziz. And then I missed another important shift in the intensity of the surrounding bio-acoustic fabric — something I might have caught had I been more present. It wasn't until later, when listening to a playback of the tape, that I recognized the signal's message.

Quite literally out of nowhere, a quick succession of chest beats from one of the apes broke the spell of the remaining ethereal ambience. Because stereo signals only reveal right and left perspectives in a set of earphones, I was only capable of perceiving sound sources coming from either side of the acoustic field. Pablo, really pissed, hammered out a rapid-fire exchange on his thorax with cupped fists, like a series of rim shots on a snare drum. There was a deafening scream and an explosive crash of vegetation as he cleared a path between himself and his more dominant rival — altogether an overwhelming sonic burst that overloaded my recording. It was impossible to tell that the terrifying uproar was coming from behind and rapidly getting closer. While others in the area obligingly got out of the way, I remained seated, awkwardly weighed down with more than forty pounds of equipment. Then a massive, hairy black hand tightly gripped my right shoulder. In one effortless motion, Pablo picked me up — recorder, backpack, and all — and flung me fifteen feet through the air in a blur of sky, vegetation, and whooshing Gore-Tex. The flash of weightlessness ended when I landed facedown on top of my equipment in a patch of stinging nettles, gasping for air that had been knocked out of my system. My body and recorder somewhat unscathed, I was lucky to walk away. All the warning signs were there, had I known to listen more attentively.

• • •

When I was growing up in Detroit, and my parents and their friends and family listened — really listened — to something that was outside the ritual buzz of their daily lives, they mostly turned to music. And, when I was present, they usually chose forms within a very narrow range of expression deemed appropriate for young, impressionable ears, a rather pretentious mix of the classics and a wee bit of jazz. Tolerated but never really acknowledged were all the extraneous noises that also penetrated our environment.

So with either certain kinds of music or irksome noise as my early listening template, imagine my sense of wonder when I discovered for myself — lying alone in my room during those spring and summer evenings — that all the living organisms outside my window were singing melodies that merged into parts of a much larger choir. The joy was a secret that I was certain no one else would understand.

It was only a good deal later that I recognized all living organisms generated a unique sound signature. For instance, when viruses let go from a surface they've been attached to, they create a detectable sonic spike — a sharp, quick change in amplitude measurable by only the most sensitive instruments. Then there are the low-frequency moans and clicks — far below what humans can detect unaided — of the largest living animal on the planet, the blue whale.

For one of my first jobs in Hollywood, I was hired as part of a sound crew during the filming of a B movie. Trying to encourage me to quit, the film director exiled me to Iowa in August and charged me with recording the sound of corn growing. He wanted me off the set, he explained, because he didn't need two sound recordists and, as I was working under union contract, I couldn't actually be fired. So off I went, ever dutiful and on a mission. Like Brer Rabbit in the briar patch, I obediently sat in the middle of a cornfield about fifty miles west of Des Moines all night long with my microphone held up to a stalk of corn, waiting for some event to occur—I had no idea what. It turns out that corn makes a sound as it expands telescopically, the staccato-like clicks and squeaks reminiscent of rubbing dry hands in quick, jerky movements across the surface of a well-inflated rubber party balloon. The sound of corn growing.

And the sounds little things make! The first time I heard ants "sing," I was nearly fifty years old. I was speechless for hours. Ants "sing" by stridulating—rubbing their legs across their abdomens. While working on a project in the American Southwest desert, my team and I were filmed by National Geographic as we recorded fire ants attempting to remove a pair of small lavalier microphones I had placed over the entrance to their nest. The ants' actions—the command signals to workers to remove the impediment from the entrance—were communicated entirely by sound.

I've often heard people say that the voice of a creature depends on its size—that small creatures have tiny, soft voices, while larger animals are somehow louder. But careful listening will quickly explode this myth. The Pacific tree frog outside my bedroom window is about the size of my little fingernail. Its voice can be heard more than a hundred yards away. One evening this spring, it registered 80 dBA at ten feet! Baby vultures in the forests of Ecuador have bodies so small that they would fit neatly in the palm of your hand, yet their roar is so loud and fierce that it would be great in a horror movie. On the other hand, many large animals have relatively soft voices—for example, the giraffe (except for its low-frequency sounds), the California gray whale, the tapir, the capybara, and the anteater. When it comes to natural sounds, there are few rules. Our preconceptions are almost always trumped by the incredible diversity of life on earth.

Anemones produce unusual sounds, although we have no idea how or why or what the sound might mean to other organisms in the vicinity. On a soundscape trip around Southeast Alaska, my group found a tide pool filled with barnacles, rockfish fry darting from place to place to hide, small crabs, clams, and some brilliantly colored anemones. One, whose mouth part (the center cavity) had grown to nearly five inches in diameter, looked particularly inviting for an experiment. I gently lowered a hydrophone into the cavity. Immediately the fleshy core of the creature sucked the instrument deep into its middle while the tentacles engulfed the rest of the object, searching for something of nutritional value. Finding none, the anemone expelled the hydrophone with a couple of loud, obscene grunts. If anemones create sounds, what about other creatures we've overlooked?

For instance, why would insect larvae create sound signatures? Some do. In marine environments, where many larvae appear to vocalize, is there already a climate of competition at such an early stage?

What would motivate hippos to vocalize underwater, and how close are those utterances to those of some species of whales? In muddy river environments, it's important to remain in contact with other members of the bloat. Like gray whales, hippos are social animals that like to stay in contact, producing similar grunts and other sounds.

What causes giraffes, until very recently thought to be rather quiet, to vocalize in frequencies so low that we can't hear them with our ears alone? Is that the only bandwidth in the biophonic structure open to them? Are they taking advantage of an empty channel so that their voices can be heard by other giraffes?

Generally we have only partial answers to questions like these and are just now realizing that we have much to gain by listening critically to the natural sounds of the earth and its nonhuman inhabitants. When I'm in the field observing animals up close, I try to imagine what they hear, and how the shapes of their ears might collect sound. I want to know how they perceive acoustic information. Cup your hands behind your ears and slowly turn around. The sounds gathered by the ear extensions make the sound appear louder and more focused. You'll hear more because your ears just got bigger.

Once, while working in Sumatra, I watched amazed as a rarely seen clouded leopard circled right in front of where I was sitting, changing the direction of its ears every few seconds, then directing them straight ahead to where it was looking. I went back to our campsite and cut out some paper ears that were similar in shape to the pinnas (outer ears) of the leopard. Then I mounted a pair of small microphones on them and clipped each ear to the stems of my glasses. The difference between what I heard with my ears alone and with the faux cat's ears was impressive. I tried to listen as might some animals with proportionally large ears— such as bats, many felids (cats), and canids (foxes, wolves, coyotes, dingoes, jackals, and others)—and to understand how ear shapes and sizes help creatures locate the direction from which a sound comes and make out its nuances. Increasing the size of the sound-gathering pinnas greatly enhanced the detail of what I heard and recorded. Bird and insect sounds were brought into much closer range, and the acoustic features were much sharper. Watch how a cat navigates by sound, catching every detail with focused attention by controlling the aim of each ear or both ears together. Make a pair of cat-shaped ears for yourself. You'll get the idea.

The way an animal detects sound depends on the specific creature, its habitat, and what it has evolved to listen for. Complex listening is one of the few operations that advanced life forms can do simultaneously with other functions — the organisms interpret information that conveys complex data, can change the coding of the signal instantaneously, and perform other tasks such as determining the usefulness of the received information relative to aspects of their survival.

At first, when their numbers were relatively small, acoustically sensitive organisms merely needed to filter out the geophonic background in order to perceive other sound-producing organisms within their habitats. As the number of species increased and became more complex, they had to be able to hear and process the particular sounds that were relevant to their well-being. Over the course of many glacial periods, especially the recent ones, the total number of creatures multiplied exponentially — species filling available biological niches. Complex habitats arose that supported robust varieties of life-forms whose behavior and survival — both individually and collectively — were determined to a large extent not only by visual, olfactory, and tactile cues but by sound.

The mechanisms for hearing vary from species to species — and they depend, of course, on whether the creature lives on land or in water. Many fish, for instance, detect changes in pressure through the *lateral line,* a bundle of nerve cells that stretches from the gill to the tail, usually about midway between the dorsal and pectoral fins. When schools of fish suddenly veer off in one direction or another as a group, they are responding to pressure waves that strike their individual lateral lines at the same time.

Terrestrial mammals share to some degree consistently developed ear structures across species. Their ears consist of an outer ear, or pinna, as well as a middle ear, which is the air cavity behind the eardrum that includes the stapes, anvil, and malleus, or hammer. Sound—a wave of pressure traveling through the air—causes the eardrum to vibrate. The structures in the middle ear transfer these vibrations to the fluid-filled inner ear. Within the inner ear is the cochlea, which contains hair cells—cells with protruding hairlike structures that determine the frequency range the listener will be sensitive to. Some groups of cells are more sensitive to low-frequency signals, while others specialize in the higher end of the spectrum. Hair cells serve as both detectors and amplifiers—the motion of the cells is converted into signals that are transmitted from nerve to nerve until they reach the brain and are processed into useful information.

In marine mammals, however, because there is no need to create an impedance match with air, there is also no need for an intermediate organ—the marine mammals' physical structure allows sound to be detected in the throat, which is then directly conveyed to the inner ear. Some toothed whales, such as dolphins, actually perceive sound through their jaws. The common seal can detect sound through its *vibrissae,* or whiskers—shorter ones pick up higher frequencies; longer ones, lower signals.

Insects detect sound in one of three ways: Some—such as crickets, grasshoppers, and cicadas—sport a kind of eardrum that is exposed to the air and that can be located, depending on the species, anywhere from the thorax to the front legs. Others hear through tiny hairs—called a Johnston's organ—that reside on their antennae. Then there are insects such as hawk moths that can detect, through a hearing-specific organ on their heads, the incoming 50 kHz to 70 kHz echolocation signals of bats seeking them out as meals. (And some nonsinging insects, such as the mountain pine beetle, don't hear at all, although they are likely to sense vibrations transmitted through the ground, air, trees, or other vegetation.)

Reptiles, in general, have a tympanic membrane that is either visible on the surface of the skin or slightly recessed. It's connected directly to the middle ear, which in turn transmits vibrations to the inner ear and then on to the brain. Crocodiles produce and receive very low-frequency sounds, suggesting that this so-called infrasound is detected by their half-submerged bodies. Like reptiles, frogs perceive sound through an external tympanic membrane located directly behind their eyes. And also like many reptiles, they probably pick up vibrations through the ground and water as well. Many times, as I've silently tried to approach the shore of a pond, frogs sitting on a log will detect the motion either visually or through the ground transmission of my advancing footsteps, and will quickly disappear into the water or shoreline grasses.

Except for owls, which have the highly developed hearing and sound-processing skills necessary for sonically locating prey in dim light and dense habitats, birds don't have obvious ears. But they do have ear holes in their heads, which are located just below their eyes and are covered with feathers. This makes sense: wind noise (in flight or even while roosting) can cause interference with reception, and feathers help mediate the problem. Aside from lacking pinnas, a bird's hearing mechanism is remarkably similar to that of a human. In fact, most birds hear within the same frequency range as humans, but the way they process sound is geared to the intricacies of the songs and calls of their own species.

Animals handle sound in enough ways to fill multiple books

on that subject alone. There is a gopher that burrows under the surface of our vegetable garden, nibbling at the tender roots of our organic plantings. It will pay no attention to the sounds of our cat's padded footfalls or swishing tail raking over the ground — but it sure as hell will respond to the slithering vibrations of the five-foot gopher snake that lurks about, seeking openings to the gopher's subterranean labyrinth. The mule-deer doe and its twin fawns that graze alongside our country road each evening are unresponsive to the sound of our car as it slowly drives by. But if I am on foot, approaching them from a hundred yards away, they'll quickly bolt into the woods and out of sight. Even though this is a hunt-free zone, there must be something in their acoustic DNA that signals to them: "Humans on foot mean serious danger." But the reassuring sound of a passing automobile — as long as it doesn't stop — registers little or no consequence.

The ultrasound signals produced by bats and toothed whales — such as dolphins, killer whales, and sperm whales — are used to send and receive information related to echolocation. These high-pitched bursts of sound, from around 18 kHz to in excess of 200 kHz, are thought to provide imaging not unlike the ultrasound scan machines used in the medical profession. Some of these creatures receive an acoustic image of an object so detailed that they can distinguish between two quarter-size coins, one made of wood and the other of plastic, from twenty-five yards away underwater.

The physiological systems that have evolved to receive sound are only the first stage in the hearing process. The organism must then decode the received signals into something of value — an acoustically sensitive creature's life depends on being able to interpret the slightest nuances of complex acoustic information to determine if the environment is safe or if danger is imminent.

Like all sentient beings that sonically navigate through the world, we, too, receive a range of signatures. Some contain useful information that we call *signal;* some feature unwanted and unrelated sound fragments we call *noise.* Most sound that reaches our ears, of course, contains a mixture of both signal and noise. Those of us from industrial societies are so inexperienced when it comes to listening to the voices of the wild natural that we tend to miss the indicators that tell us about events taking place within earshot. If we knew how to read the exacting signs that inform the acoustic narrative, we might have a better sense of the dynamic energy of each habitat. Sometimes, though, the signs are not so subtle at all.

Most of us hear the sound of crickets, katydids, frogs, or various insects as a cacophony or din of noise. It is much harder to filter out useful information within these clusters. But when you listen closely you begin to discern a wealth of data from sound-producing creatures. When neighborhood kids come by during summer evenings, I like to play a game with them. "Anyone know how crickets tell us the temperature?" I ask.

The tempo of the stridulation—or number of pulses in any given period—is based on the ambient temperature, which affects the body temperature of the cold-blooded crickets. As we begin to listen more carefully, most of us realize that when hot days begin to cool down, the pulses the crickets produce are not synchronous. Crickets generate sound by rubbing their wings together, stridulating like the singing ants I described earlier. One cricket wing has a *scraper,* the other a *file.* Sound occurs when the wing containing the scraper rubs against the wing with the file. The crickets are inconsistent with the timing of their chirps because ground temperatures vary depending on where the cricket is located within the local territory. Shadier areas run cooler than those that have been in direct sun, so crickets in cooler areas chirp at a slower rate than those in hotter ones. Eventually, as the evening progresses, temperatures on the ground even out, and all the crickets perform their wing rubbing in phase—that is, perfectly synchronized.

You can actually determine the temperature by counting the number of chirps made by certain crickets. With the snowy tree cricket, for example, you can count the number of chirps that occur in fifteen seconds, add forty to the number, and arrive at the temperature in degrees Fahrenheit. Other species have different formulas that are just as easy to calculate (i.e., you can add the number of pulses that occur in fifteen seconds to a prescribed number, depending on the species).

A few years after my Rwanda assignment, soundscape commissions took me to Australia and southern Ecuador, where I came in contact with the still-ancient soundscapes of the Pitjantjatjara's and Jivaro's habitats, respectively. The Pitjantjatjara live in the deserts of Central Australia and move through what appears to an outsider as flat and undifferentiated terrain. As a result, one thinks they'd rely more on visual than on aural cues. But their world is characterized to a significant degree by the sound of the biophony, particularly as an acoustic guide or map. "Travel along this route as long as you hear the green ants sing, then, when their song ends, head toward another voice (and so on) till you get to the place you want to go." The directions taken during their walkabouts are determined, at least in part, by changes in the soundscape.

The Jivaro, who live in the Amazon Basin and refer to themselves as *Shuar,* hear the language of the biophony very differently from the Pitjantjatjara. The soundscapes are dissimilar in the extreme: while the Pitjantjatjara desert landscape can be hauntingly still except for the most subtle signatures of wind, earth, and a very occasional creature, the Jivaro collective biome is one of the most acoustically rich environments on the planet and is never without creature sound at some level.

Once headhunters, the Jivaro fiercely resisted Westerners, from the conquistadores to twentieth-century missionaries. In 1599, after wiping out a Spanish town of around twenty thousand, they were considered to be so ferocious that they earned a reputation as the only South American tribe to effectively repel the Iberian invaders. They continued to rearrange the skull sizes of their adversaries until the late 1960s.

As with other tribes who live in remote locations, the Jivaro's and Pitjantjatjara's connections to natural soundscapes are quickly changing as contact with industrial culture becomes more frequent and imposing. But on my only visit, just before the Jivaro became more integrated into a cash economy, I was allowed to accompany a group of men on a rare evening hunt. I quickly discovered that they found their way through dense ground-level vegetation without the aid of torches or a clear view of the night sky, guided primarily by subtle changes in forest sounds. With startling accuracy, they were able to follow unseen animals, directed by the slightest variations of insect and frog articulation.

They also allowed me, an "outsider," to experience their sacred songs and dances. With a couple of flutes and a type of rainstick, their music bore a strong relationship to the sounds around them and often appeared to be driven by the constantly shifting "moods" of the forest's daytime or evening ambience. In one instance, the emotion of the music, in that attenuated moment before an afternoon thunderstorm, became quite somber and anticipatory. Then, prior to the evening chorus, after the squalls passed a short time later and the ambient forest sound picked up and became more lively, the performance resumed with a more upbeat theme and instrumentation. Echoing the mood of the environment, the tempo increased and the feeling was much more energetic. Whether the music was instrumental or vocal, or accompanying a dance, it drew deep inspiration from the signals emanating from the woods.

When I was trying to find a single, easy term that would define animal sounds coming from wild places, every expression seemed academic and obscure. In the human realm of noise, the terms were even more obtuse, with phrases such as *anthropogenic noise.* Nothing quite fit. Then, by accident, I hit on a Greek prefix and suffix that struck just the right chord: *bio,* which means "life," and *phon,* which means "sound." *Biophony:* the sounds of living organisms.

In addition to the sonic cues embedded within soundscapes, the biophony as a whole can give us valuable information about the health of a habitat. In an undisturbed natural environment, the richness and content of soundscapes vary from season to season, over time of day, and under different weather conditions. The organic and nonbiological elements that are unique to a location work in a delicate balance, acoustically defining each habitat, much in the way each one of us has his own voice, accent, and manner of speaking.

More than twenty years ago, I asked a biologist working for a large lumber company if I might have permission to record at a "forest management area" in the Sierra Nevada mountains, where his corporation had obtained a lease permit to begin selective logging on public forest land. The site: Lincoln Meadow at Yuba

Pass, about three and a half hours east of San Francisco. Bisected by a stream and a bit over two-thirds of a mile long and about a quarter mile wide, the meadow was surrounded by ponderosa pine, lodgepole pine, red fir, white fir, and Douglas fir, as well as a few sequoias. Multiple species of frogs could be heard there throughout the spring. It was a lovely, resonant place. At local meetings held throughout the area, the biologist and his associates assured the community that his company's new selective-logging methods — cutting only a few trees here and there and leaving the vast majority of the healthy old-growth sequoias standing — would have no adverse impact on the habitat. I asked for access to the site to record both before and after the operation.

With the company's blessing, during the summer solstice of 1988 I set up my system in the meadow and recorded an exquisite dawn soundscape expressed by a wide variety of creature sources. Figure 1 is a graphic illustration of a twenty-two-second

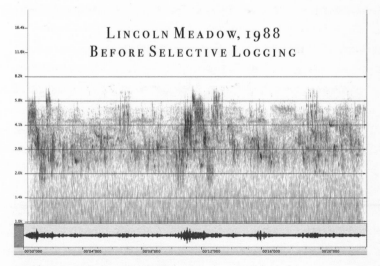

Figure 1. Lincoln Meadow, 1988.

soundscape clip from that site. (A graduate student of mine once observed that the Lincoln Meadow spectrogram reminded her of an abstract painting of a forest.) Present in the first recording were Williamson's sapsuckers (a type of woodpecker), mountain quail, chipping sparrows, white-crowned sparrows, Lincoln's sparrows, ruby-crowned kinglets, and numerous insects. Note the density throughout the illustration.

A year later, after the logging operation was complete, I returned to Lincoln Meadow on the same date, at the same time, and under the same weather conditions to record again. (The precipitation records during the winter of 1988 to 1989 had also been similar to those of the previous year.) When I arrived I was delighted to see that little seemed to have changed. However, from the moment I pushed the "record" button it was obvious that the once-sonorous voice of the meadow had vanished. Gone was the thriving density and diversity of birds. Gone, too, was the overall richness that had been present the year before. The only prominent sounds were the stream and the hammering of a Williamson's sapsucker. I walked a few hundred feet back into the forest from the meadow's edge, and it became quite apparent that the lumber company had wrought incredible devastation just beyond the meadow's sight line, where extensive patches of ground had been left exposed. While not exactly a clear-cut, many more trees were taken than had been promised. In Figure 2, the stream is represented by the horizontal light-gray section across the bottom, and the woodpecker is the cause of the vertical lines in the center of the figure. Over the past two decades, I have returned more than a dozen times to the same spot at the same time of year, but the bioacoustic vitality I captured before logging has not yet returned.

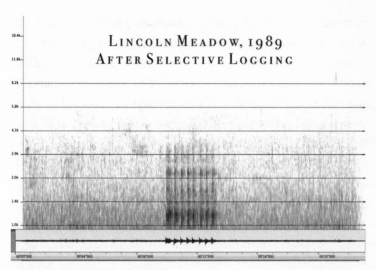

Figure 2. Lincoln Meadow, 1989.

To the easily deceived human eye—or through the lens of a still or video camera—the site even now appears wild and unchanged from the narrow perspective of the meadow. With a photo, we can frame a shot in almost any setting and, depending on what we want to catch in that fraction of a second, evoke responses from awe to horror. Still photography lends itself beautifully to the close-up shots of single animals absent the complex communities they need in order to thrive, and is thus a kind of tolerated distortion.

But even a short, unedited sound recording captured in a calibrated and comprehensive way does not lie. Wild soundscapes are full of finely detailed information, and while a picture may indeed be worth a thousand words, a natural soundscape is worth a thousand pictures. Photos represent two-dimensional fractions of time—events limited to available light, shadow, and range of the lens. Soundscape recordings, if done right, are three-dimensional,

71

with an impression of space and depth, and over time can reveal the smallest feature along with multilayered ongoing stories that visual media alone can never hope to capture. A well-tuned ear and attention to minutiae within the larger picture will always uncover any deception.

In marine environments, coral reefs tell much the same story as the meadow. A while ago, I went to Vanua Levu in Fiji to record living reefs that still produced and sheltered an abundance of organisms. In an unusual discovery, I happened to come across one that was stretched far enough — nearly a half mile in length — to contain both a living and dead component. When I dropped a hydrophone over the side of the boat to capture the part still vital, I was able to hear and record a spectacular variety of fish and crustaceans, including anemones, parrot fish, cardinalfish, clown fish, wrasses, puffer fish, fusiliers, goatfish, butterfly fish, and dozens of others. Figure 3 represents a ten-second clip of the dense,

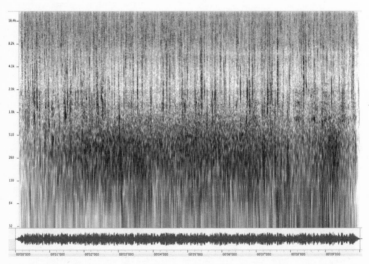

Figure 3. Vanua Levu, Fiji. Live coral reef soundscape.

healthy reef habitat. (Of course, the actual sound tells the story more distinctly than any words.) In this illustration, the noise from the wave action at the surface can be seen below 1 kHz, while all the creatures are seen above.

Figure 4 illustrates the soundscape of a nearly dead and badly stressed section of the same reef. You can still see the wave action below 1 kHz. But nearly all of the fish are gone, and only a few snapping shrimp remain as part of this marine biophony. Due to warming waters, shifting pH factors, and pollution, this sonic loss is occurring alongside the deaths of many coral reefs around the world.

Density and diversity are fundamental bioacoustic indicators when measured against season, weather, and time of day or night. If we can establish baseline recordings for any environments that

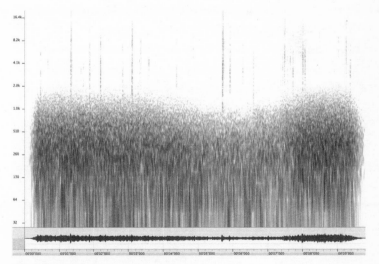

Figure 4. Dying coral reef soundscape.

are calibrated to known and repeatable standards — as I did at Lincoln Meadow and the coral reef in Fiji — then the recorded information we gather will represent a collection against which future recordings can be accurately assessed. I have always been careful to record with future comparisons in mind. When done properly, such recordings allow us to determine an expected acoustic dynamic range and to measure creature concentration and variety under an array of changing conditions. For example, we could ask ourselves: On a day with a clear dawn in late spring, just before sunrise in a remote, nearly pristine temperate forest habitat, what kind of soundscape could we reasonably expect to hear? If we record continuously over the course of a week's time, and then over a few years to account for average rainfall, wind, and temperature — assuming that the flora and surrounding landscape have not been altered — we'll get a pretty good idea.

Whole-habitat recordings of the kinds I've described illustrate the state of biomes that have been rendered ecologically transformed through human intervention, such as logging or mining; climate change; or natural phenomena, and we can make efficient comparisons — assuming we have well-collected data sets — with audio snapshots as short as ten seconds in length. Like the rings on a tree, these recordings serve as multilevel biohistorical markers. When natural cycles, disasters, or destructive acts of human intercession occur, the events are quickly and powerfully articulated through changes in the biophony. The living collective of sonic organisms responds appropriately. Nonhuman animals will try to recalibrate their voices to accommodate the altered circumstances. The resulting spectrograms either will show far less density and diversity or will appear more chaotic — that is, filled with unrelated or competing information — with very little distinction between voices, assuming any remain at all.

The presence of water and food, the climate, the vegetation, the soil conditions, the season, and the altitude all affect the biophony. And all of these combined will help determine the cumulative number of creatures living in a given biome (its density) and the number of species present (its diversity). Then there are the geological features of the landscape, which will bring out specific qualities of a wide range of vocalizations, thus highlighting the unique character of the biophony — the way it actually sounds to the ear, human or nonhuman.

A rain forest is not just the tropical ideal most of us think of. There are many different types, and they reach from the tropics to the subarctic Pacific Coast regions of the Northern and Southern Hemispheres. The densely packed vegetation of broad-leaved, straight-trunked, and buttressed trees; bromeliads; epiphytes; saprophytes; orchids; figs; and carnivorous plants, along with numerous species of animals, make up the estimated thirty million or so flora and fauna that live in tropical regions with an annual rainfall of around 160 inches (about 400 cm). At the other extreme, in temperate or subarctic zones with annual precipitation of around 80 inches (about 200 cm), rain forests also exist, although the vegetation and animal life are much more sparse, even in the warmer seasons. While some animals, such as wolves, foxes, bears, and a few species of coastal birds, are year-round residents, most tend to migrate based on when and where food is most abundant. Populated mostly with spruce, cedar, hemlock, and Douglas fir, and an understory of ferns, berries, and nettles (in temperate regions), and with tundra (in northernmost zones), these rain forests are distinctly different from those nearer to the equator. The first thing I noticed about the disparity between equatorial and Southeast Alaskan rain forests is how dissimilar they sound. They're both "rain forests." But the varieties of frogs and insects alone at the equator far exceed anything along the fifty-eighth parallel to the north. The organisms in equatorial rain forests tend to be year-round residents. Those farther to the north, in temperate zones, are seduced into song in the spring and summer months. They are more transient, or migratory, and vocalize seasonally. Meanwhile, the winter months are, in comparison, biophonically light.

Another extreme would be to compare a rain forest to a desert biome. The most noticeable difference is in the quality of the sounds. Rain forests tend to be reverberant habitats because of the high humidity and the moisture both on the ground and clinging to the vegetation. Desert biomes, by contrast, tend to absorb sound quickly because they lack moisture, and sound has nothing to "bounce" off of. While you might hear waterfalls and passing afternoon rainstorms in a rain forest, the geophonic sound signature of a desert is more likely to be wind and an occasional sand dune "singing," although violent thunder and rain sometimes do occur. And there's no comparison between the density and diversity of life in tropical rain forests versus deserts. Equatorial rain forests consist of the most densely populated biomes on the planet, while deserts and the Arctic regions — north and south — make up the least.

Tundra habitats are essentially treeless plains and are among the coldest of all habitats. Even though there's plenty of water, precipitation is fairly light and the vegetation is sparse, consisting mostly of low-lying shrubs, short grasses, sedges, mosses, and liverworts, and a few hundred varieties of flowers spread across huge expanses. The density and diversity of animals tend to be light as well. The surface is soft, cushionlike, and a bit mushy.

But underneath is a layer of permafrost—permanently frozen nonproductive soil. With the sound quality of the tundra similar to that of a desert, now and then perhaps you'll hear the voice of an Arctic fox, maybe a wolf, voles, hares, a bear, Dall sheep, and squirrels. At certain times of year, mostly during migration, you'll see caribou—thousands at a time, if you happen to be close to one of their routes, their snapping ankle tendons a characteristic sound signature, in addition to their cattlelike grunts. There are birds as well: depending on where you're located, you're likely to hear common and hoary redpolls, American robins, tree sparrows, white-crowned sparrows, Savannah sparrows, ptarmigan, ravens, sandpipers, lesser yellowlegs, warblers, terns, and wandering tattlers. Wildlife is dispersed over wide areas within very windy soundscape conditions. So, while the sonic fabric is robust overall, the bioacoustic texture is extremely delicate.

But biophonies are distinct not only from place to place—time plays a very important role as well. Although there is always some kind of performance occurring wherever there is wildlife, in places with a clear period of day and night a dynamic biophonic energy is at hand. My wife and I live just north of the thirty-eighth parallel in the Northern Hemisphere. Our biome is made up of a hilly, oak, chaparral landscape below a thousand feet, and we're forty miles east of the Pacific Ocean. From late March to late October there is hardly any rain—although over the past fifteen years the climate has started to change. During a normal rainy season, we'll get roughly thirty inches of precipitation. For several months a year—from March through mid-July—the biophony runs on a clear cycle: heavy at dawn (called the *dawn chorus*) and dusk (the *evening chorus*). By my estimate, on a scale of one to ten—with ten being the most active biophony we hear—the dawn chorus from just before sunrise to about a half hour after is a ten. The evening chorus, from about a half hour before sunset to just after the sun drops below the horizon, is about an eight. Biophonies that occur during the day, in between the dawn and evening choruses, vary anywhere from a five to a six. Evenings after dusk, given the local tree-frog and insect mix, float between a four and a five, while the time between midnight and first light usually hovers consistently around a very relaxing and soft-textured three — the best sound for sleeping.

Over the course of the summer, especially toward the beginning of August, the birds become very quiet, although they're still around, and the crickets become the dominant sound sources during the evenings and night — at times so intense that they're seemingly as loud as the dawn choruses of spring. These cricket choruses will last well into December, when the rains begin in earnest. Then they will cross-fade into the amazingly loud voices of the tiny Pacific tree frogs, signaling that it is mid- and late winter and anticipating the first bird activity of the early spring, when the cycle begins again.

Every biome on the planet expresses itself with these types of specific bioacoustic sequences and patterns, whether urban, rural, or completely natural. Climate change may be one reason that biophonic patterns are rapidly beginning to transform — some much more abruptly than many biologists and naturalists expected. There also may be other factors, such as early USGS indicators of polar magnetic shifting (as differentiated from magnetic field reversal). Currently, at the time of this writing, the poles are reported to be moving at a rate of almost eight-tenths of a mile a week. The consequences are not immediately clear, although if true this type of phenomenon alone may already be affecting some migration patterns. In locations that I've revisited throughout the world over the past several decades, the troubling muted result of human impact has been evident time and time again.

There have been acute and obvious changes in North America, notably in the areas where I have returned and recorded more than once over the past four decades. During the 1980s, a favorite spot of mine to record was a quiet but accessible site near Jackson Hole, Wyoming. From the early part of the decade, when I began visiting, well into the 1990s, the biophony remained fairly constant—the bird mix included warbling vireos, yellow warblers, white-crowned sparrows, Wilson's warblers, house wrens, and dusky flycatchers. By 2009, when I returned to sample the site after a lapse of five years, the soundscape had radically shifted. Springtime was occurring weeks earlier on average and the bird mix was now made up of hermit thrushes, Swainson's thrushes, cowbirds, grosbeaks, yellow-rumped warblers, dark-eyed juncos, chipping sparrows, and white-crowned sparrows—a very different combination. Exactly what these changes signify, we have no idea. But they correlate with reports from bird biologists throughout the United States, who have noticed similar changes elsewhere. Colleagues working in locations as far-reaching as Africa and Southeast Alaska have mentioned recent changes in avian, mammal, and insect combinations, which they've noted in biomes such as the accelerated melting glaciers on Mt. Kilimanjaro and in Glacier Bay, and in and around coral reefs.

We are discovering that the governing features of a biome's biodiversity are delicately balanced to the extreme. The biophonies of healthy habitats generally fall within a certain expected scope, meaning that given the range of the region's seasonal climate and the relative stability of the landscape, organisms that typically thrive there should reflect expected numbers of species and total population. What we have noticed is this: Whenever a biophony is coherent, or what some biologists consider "within a range of dynamic equilibrium," the acoustic spectrograms generated from recordings illustrate remarkable discrimination between all of the contributing voices. On the other hand, when a biome is compromised, spectrograms will lose both density and diversity, along with the clear bandwidth discrimination among voices that is otherwise visible in nonstressed-habitat graphic displays. Biophonies from stressed, endangered, or altered biomes tend to show little organizational structure.

When habitat alteration occurs, vocal critters have to readjust. I've noticed that some may disappear, leaving gaps in the acoustic fabric. Those that remain have to modify their voices to accommodate changes in the acoustic properties of the landscape, which may have been altered by logging, fire, floods, insect infestation, or other shifts in the nonbiotic components of the habitat. All of these variations mean that the natural communication system evolved within a soundscape breaks down and becomes chaotic until each creature's voice once again finds a place in the chorus. This could take weeks, months, or, in some cases, even years. At Lincoln Meadow the biophony at the last visit (2009) remains relatively quiet, with very light density and notably altered diversity, even after almost a quarter of a century of supposed recovery.

Listening closely to the soundscapes of wild habitats, you can immediately hear sound coming from three basic sources: (1) nonbiological natural sounds—the *geophony;* (2) sounds originating from nonhuman, nondomestic biological sources—the *biophony;* and (3) human-generated sound—*anthrophony*— where it intrudes and, in a few cases, blends. As recently as the turn of the millennium, the field of bioacoustics was still focused on the notion that there was nothing much to be found beyond the single-voice abstraction of individual organisms. It would never have occurred to most biologists to evaluate the health of an entire biome by listening to and studying in greater detail the total acoustic community. But, as my archive was beginning to uncover, there are multiple layers of consequence mixed into that collective voice.

Within soundscapes are manifold narratives—encoded stories that expose long-held secrets, what Samuel Coleridge once referred to as the "mighty alphabet of the universe." And as Loren Eiseley reminds us, we were originally readers long before we were writers, and for me the biophony has always held the most exciting surprises.

CHAPTER FOUR

Biophony: The Proto-Orchestra

In the early 1980s, soon after I received my doctorate, a friend working in the Exhibit Design Department of the California Academy of Sciences called to ask if I'd be interested in collaborating on the re-creation of an African water hole that he was crafting. In the field of animal recording, this request was unusual, since most exhibit models were the then thirty-year-old push-a-button/hear-a-sound types. In this case, the designer had in mind a much more holistic approach to the overall presentation—one very different from the common single-species list. Kevin O'Farrell was a design visionary who imagined a water-hole soundscape that featured a whole host of animals, removed the glass separating the visitors from the creatures, and brought the diorama itself out into the hall—a radical shift from the museum-design paradigms that had been in place for more than a century. Running for fifteen minutes, the audio performance would cycle through the events that occur at typical water-hole sites over an

82

entire twenty-four hour period. The sound track would be synchronized to lighting that would match the times of day represented.

O'Farrell's request meant planning and executing a more comprehensive field approach than I had ever considered previously. While I had worked in the wild on shorter trips, both on land and in water, this was the first concentrated, long-term, faraway field adventure I had ever undertaken. After experimenting for more than a month with various types of gear—there was absolutely no one to consult other than a few film sound recordists who were unfamiliar with the specifics of recording stereo natural soundscapes—I finally decided on a set of stereo mics and a portable recorder that was more frequently used for recording indoor orchestral performances. Through friends in Kenya, I was introduced to a patient and informed guide, one who needed to arrange the trip to the special requirements of capturing soundscapes. It was to be the first full set of round-the-clock natural soundscapes in my archive—or any other that I knew of—aimed at collecting not only dawn, daytime, dusk, and evening choruses but also single species' recordings.

About a week into the trip and several hours after midnight at Governors' Camp in the Masai Mara, I set up my gear and began to collect extremely rich natural sound from a nearby old-growth forest—one typical of what early humans might have encountered. After the camp's generators had been shut down and the staff retired, it finally became quiet, except for the forest ambience itself. If sound was going to be this glorious everywhere in the Mara, I realized, I needed to conserve the limited supply of tape I had brought and record at half speed, so that one reel would last for forty-five minutes instead of the usual twenty-two, even if I was at risk of losing a small degree of quality. The magnificence of creature voices was enhanced, no doubt, by my total exhaustion. I felt like I was hallucinating. The sonorities shifted like waves of Möbius strips wafting by in the still evening air, anchored by the throbbing rhythm of the insects.

My mics were mounted on a tripod just outside my tent by the river, where I had settled into my sleeping bag wearing a set of earphones. I didn't care if my batteries went dead—I was hoping to lull myself to sleep with the gentle predawn atmosphere as background. It was in that semifloating state—that transition between the blissful suspension of awareness and the depths of total unconsciousness—that I first encountered the transparent weave of creature voices not only as a choir but as a cohesive sonic event. No longer a cacophony, it became a partitioned collection of vocal organisms—a highly orchestrated acoustic arrangement of insects, spotted hyenas, eagle-owls, African wood-owls, elephants, tree hyrax, distant lions, and several knots of tree frogs and toads. Every distinct voice seemed to fit within its own acoustic bandwidth—each one so carefully placed that it reminded me of Mozart's elegantly structured Symphony no. 41 in C Major, K. 551. Woody Allen once remarked that the Forty-first proved the existence of God. That night, listening to the most vivid soundscape experience I'd had to that moment, I came as close as I would ever come to said revelation.

In planning my first long-range biophonic assignment, I had anticipated recording perhaps fifteen hours over the course of two weeks. At the normal high speed of the tape machine, that would have meant carrying forty-five reels weighing a pound apiece in addition to three sets of twelve D-cell batteries. I had already decided to record at half speed, but it turned out that I could have used a hundred more reels if I'd been able to manage the additional weight of batteries and packing boxes. On the flight home, for as long as my remaining power supply held out, I impatiently began reviewing the breathtaking range of material collected during my time on the ground in Kenya. Since so much in the field depends on luck, I couldn't believe the quality of the recordings I had captured, but at the same time I was disappointed that I hadn't had time to record more. My depression was tempered by the hope that what I heard could actually be visualized and that I might someday return, now that I knew what to expect.

When I arrived back at the lab in San Francisco, one of my first tasks was to transform the recorded samples into spectrograms — graphic displays of sound showing time and frequency, where time is represented from left to right on the x-axis, and frequency from low to high on the y-axis. When I listened to playbacks of my audiotapes and looked at the related spectrograms, my heart began to race with anticipation.

Just as black-and-white photographic images gradually appear on photo paper during the development process, unmistakably clear patterns materialized from the printer representing the audio sequences I had recorded. As the images slowly emerged, the überstructure of the soundscape plainly showed distinctive shapes not unlike modern forms of musical notation — the bat was vocalizing in the highest frequency range, insects in the middle, hyrax and hyenas a bit lower, and elephants down at the lowest end of the biophonic score. And each representation was unique. The bat was echolocating, sending out brief, high-frequency pulses of sound shown as two sharp lines in the upper-right-hand side of Figure 5. The hyrax, the "soloist" of the moment, sounded like a windup toy — a series of progressively slower grinding sounds followed by high, breathless screams. The tracery of its voice is illustrated midway across the page, beginning at the left-hand side. Once it completes a phrase, the hyrax repeats its vocalization all over again. A distant hyena found a location in the forest that resonated like an echo chamber—probably a water hole—and its voice reverberated, hanging over the soundscape in a different way than the other animals'.

Before I printed those first spectrograms on my return from Kenya, I had considered natural sound to be a chaotic random expression. The reductionist single-species method we had all been taught had us coaxing each animal voice out of its coherent context and trying to derive meaning from the sounds we abstracted from the natural world. Most of the international bioacoustic community felt the same way, as the great bird and mammal sound collections at repositories such as the British Library of Wildlife Sounds and the Macaulay Library at the Cornell Lab of Ornithology attested until very recently. But after Kenya, as I

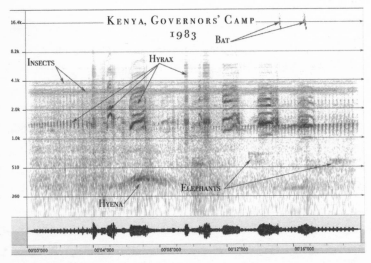

Figure 5. Masai Mara predawn example.

began to look more closely and found new acoustic software tools to work with, the patterns suggesting musical structures in the natural soundscape became too obvious to dismiss.

Based on the recordings from that first commission, no matter which 1983 Kenyan habitat I looked at or what times of day or night the recordings were made, niche discrimination plainly appeared on the page. Insects set the stage for every other sound, some by establishing uninterrupted drones that sounded continuously throughout each day and night, others by setting up rhythm patterns. Every bird species appeared to mark out its own acoustic turf. Mammals filled other niches, as did reptiles and amphibians. Before that night in the Mara, it had all sounded like anarchy to my ears. Now, for the first time, certain patterns within the structure became clear.

When I saw the first soundscape spectrographic images reproduced from rather primitive gear in the 1980s, I was reminded of William Turner's late seascapes. The early-nineteenth-century English Romantic artist's impressions only half suggested detail, teasing and drawing us into his mystical reality and letting our minds fill in the otherwise evocative representations. Even then I dared to think of the spectrograms as contemporary graphic musical scores—not that different from those written by the Canadian composer R. Murray Schafer, for example (Figure 6).

Discovering an ordered soundscape in Africa was astounding and never expected. I felt how amateur astronomers must feel when uncovering a major new galaxy or planet, upstaging the "experts." Ecstatic and armed with several dozen recordings, spectrograms, and other material for support, I couldn't wait to share my findings with my colleagues at the California Academy. Unfortunately my idea of the acoustic collective was dismissed out of hand. Alas, this wasn't a collegial nest of astronomers, and

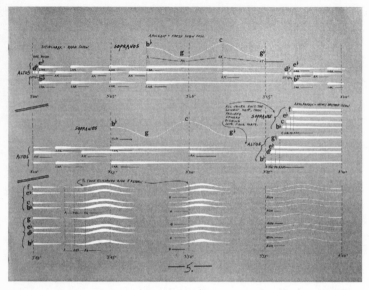

Figure 6. Page 5 from the score of R. Murray Schafer's "Snowforms," a choral composition for children (Arcana Editions, 1983, used with permission).

no one looked too deeply. My superiors made it clear that they had sent me to Africa on a mission to collect soundscapes for an exhibit, not to come up with new hypotheses. I was dismayed but not by any means dissuaded. I knew what I had heard and seen, and I felt the significance with certainty.

Gradually the growing body of my work validated the idea that creatures vocalize in distinctive kinship to one another, particularly in older, more stable habitats. Every subtropical or tropical old-growth habitat I recorded confirmed the partitioning model. Colleagues such as Ken Norris at the University of California, Santa Cruz, who immediately saw the potential and encouraged more comprehensive research, helped the concept gain footing by arguing in its favor with mutual associates and having me present the thesis at various forums that he, too, attended.

As my work garnered more support, I continued to investigate what was known of composition of natural soundscapes. Of course, regardless of the time it takes for academics to come around to an idea different from the ones they have invested in, it turns out that many human groups have likely understood how wild sound is layered since our ancestors first began to hunt and forage for food. The ability to correctly interpret the cues inherent in the biophony was as central to our survival as the cues we received from our other senses. Through the nuanced textures of natural soundscapes in the thickest vegetation, where sight lines were limited by density or darkness, we tracked prey, determined its location and direction of travel, and imitated sounds that had both practical and symbolic meaning. Forest-dwelling groups understood these signals and utilized them long before the last ice age receded. It was a time when natural soundscapes were "read" in much the same way that recipes are followed in cookbooks and routes traced on a road map.

Having heard about my work in Africa, Michael "Nick" Nichols, a *National Geographic* photographer on a combined assignment from the magazine and the Aperture Foundation, reached out for additional media to accompany the images that would result from his trip. He was in Rwanda in 1987 to shoot one of the great ape families, mountain gorillas. For his second excursion to Karisoke — the late Dian Fossey's aforementioned camp — Nick invited me to join him for a month to record the soundscapes of the Virungas and the biomes where the gorilla groups lived. These soundscapes, in turn, would become part of a traveling exhibition of his photographs, sponsored by Aperture.

During the trip I learned from Nick that none of the other sites where he had photographed had been recorded either. In order to get a complete picture of great ape habitats, I felt strongly that it was important to capture audio from those as well. I couldn't get sufficient funding from institutional or corporate sponsorships, so I sold personal items, took out loans against my small San Francisco condo, and set out to record those sites, first at Gombe — Jane Goodall's research camp on the northeastern shore of Lake Tanganyika in Tanzania — and later at Biruté Galdikis's site, Camp Leakey, in Borneo.

The first thing I noticed at each location was how much emphasis the other researchers on-site — each concentrating on a narrow topic — placed on the visual aspects of their study animals. For those whose scope of work involved sound at any level, the biophony — and in many cases even the individual species' sounds — was completely overlooked. Yet I realized quickly just how varied and rich the natural soundscapes were.

As my thesis gained traction, I no longer had to rely so heavily on my own resources and was frequently commissioned to go to various sites to collect sound for museum-exhibit installations. These adventures allowed me to further test and refine the concepts, bringing back more than just a collection of field recordings that would otherwise have limited purpose.

In Borneo — the third largest island in the world — a small riverboat took us the eighty or so kilometers from the Indonesian city of Pangkalanbuun to Camp Leakey on a slow two-day journey. Ruth Happel and I had just got off the boat and were walking on the trail from the dock to our cabin when we heard the call of an Argus pheasant. Not a second later I was looking down at the ground and found a huge feather from the same type of bird. The feather was one of the most beautiful I'd ever seen; the bird is called an Argus pheasant because its feathers have patterns that suggest eyes — the etymology refers to the giant Greek mythological character Argus, who had a hundred of them. Sometimes more than a yard in length, the feathers' main shafts show off mesmerizing yellow-brown circular patterns. Highlighted in white, these "eyes" are framed by perfectly inscribed kohl linings, not unlike the eyes of our tabby cat, Seaweed.

It was midafternoon, and the forest was filled with the voices of insects, trogons, forktails, laughing thrushes, kingfishers, barbets, hornbills, mangrove pitas, green magpies, and so many other species that we quickly lost count. We had to get out there. Before signing in with the camp biologist and unpacking, we grabbed our gear and set out in a dugout canoe that we found by the dock to find a mangrove swamp we had passed on our way in. It was a delicate operation—we weren't used to paddling dugouts with waterlines mere inches from the brackish river, and we were a bit nervous about protecting our equipment. But after about half a mile of cautious travel, we found the mangrove biome we were looking for—a perfect site, we thought. We tied the painter of the boat to an accessible branch and began to set up our gear.

It was now late afternoon, a couple of hours or so before dusk, and the forest was booming with sound. I pushed the "record" button. The first sound I noticed in my earphones consisted of maybe ten or twelve small splashes. I couldn't tell what direction they were coming from because I was recording in stereo—but I did know that the noise came from something nearby. Then the soundscape shifted noticeably—insects became quiet, birdsong became lighter. A signal? We had been recording for not more than a few minutes, but when I looked over the side of our canoe into the dark, tannin-colored water, I could already see several three- to four-foot shapes swimming in circles close to the boat, although I couldn't make out any detail and was unable to get an accurate count. Things were happening fast, and there was a feeling in the air that didn't seem quite right. Then one that I didn't see before broke the surface, and I heard Ruth, a woman of few words, mutter louder than usual, "Crocs!"

"I don't think I like this," I responded, trying desperately to sound calm. Pulling in our gear and cutting the painter, we made a quick run back to camp, never venturing out on the river again during our entire stay. When questioned by the staff, our excuse was that we found too many places to record on land — more than a half-truth, as it turned out. The gibbons of the region are the star soloists of the habitat.

It was just before dawn in a tower at the end of the Camp Leakey orangutan rehabilitation site's dock. The lookout rises some fifty feet above the black-water Sekonyer River that flows by the site, just high enough that it aligns midway up the sumptuous canopy where gibbons and other primates in the area spend most of their lives. The gibbons of Indonesia are sunrise singers. Their songs are so beautiful that ancient Dayak myths speak of the sun rising in reply. In the remaining viable rain-forest habitats of Borneo and Sumatra, every dawn chorus is filled with the near-field and distant strains of long descending and ascending vocal lines as bonded gibbon pairs connect through elaborately developed vocal exchanges unique to each couple — alluring duets of affectionate concord.

The morning after our arrival, as we recorded the languorous glissando-like lines of the gibbon choruses, I was reminded of the many melodic and poignantly arranged operatic and folk vocal duets I had heard and performed over the years. When I returned home, I came across a short fourth-century Chinese poem that expressed exactly what I had been feeling:

Sad the calls of the gibbons at the three gorges of Pa-tung;
After three calls in the night, tears wet the [traveler's]
  dress.

Unhappily, gibbons are now extinct in China. In Indonesia they, like several close subspecies, can still be found in dwindling numbers throughout the north part of Sumatra around Aceh Province—the location of the December 2004 tsunami—and in Borneo. Their duets can cover more than three and a half octaves, yet remarkably the gibbon voices become a perfect fit within the rest of the biophony.

Each discovery became a small revelation, but there were others. I finally realized that the biophonic behavior I was witnessing on paper probably wasn't unique to Africa or Borneo. I found signs of temporal distinction in our own backyard. Northern Pacific tree frogs will vie for acoustic bandwidth, time- and frequency-wise: one frog will call, followed immediately by another at a higher pitch. Sometimes their calls overlap when they are fighting for sonic territory or when the result is (hopefully) an attractive mate. The three around our small lap pool have defined their respective territories—one at each opposite end, and one in the grass about midway between the other two. Even though their vocalizations are at slightly different frequencies and might be distinguishable as a chorus, they rarely overlap in time. Instead, they set up a neat, well-paced ¾-waltz-like rhythm, with the alpha frog setting the pace. No matter how fast the alpha frog croaks, the others fill the spaces in between in quick succession with their separate but distinctive croaks, no one masking another. When they really get rolling, it's a fast ⁶⁄₈ meter. I have no idea which frog got the desired companion, but one year the alpha frog was still croaking solo well into early June. Apparently still accommodating elegantly for competition, he performed measures with a single croak and rests on the other beats, where the other frogs, had they not disappeared by late May, would have fit in. And other examples of differentiated bandwidth were showing up everywhere in the numerous spectrograms I printed out, in recordings from Equatorial Africa, South Asia, and South America.

In older, healthy habitats, where the biophonic bandwidth is well established and all the animals are more likely to vocalize together, each call is heard distinctly and each creature thrives as much through its voice as through any other aspect of its behavior. The connections of a particular species' vocalization to survival and reproduction only become clear when we understand the function of an animal's voice and its relationship to all others in its natural habitat. If an organism needs to be heard to successfully defend its territory or to communicate its viability to potential mates, then it requires clear acoustic bandwidth or noise-free time to do so. The same kinds of relationships occur in marine environments, such as flourishing coral reefs, where multiple species of fish and crustaceans thrive and generate acoustic signals.

Perhaps more surprising—yet in complete accord with this idea—is the fact that many animals communicate in an almost "underground" way that appears somewhat subtle to us; to them, it's stealth. In 1990 a colleague and I had just finished three weeks of work at Jane Goodall's earlier referenced chimpanzee research site, Gombe. We had a few extra days to wander about before our scheduled flight back to the States, and Goodall suggested that we check out a great hippo site in the Selous Game Reserve, along the Rufiji River in the middle of the country. Our camp, a typical African tourist and big-game-hunting facility, was located on the waterway, where we could see, from the high banks, large gatherings of hippos both on the shore and wallowing in the water below us. In an aluminum rowboat provided by the lodge, we drifted downriver with the current so that the river's flow rate would equalize with the velocity of the boat and wouldn't interfere with the hydrophone we had dropped over the side. As we passed submerged families of hippos, recorder rolling, it became immediately apparent that they vocalized underwater, their satiric, buffoonlike punctuated grunts revealing a fairly extensive and intricate vocabulary. As briefly mentioned earlier, hippos are social animals. In murky, crocodile-infested environments, this type of contact for animals with a highly developed social structure is germane to the safety of individual members and the bloat. When the family is submerged, members constantly vocalize to retain social contact with the others, mostly for protection since crocodiles share much of the same habitat.

Plains and forest elephants of Africa have found low-frequency transmission channels and a vocal syntax all their own. Over the wide-open grasslands and through the forests, their infrasound voicings are low enough—and their waveforms long and loud enough—that they can be detected at several kilometers distant throughout the territory, clearly signaling to others concepts such as "Join us" or "Let's meet at such and such a location soon." Likewise, wolves and coyotes, both extremely vocal animals, howl to remain in contact with other members of their respective families. Freshwater dolphins of the Ganges and Amazon, and places such as Lake Baikal in Russia — the world's deepest lake — have evolved highly developed and successful echolocation processes that are specifically geared for the less dense and more murky waters they inhabit.

Mating and territory. Mating and territory. We've always been taught that the function of acoustic behavior by birds, amphibians, fish, and nonhuman mammals is about mating and territory. But hippos, elephants, cetaceans, and other animals clearly have extra motivations for vocalizing. In addition to using social vocalizations that enforce cohesion within groups throughout and across many species — especially mammals — some species have gone even further, evolving methods using sound itself as a tool. Many toothed whales, for example, send out bursts of sound that are sometimes referred to in marine bioacoustic jargon as the "big bang" — a highly focused eruptive beam that stuns their prey and slows it up enough so that the whales can snag their meal without expending too much energy in the process. In a clever adaptation, the snapping shrimp closes its large claw so fast that the speed forms a cavitation bubble, which bursts with an impact noise so loud that the sudden *bang* stuns the fish, giving the shrimp a quick, effortless snack.

The list of adaptive acoustic behaviors goes on. I have a recording, made in the fall of 1979, of a killer whale mimicking a barking sea lion, ostensibly to attract one through sound. The American dipper, mentioned earlier, is driven by ancient instincts to nest under waterfalls, yet its songs and calls pierce even the most raucous cascade. Meerkats, members of the mongoose family that live in Africa's Kalahari Desert, fear sky-borne raptors more than almost any other type of predator. For protection, they've developed a specific alarm call that, when produced, immediately signals the other members to bolt for the cover of the nearest hole. Moths, mentioned earlier, have evolved to outsmart echolocating bats by jamming their signals. But in another adaptive solution, some bats, like *Barbastella barbastellus,* have managed to figure out what the moths are doing and have adjusted their echoing signal from a loud ping to a soft whisper. This allows them to creep up on their prey, drawing to within a wing's length without being detected.

Whatever the objective of a signal—whether it's mating, protecting territory, capturing food, group defense, play, or social contact—it must be audible and free from interference if it is to function successfully. Aldo Leopold almost got it right when he poetically described the call of a crane in *A Sand County Almanac* with these words: "When we hear his call we hear no mere bird. We hear the trumpet in the orchestra of evolution."

What about that orchestra—the entire animal ensemble within which the crane is but one performer? In biomes rich with density and diversity of creature voices, organisms evolve to acoustically structure their signals in special relationships to one another—cooperative or competitive—much like an orchestral ensemble. That is, over time, unlike the vocalizations that occur at various stages of recovery in stressed or compromised habitats, natural selection has caused the animal voices that occur in many undisturbed regions to appear "organized." The combined biological sounds in many habitats do not happen arbitrarily: each resident species acquires its own preferred sonic bandwidth—to blend or contrast—much in the way that violins, woodwinds, trumpets, and percussion instruments stake out acoustic territory in an orchestral arrangement.

The beautiful spectrogram in Figure 7, taken from a ten-second

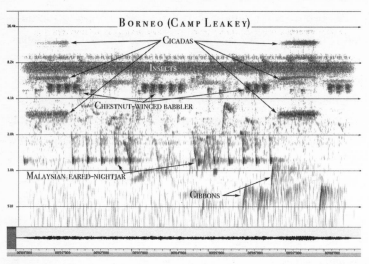

Figure 7.

dawn chorus recorded in Borneo, clearly shows a complex bio-phony. It's drawn from a habitat rich in vocal density and diversity. Look at this graphic from left to right as if you're reading an extended bar of music. Birds, insects, and mammals each form their own temporal, frequency, and spatial niches. (Note that the cicada fills three slots at the same time — a remarkable feat that must have taken a long time to evolve successfully.)

Where disparate groups of animals have evolved *together* over a long period, their voices tend to split into a series of unoccupied channels. So, each sonic frequency and temporal niche is acoustically defined by a type of vocal organism: insects tend to occupy very specific bands of the spectrum, while different birds, mammals, amphibians, and reptiles occupy various other bands, where there are fewer chances of frequency or temporal overlap and masking. Animal voices in many habitats have evolved so that they can stay off the acoustic turf of others. When that

partitioning occurs, individual voices can be clearly differentiated from one another, and the benefits of their vocal behavior
are maximized. And when there is occasional conflict, the acoustic territorial disputes are sometimes solved by timing: first one
bird, insect, or frog might sing, then others when that one quits.

It turned out that nearly every tropical and subtropical habitat I
had captured on tape was made up of a variety of partitioned voices
that formed collective sound signatures, each of which uniquely
defined a place and time and served as a unique voice print—a
territorial sound-mark. I had made thousands of recordings before
my Kenya trip, and subsequent travel to many wild sites over time
added weight to my thesis, which, by the late 1980s, I had renamed
the *niche hypothesis*—thanks in large part to the inspiration of
Ruth Happel, who was still a graduate student at Harvard studying
primatology during our trip to Borneo. Ruth quickly drilled down
to the essential questions that were necessary to uncover the mysteries of wild voices. While floating down the river heading home
from Camp Leakey in 1991, she asked out of nowhere, "How do all
these animals hear each other if they're all vocalizing at the same
time?" From that sensibility she arrived at a hypothesis that defined
collective vocal behavior as possibly more germane to survival
than were single voices. With a rare ability to think like the organisms in the animal world she studied, Ruth understood intuitively,
without knowing at the time exactly what the operational mechanism was, that nonhuman animal voices must have evolved so that
each can be heard unmasked and without interference. Her insight
gave me a new theoretical map to work from.

The radius within which a frog, bird, or mammal voice can be
heard is a mark of many complex factors. Food and the availability

of mates have significant influence over where creatures live, but we also know that the geological and botanical features of the landscape, combined with time of day, weather, and climate, play important roles as well. We know that higher voices tend to travel shorter distances—because the wavelength is shorter, and it takes more energy to project a shorter sound wave—and lower voices travel farther. What, then, might be the additional acoustic factors that would cause a creature to choose one location in which to live over another?

While few studies have focused exclusively on the influence of sound on territory, it is now becoming apparent that every wild site I've recorded generates bioacoustic boundaries that define its territorial limits. So what exactly are the boundaries of these biophonies? From a set position, how far out do the acoustic characteristics of the biophony remain intact before they begin to shift? If indeed they do shift, what sonic components have changed?

Little by little, with more time in the field, I discovered that new pieces of the niche hypothesis puzzle began to fit, and I found evidence that it is possible to define animals' geographical territory through an analysis of biophonic expression. When the thought of acoustically defined territory occurred to me, I set out to determine if there were ways to experience the phenomenon. The idea for acoustic mapping was inspired by a couple of groups performing aircraft noise studies. One, Harris, Miller, Miller, and Hanson, a Massachusetts acoustics firm headed by Nick Miller, had created an animated model for the National Park Service (NPS) at the Grand Canyon, showing how single- and twin-engine aircraft noise penetrated the surrounding landscape as the planes passed over different natural settings. The aircraft sound signatures were detected by numerous monitoring stations set up throughout the study territory. When an aircraft flew over the park, the display would show a cartoonlike colored moving over-lay with the symbol of an airplane and a radiation pattern representing the output of its sound, thereby defining the range over which the signal could be detected.

The intention of the study was to show park managers how they could oversee the soundscape experience of visitors. Aircraft noise, however, is a lot less subtle than the myriad sounds of a biophony.

Usually, when I wish to know how a territory is defined—whether by geological features or by boundaries of cities, parks, or private land—I reach for a map filled with grids or turn to imagery from services such as Google Maps. But in order to show how the natural soundscape can be used as a different means of defining a biome's borders, a few colleagues and I initially worked within the limits of 100 square meter grids that had been meticulously laid out by etymologists, botanists, ornithologists, and herpetologists at several subtropical forest research sites, such as La Selva in Costa Rica. We looked for periods of day or night when the biophonies remained constant and then we walked through the grids, crossing them at different angles, listening for zones and recording where the mixtures began to change.

On listening to playback, analyzing the notes from on-site observations, and comparing spectrograms, we found that the combined creature voices defined territorial boundaries quite differently than the geographically detailed maps we held in our hand. For one thing, it was clear that the margins characterized by the soundscapes didn't align with the human grid lines or other rational borders we might create. Nonhuman animals don't understand 100-meter-square grids or, for that matter, county, state, and country margins. At the point where the spectrogram partitioning began to show changes in biophonic structure, we knew we had reached an acoustic perimeter. We redrew the charts with overlays that reflected these new findings, then plotted a number of acoustic sectors and replaced the square grids with our new boundaries—borders that partitioned the map into amoebalike shapes, each an acoustic region that, while mutable, would tend to remain stable within a limited area over time. Working within the technical limitations of our first attempt, we realized that in order to derive more accurate information, we would need a vast network of stand-alone, data-rich, synchronized monitoring devices spread out at regular intervals throughout the habitat as well as more detailed spectrogram software—practical technologies that had not yet been realized but that are now becoming commonplace. Nevertheless, the initial implications from the data we did collect were striking.

The unique characteristics of each separate habitat are reminiscent of the signature sounds that permeate the body of a composer's work. Anyone even vaguely familiar with Mozart and Aaron Copland can instantly tell the difference between their two styles. No less passionate, the carefully structured compositions of Mozart are extremely formal and constricted in comparison to the more open neoclassic and symphonic themes generated during the early twentieth century. Just as a dedicated listener of classical, pop, or jazz music can identify the individual sound signature of a group or composer, those of us who have enough acoustic and dynamic detail stored in our heads can determine the time of day or night and the precise region we're hearing by simply listening to an audio recording of a biome for a few seconds. The natural voice themes become as clear as the main theme in Beethoven's Ninth Symphony, fourth movement.

While mapping, we noticed again that insects tended to create niches that remained constant in each biome for long periods during each day and night. Also, when one sound source dropped out at the end of its cyclical performance, another usually began to vocalize, typically within seconds, leaving the impression that replacement was necessary to keep some underlying acoustic-bandwidth structure intact. Over these "group" performances we could hear animal "soloists" who appeared for brief periods — often transient birds, mobile amphibians and mammals, and other organisms that would move in and out of the primary acoustic field. Like an eight-bar blues solo on guitar, their voices, too, seemed to fit into acoustic channels or temporal niches where little or no conflicting aural energy was present.

One great adaptive advantage of having all of the contributing voices of a habitat partitioned into niches is that the whole within an entire niche configuration often sounds more vital, rich, and powerful than the sum of its parts. The harmonic content of the drone voices — insects and chorusing frogs, for instance — sometimes adds what in music terms is called *frequency* or *amplitude modulation*. Another example of frequency modulation is vibrato added to a note played on a violin. If a violinist is playing a C-natural in the second position on the A string, she can modulate the C seven or eight times a second by rolling her finger back and forth, a bit flat and sharp of C's 523 Hz, adding an effect that musicians call *vibrato*. If the violinist periodically varies the volume of the C in much the same way, she would be modulating the amplitude.

Sometimes all that insect and amphibian racket creates *intermodulation,* where two or more signals are so close in pitch that they occasionally beat against each other, momentarily canceling each other's signal — a totally different acoustic effect than any of the original sources sounding individually.

Each cohesive habitat expresses itself through its own special niche composition—its unique voice. Think of moving from one biophonic territory to another as moving along the path of an acoustic spectrum—from low to high frequency, from one point in time to another through space. In the case of biophonies and geophonies, the bioacoustic spectrum is completely biome-dependent—biophonies are universal only in the sense that they exist nearly everywhere natural soundscapes are experienced. Each biophony is as different in texture as our own vocal signatures.

When modern humans first appeared in the tapestry of the biosphere, they had to be quick studies, categorizing their knowledge of the acoustic environment in ways that could be useful. Our ancestors would have understood that some sounds could be a practical means for survival. To the extent that people's existence depended on a harmonious relationship with their surroundings, a dialogue with the forest became an imperative. Louis Sarno, a musical anthropologist from New Jersey who has been living with and recording the music and natural soundscapes of the Babenzélé pygmies (Ba'Aka) in the Dzanga-Sangha forest of the Central African Republic since the mid-1980s, often tells the story of how the young children of the Ba'Aka seem to know, almost instinctively, not only the practical meaning of sounds within the forest soundscape—as related to sources of food and danger—but also the social signals (spirits, inspiration for music, and even occasional linguistic expression).

Close links between humanity and the soundscape have always been an essential lens through which we understand the world. Our knowledge of biophonies and how they change over long periods of time and under a variety of climactic and seasonal circumstances enhances our modern geological, topographical, and floral distribution scope of understanding, providing details not likely to be captured in satellite imagery or topographical mapping sequences. Those of us living close to the natural world have learned the permutations of these dynamics well. It is likely that buried deep within the human limbic brain is ancient wiring that springs to life every time we reconnect with these delicate webs of acoustic finery—the multiple layers of resonance that still exist in parts of the wild.

It didn't take early humans long to find useful ways of incorporating biophonic information into hunts, ceremonies, language, and the dialoguing exchanges of music—our first organization of sound.

CHAPTER FIVE

First Notes

Each of us consumes a world of sound, but our primary sound-scape defines our environment. As a child, mine comprised the range of sound from our home and the surrounding open fields and woods. When I was around two years old, my family moved to what was then a transitional zone between urban and rural Detroit—former Midwest farmland where bird and insect sound still flourished but where the remaining landscape would be altered shortly after World War II into modest, middle-class, red-brick housing. This was an epic transformation from the vast, heavily wooded moraine shaped by the last glaciers to the compressed mass that would define much of postwar urban America.

Our unassuming home was badly insulated for weather and sound. Even with the windows shut tight, birdsong from the fields and occasional traffic from the street blended with the interior clamor of the Krause family. Because of my compromised vision—the result of astigmatism and farsightedness—sound was the sensory element that most captured my imagination and helped me find my way in the world. Despite our location at the corner of what would soon become a busy intersection, when we first moved I would listen to exotic dawn and evening choruses — birds, insects, and occasional frogs from the surrounding fields, which hadn't yet been dissected into lots for more homes like ours.

My tiny room, just large enough for a crib or a small single bed, was located on the second floor, in the back of the house above the kitchen. It was the farthest from the street, facing northwest and looking across what, to a young child, were vast open fields. During spring it was infused with daybreak and dusk songs of mourning doves, wood warblers, cardinals, chickadees, vireos, robins, starlings, pheasants, amphibians, crickets, and a variety of insects. I came to know the sounds of the nonhuman creatures of my youth very well. They were mixed with doors that would creak, click, and snap open and shut as the humans in the house rose each morning. Plumbing would spring to life from the bathroom down the hall. The sounds of clattering pots, plates, and silverware would rattle up through my floor with a reassuring timbre when my dad got up early and ate breakfast before heading off to work. Most evenings before bedtime, crowning the normal sounds that filled each day, an announcer's voice or the sound of music would rise from the old Philco radio and record player sitting in the far corner of the living room.

After everything was shut down for the night, my dad would come to my room and read stories. I especially liked the tales that evoked acoustic events — pirate yarns; legends of giants, their huge feet thundering across the landscape; ancient battles; children lost in the woods, obsessed by mysterious noises. In the end, however, it was the faithful combination of the whip-poor-will and crickets outside my window that finally lulled me to sleep.

The house itself, a fifteen-hundred-square-foot home typical of many prewar dwellings of the time, had its own voice: the walls oscillated and thudded slightly with a low-frequency shudder—felt more physically than aurally—when it was windy and the pressure on one side of the building was different from that on the other. And as the wartime Detroit industrial population exploded, other houses filled vacant lots where we once kept a victory garden, streets were paved, birdsong disappeared, and we found ourselves surrounded by the din of ceaseless human enterprise. All of those early soundscapes are still clear in my mind—I'd recognize them instantly if I heard them again. No picture of our family, our home, or our surroundings can even begin to convey the animation of that environment as well as my memories of the sounds inside and outside that house.

Before I was five years old, my first soundscapes were replaced with music. I began to study violin and composition. Beethoven, Mozart, and Vivaldi, my favorite composers, were soon traded for a world of jazz that my parents' friends introduced me to. As that domain opened up and I began to ask questions about the nature of sound and music, my queries were mostly met with blank stares from my parents and their friends. Even my violin and composition teachers knew little beyond the notes on the page, the accepted range of their principal instruments, and the literature they had been exposed to. The instrumental choices my parents imagined for me—violin and piano—were as conventional as their future academic and professional visions, which centered on either law or medicine. They would never understand or quite accept why I chose the path I ultimately settled on.

As a teenager, I switched to guitar and became fluent in all styles. My choice to leave the violin behind was met by expressions of dismay and a historic number of pursed lips. From that moment on, my parents never looked forward. I never looked back. When I applied to the schools of music at Eastman, Juilliard, and the University of Michigan in 1955, I was essentially rejected on the grounds that the guitar was not a musical instrument.

A couple of years after graduation from college, while I was working as a professional studio guitarist, the folk music quartet the Weavers invited me to audition for the venerated Pete Seeger tenor slot. I was one of many artists who sent in performance tapes and risked a live audition. To my great surprise, I made the final cut and debuted with the group at their historic 1963 Carnegie Hall reunion concert, where—with Pete, Ronnie Gilbert, and Fred Hellerman—we introduced "Guantanamera" to the American public.

Around the time of the Weavers' split in early 1964, musicians began experimenting with modular synthesizers such as the Buchla and the Moog. From the moment I first heard one, I knew that that was the kind of innovation I wanted to learn about and use. That's when I moved to California and began to work with Paul Beaver. Through the questions that arose during our L.A. synthesizer workshops, we constantly challenged old assumptions and definitions of music.

By the time Paul and I wrote and recorded *The Nonesuch Guide to Electronic Music* in 1967—an introduction to analog synthesis and performance—we also felt compelled to address the ways in which the synthesizer shed new light on long-held ideas about sound and music. Foremost on our minds was a basic question: What is music? Definitions of music vary widely from culture to culture, within given societies, and even from person to person.

With the advent of sound synthesis, Paul and I thought we could reduce complicated definitions of music to a single fundamental equation, like $E = mc^2$, by asserting that music, in the human realm, is simply nonlinguistic and conscious *control of sound.*

There were many reasons we arrived at this controversial explanation. For one, it seemed to fit all societies that venerate music and musicians, since a performer must—in order to create music as we know it—at the very least decide on which sound sources to control and how loud and long each sound in the sequence will be heard and expressed. In the end, it turned out that our definition was missing at least two other important factors: structure and intent.

As I became familiar with music of all types, I realized that fundamental to each form are vertical patterns—that is, instrumental texture and layering—and horizontal, or time, patterns. A particular combination of vertical and horizontal patterns gives each musical form a unique definition. A modern Greek band, for instance, might consist of a bouzouki (a three-stringed lutelike instrument), a toumbeleki (a small metal drum), a regular Western guitar, a defi (a tambourine-like percussion instrument), a violin (Western style), and perhaps a tambouras (the ancestor of the toumbeleki but with up to six strings). Central to the structure of the sound are stringed and percussion instruments, along with lead and occasional backup vocals.

A Balinese gamelan orchestra, on the other hand, stresses the sound structure of metallophones, xylophones, gongs, flutes, and the human voice. The Greek vertical structure is based primarily on Western twelve-tone musical tuning, while the gamelan orchestra tunings feature either five or seven notes to an octave. The plucked and bowed string textures of the Greek band will sound very different from the hammered metallic fabric of the Indonesian ensemble.

Horizontally, the structures of many Greek folk songs are

propelled along with lively tempi and ⁵⁄₄ and ⁷⁄₈ time signatures. Gamelan music, alternatively, consists of several basic rhythmic styles of interlocking beats that unfold in hypnotic patterns throughout each piece. When these two structures are compared to American country music, with bands typically made up of guitar, bass, mandolin, fiddle, five-string banjo, a drum set, lead vocals, and tight backup harmony, vertical and horizontal organization becomes quite clear. Structures of these types are inherent in and seminal to all musical forms and have been one of the defining variables of every sonic performance humans have engaged in.

Intent is the easy part. How many of us have ever picked up or sat down at an instrument without intending to generate some kind of sound—especially when we discover that the object of our momentary curiosity produces one? When a two-year-old child sits on her parent's lap at a piano keyboard and strikes those first notes with her fist, she realizes that she's created something engaging and immediately becomes fascinated with trying to produce a similar result by doing the same thing again. Then she'll strike a higher or lower fistful of notes on the keyboard. Soon enough, if she's encouraged in the right way, this young Björk will find a melodic or textural line she particularly likes and adopt her own filters through which to project her own special voice.

While switching from electronic music to recording natural sound, I found my curiosity evolve from questions about the elements of music to questions about its origins. Each question drew me farther down the rabbit hole of musical mysteries. Where does our urge to make music come from? What might be the connection between biophony and human music? Does the emotional content of animal vocalizations shed any light on the fact that music is a primary means through which humans express emotion? When studying animal voices, I realized that not acknowledging the context in which animals vocalize—the biophony—caused us to miss a crucial part of the big picture. Could the same be true for music? When seeking explanations for the structure and intent in our music, have we been ignoring the context in which humans first began to control sound? How did the sonic structure inherent in biophony impact human expression to take the form of music? Did murmurs from the wild that suggest rhythm, melody, polyphony, and design serve as the organizational basis of musical expression? My fascination with these questions has animated much of my life to this day.

With the advent of the ecological consciousness that has sprung up in the last half century, only occasional attention has been paid to natural sound. But in response to the primary focus on recording, archiving, and studying the voices of individual, out-of-context creatures, a more holistic sense of the biophonic world is finally beginning to flourish. Studies of natural sound and its connection to human expression in the form of music, however, have been even slower to materialize. The great preponderance of research, articles, and books on the subject are still primarily anthropocentric and solipsistic, essentially stating that music springs from us alone or that we are the ultimate judges of what is musical in the world. Perhaps we are. But we're starting to see research that suggests a wider field of influence.

At a Google-O'Reilly Science Foo conference held in Mountain View, California, in 2008, Aniruddh Patel and a few of his colleagues showed a video of a cockatoo, its head and body weaving and bobbing, its feet shuffling from side to side in pretty close sync to the beat of a pulsating sound track. When the tempo shifted, so did the response of the bird, suggesting that non-human animals respond to rhythm (ours, of course). And many articles — including one in *Wired* — have focused on the seemingly innate rhythm of newborns, learned at the embryo stage from the heartbeat of the mother and from music detected outside the womb. Almost nothing has been said about the non-human rhythms of crickets or chorusing frogs, or ocean waves, or dripping water after rain, but one researcher, Björn Merker, along with some colleagues, has tentatively crossed the line to factor in other species, some closely related to humans, when considering the "evenly paced" group synchrony model (i.e., tapping or dancing to the same beat). While he concludes that the actual mechanisms of the behavior are poorly understood, there is some evidence to infer that at least synchronous rhythm structures in humans may have evolved from other species.

Nils Wallin, a Swedish scientist, coined the term *biomusicology* in 1991. Around that time, researchers were beginning to dig deeper into our past, searching for the links between acoustic configurations that occur in the natural world and the evolution of human music. Reflecting on the possibilities, Wallin speculated that "our forebears might have been singing hominids before they became talking humans.... If so, that... would have some bearing on the way we approach the question of the origins of music."

Of course, there are no hominid species other than Homo sapiens that exist in the present. But for clues about music's origins, we can look to our cousins, the primates, as well as to other mammals. When I was in Rwanda recording mountain gorillas and their habitat, for hours I'd listen to them "sing" and watch their behavior. The gorillas expressed all kinds of emotions with sound. They would exchange greetings by a kind of soft, two-grunt clearing of the throat. Basically this meant that all was OK—a signal that all were feeling emotionally secure for the moment. If you articulated the sound just right, your presence would likely be accepted by the habituated groups. Females, particularly when grooming, often "sang" with an unself-conscious humming of short phrases—a sweet, easy series of random-sounding notes. These classes of vocalizations have been dubbed "singing" by field observers because they sound very much like human females absentmindedly humming to themselves.

The whole scene would change when young-adult males, awash with testosterone, would look for a receptive female to practice with. Silverbacks, the dominant males, never take kindly to that behavior. Always focused on passing on their DNA to future generations, they respond with an enraged series of loud screams, chest beats, and full-body charges that no sentient being in his right mind would dare challenge. These vocalizations are not songs but dominance signals and warnings that are bursting with emotion. The aggressive screams that come from a pissed-off gorilla are the loudest mammalian utterances I have ever heard on land. If you happen to be nearby when a silverback lets loose, you might be deaf for a while. Those alpha warning screams carry emotional content that you can only hope is not directed at you. I've also watched female chimps and gorillas whose babies have died; they carry the bodies around for days. Whimpering and crying sadly to themselves, they sit apart from their family groups, inconsolable.

We primates are well-known for our affinity to song. Researchers have characterized the vocalizations not only of mountain gorillas but of chimps, lemurs, lorisids, and monkeys as "singing." Bonobo and gibbon "singing," loaded with messages of intense sexual desire, can be heard throughout the forests of Africa and Asia, respectively, where healthy groups still thrive. Some of their singing reminds me of the unconscious humming I've caught myself in the midst of during my early-morning runs, when I'm transfixed by the rhythm of my breathing or footsteps, completely calm and relaxed into a natural tempo.

The songs of all the primates—humans included—are likely a transformation from loud calls that defined territory and expressed alarm to intricate patterns that express social connections. Through observations in the mid-1980s, John Mitani and Peter Marler found that gibbon male songs, while rarely repeated, nevertheless follow strict rules of modulation and delivery in order to successfully attract females. But what are the elements that qualify these primate vocalizations as "songs"? Since the field of animal communication is so new and research so recent, the best we can do is consider the underlying fundamental ideas of song to arrive at answers. We define the vocalizations of male humpback whales as "songs"—sequences of acquired expression repeated over and over during each mating and calving season and in fragments during summer feeding. Sitting among wild chimps and gorillas for long periods of time, I found that the distinct modulation of their random vocalizations as they're grooming, playing, or foraging—those combinations of sound described by researchers as "singing"—generates an emotional state within the group that pacifies even a wary human. Whenever the gorillas allowed me to join them for their afternoon siestas, those vocalizations would ease me to sleep.

We can also find emotional expression in the sounds of other mammals. Killer whales live in highly social pods where syntax and "vocabulary"—that is, different kinds of whistles and screams—signal mood, food, and their relationships to pod members and other marine species. They have a special foraging sound when the pod is chasing after fish. And when attacking other marine mammals (which they occasionally do since they are carnivores), killer whales have unique aggressive vocalizations. These forceful, punctuated, and animated sequences are quite different than the normal syntactic social contact and feeding sounds that are more generally expressed between members of resident or transient pods. During August 1979, I recorded the vocalizations of three orcas attacking a humpback in Glacier Bay in a small cove (Fingers Bay) to the west of Willoughby Island. It was a unique and rare vocal exchange, never before captured on tape.

The most obvious example of orca emotion I've ever observed, however, came from a comparison of expressions between two whales that had been held in captivity at a theme park and those of the still-wild pod from which they were originally taken. While working on my doctorate, I had an opportunity to record Yaka and Nepo, two captive animals at Marine World, then located in Belmont, California, just south of San Francisco. Wanting to compare syntax and other vocalizations, I set out in the summer of 1980 to record the wild pod from which they'd been taken, which still lived in the channel between Vancouver Island and the mainland of British Columbia. While syntactic similarities existed between the captives and their wild family, the ways in which the vocalizations were expressed felt quite different. The wild animals' vocalizations were nearly always filled with energy and vitality. Quickly paced and assertive "up-screams" and "down-screams"—types of loud ascending and descending whistlelike vocalizations—were urgent and forceful. The captive vocalizations, by contrast, were palpably lethargic and slow.

Of course, there's no precise way to quantify animal feelings or our impressions of their emotions, which is why researchers tend to stay clear of the subject—a scientist cannot be caught with his or her anthropomorphic pants down. I would guess, however, that most people who have pets would immediately agree that their animals show emotion. When our cat YoYo Meow wants something such as food or to go outside, he uses a particular plaintive, high-pitched voice, the meaning of which is unmistakable. But if you stroke his fur the wrong way, the voice converts to a low growl, a warning of "If you do that again…" My wife and I are fully trained.

Truly, the saddest vocalization I've ever heard emanating from a nonhuman didn't come from a primate. It came from a beaver. A couple of years ago, a fellow recordist from the Midwest sent me an audio clip of an event that took place at one of his favorite recording and listening sites—a small remote lake in central Minnesota. While recording one spring day, he watched in stunned silence as a couple of game wardens appeared on the scene, planted some explosives, and blew up a beaver dam that had helped establish and maintain the subtle ecological balance of the habitat at the lake's outlet for years. Since there were no houses or nearby farmland to be protected, it seemed like an act of willful violence and unnecessary authority. The beaver family, its young and female, were decimated when the dam was blown apart that day. Remaining behind after the wardens left, my friend captured an altered habitat that no photo could have revealed. After dusk, the surviving and probably wounded male swam in slow circles around the pond, crying out in obvious pain for its mate and progeny. Its voice is so forlorn and heartbreaking that the recording is always emotionally difficult for me to hear. Although tail slaps and moaning sounds of beavers in and around their dens have been heard and even recorded on a few rare occasions, that's the first and only time I've heard beaver vocalizations of this type. I hope I never witness cries like those coming from a living being again. The most heartrending human music I've ever heard doesn't come close.

My experience in the wild has yielded countless examples of emotional expression in many mammals — sounds that thus have become part of the fabric of biophonic structure. In fact, sound is one of the principal ways in which animals show emotion. Humans, too, with our voices and with music.

In *The Descent of Man,* Charles Darwin imagined the evolutionary connection between human music and emotion. That some of the meaning of music is sexual, as Darwin suggested, became clear to me the minute I switched from violin to guitar as a teenager. But music also has meaning in times of war, when seeking relief from stress, in spiritual settings, in communal contact and identification, and when expressing a wide range of emotion, from joy to sorrow. Often I don't need to understand a single word of a person's native language to know how they feel. They can just hum a melody or even utter a series of nonverbal sounds, and I'll know more about their mood than any words could express. It doesn't matter if the person comes from remote groups living on the North Slope of Alaska or in the rain forests of Papua New Guinea.

Does this mean that for humans the urge to make music is innate? Debates on the evolutionary basis of music are notoriously heated. Darwin seemed to think that music was an evolutionary adaptation, but not all contemporary scientists are so sure. The MIT cognitive scientist Steven Pinker famously dismissed the idea by calling music "auditory cheesecake." We like cheesecake because we evolved a taste for fats and sugars, the components of cheesecake — we didn't evolve a desire for cheesecake itself. We like music, the argument goes, because we evolved a liking for some of the components of music, which presumably have functions related to language. Music itself, however, is not an adaptation. "Music is useless," he wrote in *The Language Instinct* in 1994.

But in the 2006 book *The Singing Neanderthals: The Origins of Music, Language, Mind, and Body,* the archaeologist Steven Mithen elaborates on the possible evolutionary origins of music by suggesting that language was preceded by something neither specifically linguistic nor musical but an amalgam he termed "Hmmmm": Holistic, multimodal, manipulative, musical, and mimetic. Another researcher, Christopher Small, devised an even better term, *musicking,* by which he meant "to music." He asserts that singing, humming a tune, tapping one's feet to a rhythm, playing an instrument, performing in an orchestra, and composing music all reflect a single activity that can be captured with the verb *to musick.*

In a review of Mithen's book, William Benzon, a cognitive scientist and musician, walks us through his own discoveries and hypotheses on the origins of music. His explanation begins with rhythm, specifically that of walking, where the coordination of biped muscles is central to balance and pacing. Drawing from rhythm, members of modern human groups would synchronize their pacing, clapping, shuffling, walking, or leaping in coordination with one another, a kind of musicking that resulted in the uniting of individual personalities and in their merging harmoniously with the group—a cooperation with reciprocal benefits. I would guess that most of us have experienced this synchronization to music at some point in our lives—such as when we dance or tap our feet to a particular rhythm.

When I was in my early teens, I experienced a moment that could have occurred at any time in human history. It was summer in the early 1950s, and my parents unloaded me at a camp located in the middle of Algonquin Park, Ontario. The usual eight weeks of summer activities—baseball, swimming, tennis, and team competitions—temporarily distracted most of the inmates in our coed enclave (those not otherwise struck by the onslaught of coming-of-age stirrings, that is). Yet ten days that summer stand out above all. Twelve of us—a Native guide, two counselors, and nine anxious, citified, testosterone-driven teenage male campers— took a twenty-mile canoe trip a few days' paddle away from our base. To get to our destination—a remote lake—we traversed many wilderness waterways and endured long portages through swarms of leeches, mosquitoes, and the nasty biting black flies of the Canadian boreal forest, with our mighty ninety-pound, cedar-ribbed, canvas-covered Chestnut canoes and all our gear.

Within a few hours on the water, we learned to temper our egos and to work together as a group—imperative if people are to survive in anything like the wild. Every now and then, when we got tired, our counselors urged us into song, the tempo of which set the pace for our collective paddling. Together, we slogged on. With cupped hands, we drank water so pure and sweet from the lakes and streams that even we noticed the contrast in taste between this natural liquid and what we had known in the cities and suburbs, where most of us lived. The water was clear enough that we could spot huge lake trout swimming ten or fifteen feet below the surface. To supplement our basic supplies, we caught fish and cooked and ate them as we traveled—often snagging those that we saw lurking in deep pools as we leaned over the gunwales of our canoes. Guided only by a few paper topographical maps, the sun, the stars, and the moss that grew on the north side of trees, we managed to navigate quite safely to each night's campsite.

I clearly remember the complete sense of tranquillity. Even my peers managed to button it up for long periods of time out of fear of breaking the natural hush, or out of newfound reverence, or both. In more than a week on the water, we never heard a plane, motorboat, car, chain saw, or radio. We never saw another person outside our immediate group. Sometimes we felt lost and not lost—right at the level of tension that makes one feel alive and alert.

At night, camping along the shorelines, we'd build a fire and burn pine boughs to keep away the incessant mosquitoes and flies. Otherwise we were surrounded by real darkness broken only by the brilliance of the night sky. The counselors would break into loud song when they were anxious, beckoning us to join in. We needed to make our human presence known to the lingering animal spirits that we vividly conjured up in our minds.

Group singing is particularly reassuring during those moments when everyone joins in and lends power to the chorus. Mithen, who believes that music is deeply rooted in human evolutionary history, explains that it enables social bonding and the communication necessary to signal the direction of existing game, the organization of a hunt, a coming-of-age ritual, sexual attraction, and just plain expressions of joy or sadness.

I think that we can look at music as an acoustic mirror—it reflects our culture and our surroundings at any point in time. If Mithen and others are right in claiming that our urge to make music is innate—that humans may have even been making music before they were using language—we can look to the context in which we evolved for clues about music's origins.

Of course, we are now far removed from our origins—that is,

our acoustic environments have radically changed—and our musical forms elegantly reflect this break from our past. Starting in the 1950s, for example, a few avant-garde composers—including John Cage, Vladimir Ussachevsky, and Otto Luening—picked up on philosophical vestiges of the Italian futurists and utilized the combined sounds of urban environments to create experimental sonic works. When taken out of their original milieus and placed in new ones, fragments of noise became structural components of composition.

Later, Pauline Oliveros, Morton Subotnick, and many others experimented with the textures of human-generated sound. For *In a Wild Sanctuary,* Paul and I included fragments of San Francisco urban noise—the rhythmic clicks of cable cars' underground towropes as they pass over the control guides beneath the street, for example. We also used the Doppler shift of buses as they rounded corners downtown, and we incorporated the sounds of war.

A number of other composers recognized the aesthetic value of selective "noise," among them the Beatles and Frank Zappa. The orchestral structure of *Sgt. Pepper's Lonely Hearts Club Band* could not have been accomplished without the consummate musical knowledge of the Beatles' producer, George Martin. Under the pseudonym Ray Cathode, Martin had experimented with audiotape and electronic manipulation as early as the early 1960s as part of the U.K. music scene and the BBC's Radiophonic Workshop, which produced, among other projects, sound effects for radio. Through this work, he honed techniques that were a perfect sonic fit for the Beatles. Martin brought with him a sensibility to the emerging electronic soundscape, something that the four members of the band hadn't previously experienced, resulting in the timeless sonic textures heard throughout the album. Zappa generated a masterly combination of sounds on the album *Freak Out,* directly countering the music of the "flower generation" with a driving mix of urban sound, political and social commentary, and pop and psychedelic arrangements.

While technically interesting and notable — the carefully chosen sound fragments were transformed into "music" by laborious editing, tape manipulation, and filtering — these experiments achieved only limited cultural acceptance at the time, except for the Beatles' effort, of course. Far more compelling and immediately responsive to our urban environments have been hard-rock and heavy-metal artists such as Jimi Hendrix, Led Zeppelin, the Who, AC/DC, and Black Sabbath, and later groups such as the Art of Noise — also the musical styles of punk, industrial, rap, and hip-hop. As Joel Selvin, bestselling rock-and-roll history author and former music critic for the *San Francisco Chronicle,* told me, "The elements of noise [from those groups] were an important undercurrent in certain styles of hard rock or heavy metal. Musicians drew consciously and unconsciously from the audio clutter of modern urban life — from automobile traffic to claustrophobic city dwellings, from feedback squalls to breakneck tempi, it was all fair game to be incorporated in the bombastic and often frantic music these pioneering rock musicians of the '60s and '70s made."

Unlike contemporary musicians, our early ancestors would have had only the wild natural surroundings as inspiration. We can certainly speculate about the natural soundscapes from around fifty thousand years ago, the time from which the first known bone flutes have come down to us. And in some viable habitats, where things have changed relatively little over the long arc of time — the remote parts of the Amazon, the Dzanga-Sangha (of the Central African Republic), the jungles of Papua

New Guinea, and Borneo come to mind — we can still catch an echo of the acoustic textures of our ancient past. Listening to the archive recordings I've collected from these locations over the past several decades not only takes me back to when I made them but sends me many steps beyond, delineating the sonic timelines of evolution. When these ancient voices were first expressed and our ancestors first heard them, the vocalizations were infused with acoustic textures unique to each type of organism, and every voice stood out in relationship to others.

And each had its primal place. The spectrograms of my recordings at Borneo and Kenya clearly show a well-defined acoustic anatomy marked by very discrete bioacoustic partitioning — probably much the same now as it was thousands of years ago. Looking at things in that light, we see that it's a bit like uncovering living acoustic fossils.

In fact, it is possible that we can hear ancient soundscapes even in present-day North America. Kristin Junette, at one time a Montana State University graduate student studying with dinosaur expert Jack Horner, reasoned that, based on the fossil record and the known sounds of insect species still abundant today, we might be able to partially reassemble their individual signatures to get an idea of the basic insect ambient sound as far back as the time of duck-billed dinosaurs — about sixty-five million years ago. So piece by piece, creature by vocal creature, niche by painstaking niche, we reassembled an approximation of a viable soundscape for the hadrosaur. When we got all the parts together, the soundscape turned out to be similar in acoustic structure to late-summer old-growth sites we had recorded in the Adirondack Mountains of upstate New York. Then, based on the acoustic physiology of the animal skull, we re-created a representative hadrosaur vocalization that sounded somewhat like a slowed-up recording of a great hornbill — a bird that lives in the rain forests of Sumatra and India.

Imagine being able to hear what life sounded like in Africa two hundred thousand years ago. According to a recently published study headed by Tim White — who discovered "Lucy" with his UC Berkeley colleague Donald Johanson — modern humans didn't materialize in Africa's plains; rather, it is more likely, based on fossil and isotope evaluation, that we emerged from forest habitats densely populated with all kinds of wildlife, many habitats of which still exist today, just in smaller fragmented forms. We have places where mountain gorillas, orangutans, wild cats, lemurs, birds, insects, elephants, eland, jackals, amphibians, and reptiles thrive, and that consequently may still be suggestively radiant with ancient sound, an eloquent sparkle that emanates from the wings, feet, beaks, and thoraxes of thousands of simultaneously chorusing organisms.

Other studies, like those that address the first human symbolic graphic expressions, suggest that early modern humans populated a wide range of forest, grassland, and coastal habitats throughout the entire continent of Africa. Bonded closely to the natural world, early humans would have first imitated the voices of these soundscapes.

Back then our engagement with natural sound was exactly the opposite of what most of us now experience in the wild. Travelers and hunters would have found solitude among the nonhuman animal and geophonic landscapes: the creature world of whirs, shrieks, scratches, hisses, bleats, clicks, barks, howls, moans, buzzes, and crunches; the drones and pulses of insect and frog choruses; the effects of wind exciting into action the chafing of leaves on trees or wafting through grasses; the sounds of water gurgling in tiny rivulets or rushing downstream; or the crash of waves at an ocean shore. All day, every day, they would have been enveloped in the soundscape of the surrounding environment, listening as it changed from day to night and back again, or as they moved from one location to another or through the course of the seasons.

In instrumental music, timing is everything. So it is with the natural world: The day is split up into temporal segments, from macro-time to micro-time. It begins with the entire cycle of the day and night. Within that is embedded the dawn chorus, the daytime chorus, the evening and night choruses. And within those are the spaced utterances of birds, mammals, and frogs. An even finer resolution would be the twelve or so vibrations every second of a single cricket's chirp each time the scraper is drawn across the file of the insect's wings. In the healthiest of habitats, all of these sounds coalesce in an elegant web of organized signals that are full of information about each organism's relationship to the whole. From this ensemble comes the music of nature.

Humans have a well-established aptitude for mimicry. The French psychologists Henri Wallon and Jean Piaget highlighted the role of imitation in early human ontogeny and partially characterized the human species by this ability. Piaget suggested that we begin to mimic because we want to make ourselves understood, to make our presence known to others. It would have been natural for us to seamlessly integrate these protomusical voices into our lives, which were maturely in balance with the rest of existence around us.

Emerging from the Pleistocene, wherever we found ourselves, we would have been encircled by wild habitats filled with the radiance and sensuality of natural sound tracks: Seasonal bird and mammal voices joined with the throbbing rhythms of insects in ancient forests. We listened intently as wind, storms, and water added their own special dynamics to the sonic mix. As a means of protective cover and an atavistic desire for connection, we watched and listened closely as birds sang; insects divided time with regular beats; primates swung through the canopies, intermittently drumming rapid staccato chest "pops" with cupped fists; and frogs chorused their individual and collective ways through the sweep of each passing day. The lyricism of these voices conveyed crucial information about the events transpiring in the habitat, reflecting a range of communal sensations whose significance would have been felt, in turn, by every living organism.

Humans would have first heard sounds to imitate within the sumptuous tapestry of biophonies. Our imagination and our innate need to hear relationships between sounds would have been first stimulated by the voices of the tropical and temperate forests, deserts, high plains, tundra, and coastal regions, where we camped, hunted, and listened. As I stated in the previous chapter, when a biophony is intact, the distinction between critter voices is clearly expressed. It is a communion of sources in which these acoustic slots have taken time to evolve—perhaps millennia. Through mimicry, we would have transformed the rhythms of sound and motion in the natural world into music and dance— our songs emulating the piping, percussion, trumpeting, polyphony, and complex rhythmic output of the animals in the places we lived.

But how would we have joined the "orchestra"? Our ancestors' method-oriented minds would have perceived this elaborate interactive process in which animal voice found an open channel, or time to perform. This would have served as a template from which to arrange our own sounds—made with our voices and early instruments—in much the same way.

While we were carefully listening, we would have transformed what we heard into expressions that reflected immediate links to the world around us. While imitating the sounds of the natural world, we would have found that almost any object will produce a sound: a pair of hands coming together or striking our bodies in different ways (à la Bobby McFerrin), or banging together different lengths and types of stone, wood, and bone, or beating on skins stretched over a hollowed-out log or an animal shell.

It is easy to imagine how, in addition to using early percussion instruments to reproduce what we heard, we would have blown air through the hollow of wood or bone tubes to produce a broad range of resonances. A bone flute found in a cave in Germany and fabricated from the wing bone of a vulture dates back nearly forty thousand years. Yet the five holes carved in the length of the tube generate a crude pentatonic sequence of notes, and the V-shaped notch at one end presumably allowed the musician to create various tones and textures.

The pentatonic scale itself comes directly from the wild, reflecting not only the rich biophonies of the forest but also certain animal soloists such as the common potoo and the musician wren, shown here in Figures 8 and 9. The scale is a noticeable feature of traditional music associated with soundscapes — a five-note musical series generally consisting of the first, second, third, fifth, and sixth notes of a Western major scale. (For a common pentatonic phrase in Western music, think of the opening bars of "Oh! Susanna" or "Amazing Grace.") The Ayahuasca songs of the Peruvian Amazon, for example, take up the pentatonic polyphonic drones and melodies found throughout forests of the world, which have also made their way into traditional music of Africa and New Guinea, as well as that of the Nùng An in Vietnam; the Sena songs of Nagaland, India; and the Peuls Bororo of Niger.

COMMON POTOO

Figure 8.

MUSICIAN WREN

Figure 9.

But the common potoo, widespread throughout tropical Meso- and South America, was playing it first, bending the sixth note of the scale slightly sharp in its song, giving it a bluesy feel. (Here the musical notation is transposed up a half step to the key of C major.) The timbre of the potoo voice sounds like an ocarina, an instrument that was in use among the Aztecs when the Cortés expedition discovered it in the early sixteenth century and introduced it to Europe (and which is now one of the iPhone's most popular apps).

The musician wren's whistlelike voice sounds like it is made up of pitched white noise. (Here, the notation of its song fragment is transposed down a major third to the key of F major.) It repeats the same sequence of notes over and over, sometimes with slight variations. When interrupted by the call of a loud parrot or other bird, the wren will abruptly stop midphrase and wait for the intruder to finish before picking up the musical line exactly where he left off.

Both sequences are easy to replicate and would be recognized as musical phrases across many cultural lines. And both species will adjust the note sequence if, for some reason, one or another is not victorious in attracting mates. Each bird is controlling a series of notes, can adjust its song if it's not deemed successful (some common potoos don't sing the blues, for example), and chooses the number of times the sequence is expressed. Each structure is unique to that species, and we can recognize several levels of intent: there are the drives to impress a potential mate and to claim turf, and, of course, there is the need to be heard within the context of the local bio-orchestra.

The idea that human music has its roots in the soundscapes of the natural world has had a renaissance since the 1980s. One compelling link was rediscovered within the cultural expressions of the aforementioned Ba'Aka — also known as Babenzélé pygmies — of the Dzanga-Sangha rain forest in the western part of the Central African Republic.

Louis Sarno, the American ethnomusicologist, arrived in the Dzanga-Sangha region just before radical changes such as stepped-up logging, poaching, increased missionary pressure, and other seductive lures drew members of the group into the cash economy. With the tribe not trusting him at first, he had to spend many months "rushing" the group's fraternity — for instance, eating bowls of live grubs given to him as one of many tests, until finally he was accepted as "Oka Amerikee," loosely translated as the "Listening American."

When Sarno arrived in the Dzanga-Sangha, the link between the sounds of the forest and the music of the Ba'Aka seemed so strong that, he realized, without the biophony providing an obvious acoustic structure, their music would not have evolved as it did. Time and again, he witnessed his group break into performances, and the more he became familiar with both the music and the habitat, the more he recognized the mimetic connections between their music and the forest rhythms of the insects and frogs, the solo voices of birds, and the occasional mammalian punctuation—and the multiple ways the sonic structures of the human and animal often reflected one another. Sarno's many accounts reveal how he came to hear the compelling spiritual, social, and practical connections between the biophonies of the forest and the resulting Ba'Aka music; the biophony was the equivalent of a lush, natural karaoke orchestra with which they performed.

The wild sonic environment the group surrounded itself with was the voice of their existence since their arrival in the Dzanga-Sangha. It may have been a primary beacon that lured them there in the first place. Describing a performance in an unpublished manuscript, Sarno wrote:

This was *esime,* an extended rhythm sequence tacked on to the end of every song in a number of different dance forms, particularly those with drum accompaniment. What *esime* lacked in melody, it made up for in the complexity of its densely packed blocks of polyrhythm. Each woman had her own cry—a meaningless sound, a word, a rapidly uttered phrase—which she repeated in a characteristic periodicity. Each periodicity was unique. Some speeded up, broke their own beat, went retrograde. Tone hadn't lost all significance, either—in the array of cries and sudden conjunctions of two or more periodicities, intervals of minor seconds, of diminished and augmented sevenths, prevailed.... Two women elaborated on [these] constituent phrases with improvised recitatives of yodel ornamentations and fanfare formulae, in a mind-bending display of free-flowing counterpoint that would have astonished the likes of Max Reger.

The soundscapes of these Central African forests are dazzling and blissful; the magnificent sonic cross-fertilization straddles multiple species. Lowland gorillas strike rhythms on their chests that are surprising and intricate. Forest elephants forage in marshy open meadows, bellowing low, raspy growls—their sounds more felt by humans than heard—that reverberate over great distances. Black-and-white-tailed hornbills sail over the canopy, their raucous calls and the edge-tones of their beating wings subtly changing pitch as they find airborne purchase and pass in high arcs overhead. Goliath beetles hum and buzz. Red colobus and putty-nosed monkeys shout sforzando alarm calls to members of their groups. Hammerkops, ibis, and parrots pierce the air with their screams and calls. A wide variety of insects and frogs add a constant hum-and-buzz counterpoint to the acoustic fabric.

One only needs to listen to Sarno's lustrous recordings to hear the deep connection. Described by him as "one of the hidden glories of humanity," Ba'Aka music emphasizes full, rich voices and bright-sounding harmonies. The sonorous textures, intricate rhythms, and consonance and dissonance flow from and are influenced by their native biophonies.

Of course, we'll never be able to hear the music of early humans—but as I learned for the first time at the sacred Nez Percé site at Oregon's Lake Wallowa, geophony as well as biophony served as early sources of musical inspiration. We can see this influence in the Sami people, quasi-nomadic reindeer herders from the northern reaches of western Russia, Sweden, Norway, and Finland, where wind — that ever-elusive element that is heard only through its effects — whips across the land. Descendants of the first Homo sapiens to settle in Europe — and the only indigenous group officially recognized by the European Union — the Sami create a type of music called *yoik,* an ancient kind of throat singing that is perhaps the oldest folk-music tradition in Europe. *Yoik* is shaped, in part, to convey a sense of place through the composition of its sounds. Along with the Sami, Tuvan throat singers from Central Asia and some Inuit groups who live in the Northwest Territories of Canada emulate in their music the constant wind that roars across the open plains and tundra, the strongest natural acoustic presence of their environments. By subtle manipulation of sound's resonance as it comes from their throats, the singers can generate multiple harmonics that leave the impression of many voices simultaneously coming from one source.

For the Yanomami, the rhythms and melodies of rain striking vegetation and the surface of puddles are strong features of their traditional music, as they are for other groups living in tropical rain forests — including the Jivaro. A tribe once completely isolated in the tropical Brazilian mountains and rain forests, the Yanomami use rainsticks to incorporate their acoustic environment in their ceremonies and music. Their soundscapes include the sound that the thickest leaves in the forest canopy make as they strike one another in uncoordinated contact, oscillating in breezes that precede afternoon thunderstorms. As I mentioned previously, the forceful torrent of rain at the leading edge of rainforest squalls sounds incredibly loud — it comes on so fast that there is no way to avoid it. The sensation is one of anticipation, which is translated into music as dynamic expression contrasted with quiet passages. When the rain passes and the downpour eases off in the distance, the forest soundscape returns in a slow, transitioned cross-fade with the added feeling of reverberation, which was not as present before the storm. In the wet forest every voice echoes with extended life and energy.

At times like these, the Ba'Aka women will scatter throughout the dense Dzanga-Sangha to gather seeds and fruit, and to sing in bursts of sound, picking up on the bird and insect voices that have returned since the storm moved on. The women's singing reverberates for nearly ten seconds throughout the forest before fading out, leaving the dreamlike impression that their voices go on forever.

Of course, the Ba'Aka are a living culture, and their music remains fluid—especially when outside influences encroach on tradition. Contemporary impacts on Ba'Aka music come primarily from two sources: contact with recorded and broadcast media, and missionaries. Over the last few years, their music has begun to shift, reflecting influences of more restricted modern harmonies and rhythm. Now, with the Ba'Aka's neocolonial contact with the cash economies of China, France, Belgium, Germany, and other countries—where many forms of resource extraction are endemic—the older, more restorative societal structures are quickly breaking down, and the fragile connections that once bound the Ba'Aka emotionally and practically to their roots has been corrupted. Because they rely more and more on the economic models of civilization, members of the Ba'Aka have been forced into prostitution, poaching, the black-market distribution of drugs and cigarettes, and trafficking in rare animal parts. Contact has also introduced diseases that have proven to be particularly virulent given the group's low resistance.

In general, missionaries are fairly selective when it comes to the souls they wish to save. Because there is nothing of great monetary value to be gotten from the Ba'Aka—no exotic skins, medicinal plants, minerals, or gemstones—and access to their remote forests is difficult, evangelists, until the recent discovery of rain-forest hardwoods, have been slow to reach out to them with any fervor. But they have had some presence in Ba'Aka communities for decades, and within the past half century several denominations declared that the music and dance of the Ba'Aka weren't spiritual enough for the sensitive ears of the Trinity. Their "primitive" music was discouraged on the grounds that, by performing it, the confused converted would never be able to enjoy the benefits of eternal salvation. Finding only minimal comfort in modern spiritual certitude and the faux excitement generated by electronically produced music, the Ba'Aka are now in the midst of a struggle to temper the seductive influences of contemporary media in favor of their ancient links with the living world.

Unlike the Ba'Aka's music, Western song hasn't been inspired by the biophony for thousands of years. Rather, like many of our art forms, our music is self-referential—we continuously draw on what has already been done, traversing a never-ending closed loop that turns in on itself like a snake devouring its own tail. We have thrown everything at the medium—electronics, mathematically structured scales and composition, logic, emotion, religious constraints, combinations of instruments, indiscriminate source materials (such as sound samples of birds, mammals, vacuums, cannons, city ambience, and banging trash cans)—and yet true holistic connections to the soundscapes of the wild have hardly been tapped as sources of inspiration.

CHAPTER SIX

Different Croaks for Different Folks

Although the Muir Woods recordings were primitive in quality, Paul Beaver and I were staggered by how forceful the raw material was, just hearing it on its own. We often found ourselves in the studio, listening to the soundscapes not so much for inspiration or as a respite from our labors but for the experience of being mesmerized for long periods absorbing the ambient material, playing it over and over, conjuring images of what the sounds might visually represent. Even Paul, who had little affinity to the natural world, would sit alone in the studio quietly assimilating the tracks. I now realize that we were rediscovering by accident a part of the living world that our culture had by and large forsaken.

During the process of composing *In a Wild Sanctuary,* Paul and I were immediately faced with a dilemma. How would we integrate natural sound into musical structure, when we were so uncertain about the idea of natural sound as music? We had no clue at the time that it, too, might have structure, and we were both new to the concept of integrating a wholly foreign audio component into more familiar forms; we spent many hours experimenting with textures, relative levels, and musical timbres and rhythms before we determined that natural sound and music, as we had come to understand them, were at least aesthetically compatible.

I find it ironic that I am writing a book about something that our ancestors knew intuitively — something that would have been a fundamental part of the fabric of their lives and that needed no explanation. Early humans would have had an intimate relationship with their soundscapes; they would have learned to "read" the biophony for essential information. Their music would have been an intricate, multilayered transformation of the sounds they were immersed in — the local creature life as a collective, as well as the sounds of the landscape.

Our music always reflects our influences — our background, education, culture, and links to the environment in which we surround ourselves. Yet when composers of the past three centuries or so promoted their works as being connected to nature, our own idealized version of nature was reflected back to us in a narrowly closed loop. Mostly it consisted of single voices picked for how each might be incorporated in our compositions in a predetermined way — nothing but faint echoes of the wild. How did our music become so detached from nature? Is anyone making music today that reflects our deep ancestral links to the wild? And how would our music sound if we could somehow harness all the experience and technologies we possess and find a way to reconnect once again with the nonhuman creature world for one brief moment?

• • •

Our adversarial relationship with the natural world found traction at early stages of written history. Around the third millennium BCE, much of the land east of the Mediterranean was covered with vast cedar and pine forests—resources that supplied the people of the Fertile Crescent with firewood and building materials, sustaining the populations with abundant sources of food. It was a woodland so beautiful and rich that it is considered to be one of the possible inspirations for the mythological Garden of Eden mentioned in the Book of Genesis. But as human numbers grew and struggles for dominance over limited resources materialized, the area changed rapidly.

There is an early reference to the razing of the cedar forests in the Epic of Gilgamesh. As the story unfolds, Gilgamesh—a historical Mesopotamian character who ruled Uruk (now Iraq) around 2500 BCE but who has been transformed through many narratives into a demigod with superhuman powers—decided to ensure his status by constructing a huge wall, ramparts, and a temple. The problem was that the forests were thought to be a dwelling place for the Mesopotamian gods and therefore off-limits to human beings. The cedar forests were guarded by the demon Humbaba, who protected them from all comers. Not to be denied access, Gilgamesh and his army attacked Humbaba at a vulnerable moment and prevailed. "So Gilgamesh felled the trees of the forests and Enkidu cleared their roots as far as the bank of the Euphrates." (Enkidu was a companion of Gilgamesh who was supposed to symbolize a close connection to the wild natural world.) In the forest, they cut the tallest trees, built rafts, and floated the materials down the river to Uruk, where construction on the city gate and ramparts began.

While at first this activity had little impact on the forest, it did fuel the drive for further extraction by the Phoenicians—the gods had been overcome and the chain of protection broken—who used the timbers to construct their boats and cities. But the greatest impact didn't occur until a few hundred years later.

According to biblical accounts, around three thousand years ago King Solomon hired seventy thousand axmen and eighty thousand haulers and ordered the cedar forests of Lebanon cut down for the construction of the Temple in Jerusalem—the first literary instance of a massive and disastrous clear-cut that to this day has lingering consequences. A few patches of the cedars and secondary-growth pine forests that once stretched between Jerusalem and Bethlehem survived into the nineteenth century. Now, except for a small number of biological island reserves—such as the Al-Shouf Cedar Nature Reserve, which contains three small cedar groves representing a quarter of the remaining trees in the country—they are all gone.

Ecohistorians have determined that the great initial loss of the Lebanese forests may have instigated a regional biomic change, causing much of the area to be overcome by desert because the deforestation and agriculture so radically altered the water table, streams, and river systems. Wildlife lost its fragile hold in the region. While we have no idea what the old forests sounded like, with their special mix of creature life, we do know, from the selective and clear-cut logging I and many of my recording colleagues have experienced, that the disappearance of a land cover of trees means the destruction of relevant biophonies.

In the first and most often cited of several biblical creation myths in Genesis 1:28, we are mandated to conquer, fill, and subject the earth to our will, driving a wedge between humans and the wild and setting the stage for our culture's view of nature. But the proactive tide against "nature" advanced in earnest around the fourth century. After the Nicene Council, dance was judged to have overtones of sacrilege, hedonism, and paganism—things to avoid if one wanted spiritual purification. The human body itself, undulating and suggestive in many forms of dance—and considered evil in its wildest state—was deemed suspect and threatening to authority. While music and dance were still part of early Christian rituals in the first and second centuries, the eroticism and animism they suggested, particularly free from institutional constraints, were still a bit too liberating for an ascetic priesthood bent on controlling the newly converted and illiterate populations.

The Roman emperor Constantine asked his priests to put a label on what was considered the wild—the unknowable, uncertain, uncontrollable, dangerous, and untrustworthy. The word they chose was *natura*. (Note the Latin feminine ending.) "At enmity with God" (a common early Church interpretation of the word), *nature* was also referred to as the "carnal mind." Those who wished to live in harmony with the natural world were considered to be primitive, unenlightened, wicked, pagan, or all of the above. Given the Church's unparalleled influence on European culture, this suspicion and fear of the wild became a strong and persistent undercurrent of developing Western thought.

Different types of music were discouraged or banned outright, especially that which originated with early Christian groups such as the Gnostics—both they and their music were thought by the council to be too secular. Thus began a millennium of various degrees of musical suppression. In the Middle Ages, a notable peak in the intensity of these divine limitations, the Church went so far as to ban the augmented fourth interval—considered the "devil's note." (This is the interval from C-natural to F-sharp—

the opening two notes of the song "Maria" from *West Side Story,* for example.) Secular music was rebuffed, and only certain types of religious-based compositions were allowed. Savonarola's Florentine reign during the closing days of the fifteenth century was marked by the famous "bonfire of the vanities," a historic moment when particular music and musical instruments went up in flames along with other cultural artifacts such as books — and paintings by Botticelli, who got so swept up in the group hysteria that he tossed many of his own works into the inferno.

Until very recently a similar restriction was imposed on indigenous cultures such as the Ba'Aka, who, when first visited by European missionaries, were strongly dissuaded from performing their ancient music. According to Chuna McIntyre, a Yup'ik Eskimo singer and dancer, when evangelists finally made contact with his family in the southwestern region of Alaska a few years after the turn of the last century, his tribe's music was suppressed in favor of sanctioned Christian hymns. As the Native music was driven underground, it was furtively kept alive by the elders in his tribe — McIntyre secretly learned the old songs and drumming and dance routines from his grandmother. Shortly before her death in the early 1990s, he recorded them. More recently, Russian Orthodox and Moravian church leaders have been less resistant to the old religion and its songs, and the Yup'ik once again perform their Native music as part of the sustaining and open voice of the community.

Massing into protected enclaves such as perched villages and walled cities, Europeans ventured less frequently into the natural world, partly because forest resources near villages were being depleted (and were thus farther away) and becoming inaccessible. Their increasing ability to grow and store food necessitated the expansion of fortifications built to repel invasion and theft.

"Nature" took on a mantle of myth exaggerated through narratives of its perils—dangerous, child-consuming beasts and dark, foreboding forests where those who ventured too far were likely to encounter grave danger. Despite our deep psychic connection to the heart of the natural world, the idea of wildness that was central to the social fabric of our ancestral groups was repressed, characterized as embodying evil, and/or framed as irrelevant.

Even by the thirteenth century, when Thomas Aquinas formalized the notion that the soul was unique to humans, Westerners had no longer expressed much need to articulate music through the voices of animals. The divine had taken a different tack. The sacred message of Genesis was firmly in place. The view of the wild as a resource—one of wood, skins to make us warm, meat and selective flora to keep our stomachs full, metals to produce plowshares and weapons, and animal and fossil fuels to use for heating and cooking—was firmly entrenched.

Beginning around 1200 BCE (when music was first notated), instead of performing with the sounds of the natural world, we gradually began to express ourselves musically—both inside and outside our protected cities—by arranging solo or ensemble sound performances on their own merits. Even the musical instruments of early humans—the bone, stone, and reedlike artifacts discovered on forest floors and in caves—had ranges of expressiveness that reached, in some cases, far beyond their original mimetic intent, thus freeing musicians to expand their creations outside the limits of wild sound.

With its roots becoming more obscured over time, Western music in particular went through a medieval stage of internalized and somber holiness. The music favored by the clergy was performed in religious venues, where thick stone walls were designed in part to create the auditory illusion of expanded interior spaces through long reverberation. At the same time—intentional or not—the substantial partitions kept the sounds of the natural world from intruding. Sacred (and even secular) music became a diminished reflection of the wild aspects of a feral human soul. Although forest spirits had at one time been celebrated in early musical forms, these medieval tendencies toward inwardness and detachment were significant departures from the ecstasy that our bond to nature had once stirred.

From the Renaissance to the present, Western culture has ardently drawn its understanding of the world from the growing influence of science. Examples of such influence can be found in the work of Renaissance painters such as Giotto, da Vinci, Raphael, and Brueghel, who inserted idyllically sanitized scenes in their nature images, exacerbating the notion that humans can improve on what is inherently chaotic. This same vision inspired the reactive designs of well-crafted parks such as the Tuileries (Paris), Hyde Park (London), Central Park (New York), and the gardens at Versailles—each one marketed as a rational improvement on the wild Eden.

At about the same time that scientists of the eighteenth century began accumulating and studying animals, collecting them in large numbers from their wild habitats, curing the skins in arsenic and storing them in museum drawers, the father of taxonomy, Linnaeus, devised a way of categorizing every organism. While immensely helpful to organizing the specific details of our environment, taxonomy intensified the trend toward imposing our own sense of order on the natural world. *Nature,* for us, became a contradictory and fragmented collection of single parts in which even the word itself was a symbol of division.

John Muir—a hero among many—embodies a paradox that has become a hallmark of how we think about nature: that the wild should be preserved, yet improved upon. Before the turn of the last century, Muir strongly advocated expelling the Ahwahneechee Paiutes and the Southern Sierra Miwoks from their ancient home. His target: Native American groups that had lived in and around the Yosemite Valley for centuries in a relatively successful strategic balance with the natural world. While the tribes had had some impact on the land with controlled burns, limited agriculture, and hunting, nothing compared with the impact of their Muir-sponsored removal: the ecological balance of the previously intact site was altered forever. Muir felt that sharing space with what he called the "diggers" inhibited his enjoyment of the landscape and interfered with his shepherding tasks. He considered the Miwoks to be "dirty" and "fallen" and therefore not worthy of the stewardship they and the Paiutes — who had a hostile relationship with the Miwoks — had learned. By eliminating these "unsightly" Native residents, the well-heeled, educated members of Muir's newly formed Sierra Club could supposedly improve upon Yosemite's management. Meanwhile, Muir wrote lovely paeans to the sound of wind blowing through the High Sierra conifers, signaling a sense of place he thought only he could understand. As time passed he came to reconsider his judgment. But by then it was too late.

Musical invention reflects modern views of ourselves and our increasing dissociation from the wild. Paralleling trends in science and the visual arts, composers, too, beginning in the mid-eighteenth century, began to echo the deconstructive inclinations that had become common in the rational philosophic and scientific communities. Tied only to a vague idealized notion of wildness, many composers drew on the voices of celebrity or signature animals, or on geological and weather events, to animate their music. Claiming "nature" as an inspiration, they, too, deconstructed the environmental whole and then reconstituted a selection of acoustic elements into a culturally resonant expression, assigning special meaning to a few particular organisms or events.

For example, Mozart wrote music lionizing his pet starling. The Sixth Symphony (the *Pastoral*) by Beethoven incorporates the voices of a cuckoo and quail, while *Cantus Arcticus* by the Finnish composer Einojuhani Rautavaara features recordings of common cranes. Heitor Villa-Lobos, from Brazil, wrote a piece called *Uirapurú,* highlighting the musician wren mentioned in the previous chapter. Vivaldi voiced the seasons. Debussy romanticized the sea. Olivier Messiaen's music echoed the songs of birds he noted as "musical" while hiking in the French countryside with his wife, Yvonne. Messiaen didn't limit his work with birds to just one or two compositions. He considered himself equally an ornithologist — aside from his many stunning pieces that assumed a range of different forms, he also took the songs and calls of ospreys, flycatchers, warblers, thrushes, and skylarks and transformed them into a number of musical strophes, highlighted in works such as *Chronochromie, Des Canyons aux étoiles…, Réveil des oiseaux,* and *Oiseaux exotiques.* Americans such as George Crumb and Alan Hovhaness wrote celebrations of whales, and Paul Winter jammed along with timber wolves in *Common Ground,* dedicating much of his musical repertoire and performing life to tributes of the natural world.

Although I enjoy a great acoustic venue enlivened with a world-class orchestra and a talented conductor, I find that, however respectful, brilliant, and conscientious the performance pieces may have been, in reality few of the musical works that claim nature as an inspiration speak to the essence of any natural environment I know. By featuring signature creatures selected from outside their rightful acoustic settings—animals whose voices just happen to fit the musical paradigms that composers are comfortable with—our compositions demonstrate a creative myopia: they present "nature" in terms of what the artist thinks it ought to sound like. We assess that which is deemed "musical" in our world and reject that which is not. We critically filter out "extraneous" sounds in favor of a preferred musical palette.

Marcel Proust understood the problem when he wrote in *Swann's Way:* "Perhaps the immobility of the things that surround us is forced upon them by our conviction that they are themselves and not anything else, by the immobility of our conception of them." For me, our attempts at nature-related music evoke an intense longing for the more layered and richly textured voices that emanate directly from the wild. Either way, these music-from-"nature" performances forcefully express the cultural limits of our nexus to the natural world. Luc Ferry, the French ecophilosopher, put it more succinctly when he observed in *The New Ecological Order:* "Nature is beautiful when it imitates art."

When I was an undergraduate in college, I took a music survey course from the eminent musicologist H. Wiley Hitchcock. As part of his program, he introduced the class to the work of a British ethnomusicologist, Colin Turnbull, who in the 1950s had gone to the Congo to record the music of the Mbuti pygmies of Zaire. Hitchcock played a few recordings of the tribe's music—waves upon waves of hypnotic repetition, intricate rhythm patterns, melodies and polyphonies colliding and separating from one another effortlessly, subtle dynamics adding excitement to the performances. At the end of the three scratchy field recordings, the professor let a moment of silence go by as the class absorbed what it had just heard. The discomfort of many students in the room was palpable. They were eager to move on to the American folk music promised in the next round of subjects. (*Folk music* in the late 1950s was becoming a popular idiom.)

Still, Hitchcock held us there in the past, as if unsure where to take his point, anxiously shifting his weight from foot to foot as he considered what to say next. Then, using the descriptive vernacular of the moment to put the pygmy music in perspective, he began to assess what we had just heard first as "primitive," and second as not terribly relevant given how advanced music of the West had become. He had made his point—one that resounded throughout much of the academic and popular music world of the time. There was a general pattern here: what had been de rigueur for these hunter-gatherers over the course of thousands of years took Westerners only a brief instant to dismiss.

Despite Hitchcock's hesitation, the recorded samples he played were so unusual and rich that I never forgot that winter afternoon in the lecture hall. As it turns out, the "primitives" my university professors spoke of had a lexicon of musical expression far more intricate, dramatic, and dynamic than anything I had heard materializing from our most advanced institutions. For one thing, the musical examples came from groups that were clearly more aural than visual. And for another, their music was evocative of creatures they heard all their lives but may have never seen, such as tiny insects, frogs, birds high in the canopy, or nighttime creatures. I might add that the music of the Mbuti pygmies is filled with expressions much closer to our heart and soul—a celebration of life—than most of what I had heard coming from schools of sound-art production using the most innovative technologies and literary rationale.

After his lectures on folk music, Hitchcock introduced the

class to Charles Ives, a composer he would study and write about for the rest of his life. The professor, however, failed to make an important association that was so central to Ives's compositions.

Almost a century ago, Charles Ives, a Connecticut insurance salesman who decided to quit talking and begin listening, wrote his Fourth Symphony. Finished shortly before the end of World War I, this transcendent twentieth-century work did not get its first full performance until 1965. Still, as a reflection of music's wild origins, it is arguably one of the major contributions to American (and possibly Western) musical literature of the last hundred years. Ives, one of the few deep listeners of his time, managed to synthesize familiar landscape acoustics and weave them into a tapestry that embodies competition, cooperation, tension, polyphony, polyrhythms, release, consonance, dissonance, microtones, instrumental and human voices, and themes spatially converging and separating—just as sonic events occur within the borders of the wild. (The third movement of Ives's Fourth Symphony is one of my all-time favorite pieces of twentieth-century music.) More remarkable, the work intensely reflects spontaneous aspects of the interior human psyche as contrasted with the natural world—expressions of great energy and softness, deep emotion, surprise, uncertain resolution, and an immediate temporal presence.

Composing in the late period of the industrial revolution, Ives was still able to capture the beauty and depth of human wildness—the elements that reside deep within all of us. My guess is that when musicians and conductors first read the score, they were mystified by the power that this extraordinary work unleashed and the ideas that it expressed. The double-sharp and -flat notes on the page were so far removed from the common Eurocentric musical literature of the time that at first read-through by the orchestra members, the music could not be clearly interpreted, particularly the strings. Leopold Stokowski's 1965 recording of the piece's premier performance (by the American Symphony Orchestra and Schola Cantorum chorus of New York) shows how constrained and unfamiliar the performers were with these concepts and how uncomfortable the conductor was with the content. The reading is stiff and laborious. A later rendition by Michael Tilson Thomas with the Chicago Symphony Orchestra and chorus is less cautious. Unexpectedly, the best performance of all was the Oakland Symphony Orchestra's 1967 version conducted by the late Gerhard Samuel, which portrayed a fresh, youthful innocence and captured the vital textures and dynamics that Ives likely intended in his masterpiece. It is a recording held in archive version only, never released to the public. While not a "perfect" reading, it evokes the passion and wildness of a youthful America we can only hope to hear again.

In addition to Ives, a number of Western composers are revisiting the soundscape as a valued resource for the creation of music. Aribert Reimann's orchestral score for his opera *Lear* is one example. Its 1981 American premiere in San Francisco was received with mixed reviews, but I consider it one of the few compelling late-century Western orchestrations I've experienced. It suggested the urban soundscape textures not yet so prevalent in the European academy, and through the lush acoustic tone clustering of his string orchestrations in act 1, Reimann exposed a tension between the electronic studio music of the era and sounds from the populated metropolitan worlds in which he lived.

Numerous orchestrations by the late Benjamin Britten, such as *Billy Budd* and *Death in Venice,* are strongly influenced by the urban and natural soundscapes that surrounded him during his many travels abroad and at his home in East Anglia.

And there are others, including works by a few students at the Center for Computer Research in Music and Acoustics (CCRMA) at Stanford—where composers and innovators such as John Chowning study the intersection of music and information technology using advanced synthesizers as creative media tools through which they express what they have discovered. Some of the students have begun to reexamine the potential of natural soundscapes and early instruments as important sources of compositional stimulus.

R. Murray Schafer's Patria series, an elaborate cycle of operas written over the past three decades, features several performances that take place in remote and natural settings—far removed from ceremonial halls of culture. *The Princess of the Stars* has been performed on a lake, usually in Northern Ontario. Instrumentalists from the Toronto Symphony are scattered out of sight of the audience throughout the forest surrounding the lakeshore, while the singers, on illuminated boats, begin their musical narratives along with the changing sky just before daybreak—emerging a little after four a.m. on late summer mornings from small alcoves that encircle the lake. While the audience stands or sits on the shore, the performers are induced into action by the natural soundscape, led by the dawn chorus of birdsong. Schafer has also written an a capella choral piece about wind, arguably one of the most difficult aspects of the soundscape to convey through musical art. His piece *Once on a Windy Night* demonstrates how we can be inspired through critical listening, as Schafer gracefully captures the essence of this invisible phenomenon with stunning impact.

The Italian composer David Monacchi defines his work as being based on an "eco-acoustic paradigm," a flexible compositional model used for many of his pieces. As part of the creative process, Monacchi likely spends as much time in the field collecting material and listening as he does composing. The natural biomes that he analyzes for their biophonic partitioning directly affect nearly all of his compositions — his musical muse is derived from intensive listening and the sonic details he discovers in the related spectrograms. Monacchi's arrangements are meant to express the ecological principles hidden in the biophonies of entire wild habitats. In his own words: "The segregation of sounds into temporal, frequency, and specific niches — observable in the sonic expression of many undisturbed ecosystems — is an example of the important narrative structure that I try to convey to audiences through my sound-art and music." In his masterly revelations of nature's composition — both seen and heard — audiences are immediately made aware of our atavistic links to biophonies. Eyes flashing with excitement, David told me: "My most important role as an eco-acoustic composer is to understand and reveal nature's intricate acoustic formulas and, at the same time, to be able to interact with biophonies without disturbing the equilibrium of their delicate set of patterns."

For his concerts, Monacchi surrounds his audiences in a multi-speaker envelope of highly calibrated sound sources — a system referred to in the industry as AmbiSonic — and performs segments of the material that capture the dynamic and dramatic lyricism inherent in the original tracks. Sometimes he manipulates — that is, pitch-shifts — the ultra- and infrasound components so that his audiences can better hear the interplay of low-frequency elephant sounds at one end of the spectrum and high-frequency bat and insect noises at the other.

In his composition *Nightingale* — this is the remarkable part — he streams the spectrograms across a large screen in the center of the stage. Within the niches that define the biophony, Monacchi improvises in real time on a transverse wooden flute. "At those moments, I am transported," he says, a fact confirmed by his body language and countenance during his collaborative concerts. In another, more recent composition called *Integrated Ecosystem,* he explores the interaction of a digitally synthesized performance with a primary equatorial rain forest's sonic habitat. The spectrograms, projected again in real time during the performance, show how he aims to create a sound sculpture that is strictly within the available temporal and frequency niches of the complex bioacoustic ensemble. Performing a real-time synthesis through several sensors that detect the movements of his hands and connect to custom generative software, Monacchi adds his electronic signature to unfilled narrow bandwidths and available time windows, building a powerful metaphor of one species — the human — that comes full circle and plays within a composite animal orchestra, finding synergy and a balanced, harmonic relationship.

The natural world holds many secrets that can inform our music, yet as composers, many of us have ignored them. After hearing my presentations, musicians and composers often ask how they can learn more about the field of bioacoustics, which is otherwise so remote from their thoughts and experiences in the classroom, practice room, stage, and studio. I give the same advice to everyone: Turn down Ronnie James Dio, Orange Sky, Panic Bomber, Arvo Pärt, and Philip Glass for a moment. Try to put them out of your mind. Listen to the aural *contexts* in which the creature world vocalizes. As you would with any musical composition, engage with all of the sounds that make up the animal orchestra. Notice how the individual sources mix together. "Listen to the bass, it's the one on the bottom / Where the bullfrog croaks and the hippopotamus / Moans and groans." Be mindful of the subtle differences in the ambient flow of streams, creeks, and waterfalls; the cells of thunder and rain passing by (be sure to take your headphones off when in the presence of electrical storms); the wind in the aspens, pines, or maples; and the wave action at the shore. Try to pick out the structure of the creature symphonies conveyed by whole habitats. Notice the seasonal dynamics — rich and intricate in spring, delicate and sporadic in winter. Which high-pitched birds and insects do you hear? When do you hear them (what times of day, year)? Where do the amphibians fit in the spectrum? Who fills the mid- and low-range acoustic turf? What creatures set up rhythm patterns? Which ones rely on timing to be heard in relation to others? These are the same questions that composers address when faced with orchestrating their musical lines with the instrumentation at hand. How would you set about composing a piece of music from this palette?

In order to harness nature as a source of musical inspiration, we must be willing to make the time and find ways to hike back to wild places. For me, the process is singularly edifying. Once I've located a noise-free location, a goal in itself, I listen — sometimes with eyes closed — to the ways in which the blend of creature voices define space. Because each habitat — even those within the same biome — will express itself with an assemblage of sound signatures that form a unique collective voice, I can rarely anticipate what the sound of the landscape as defined by the biophony will be. They're always different — often in not-so-subtle ways.

The disparity between landscapes and their inhabitants is one reason why the music of Béla Bartók, the early-twentieth-century Hungarian composer, sounds so unlike the wide-open optimistic feeling of Aaron Copland's compositions, which depict an idealized American West as he imagined it in the last midcentury.

153

Each of us has at least one sound-mark in our head, a signature soundscape that defines a sense of place in our aural experience. For composers, that sound-mark is the font from which they draw the fragments that they plait into music. In the wild natural world, that mark can be very rich—it just takes time and a quiet frame of mind to unravel and understand.

A week or ten days in the field is rarely enough. Animal activity isn't framed by human time: mostly their hours to sleep, forage, and hunt differ widely. Instead, intervals are determined by the cycles of seasons, the amount of daylight or darkness, the passing of weather, the dappled shades of light on the forest floor as the day progresses, and the distinct fragrances that arise at various times. Of course, the combination of all these elements manages to evade complete capture on audio or video media. But after being present below the canopy of an equatorial rain forest for a very long time, we find that the tactile, aural, and visual elements eventually unite into a single, overall impression. Only at that point might someone begin to hear the phrases that motivate the nearby hunter-gatherers to begin an ancient chant. The forest becomes a place of worship, and we start to imagine what it must have been like to be part of the creature world. In fact, nothing can replace the experience of being there—but it's our presence itself that's turning out to be perhaps the most formidable hurdle of all.

CHAPTER SEVEN

The Fog of Noise

It's late at night, and I'm sitting in my studio listening to a recording. My working space isn't big—maybe large enough to accommodate the footprint of two medium-size cars tightly packed—but with the special techniques I've used to record my soundscapes in the field, the illusion created by the playback fills the room way beyond the reaches of its design. I'm auditioning a recording that was made in Yellowstone National Park during a fall afternoon—one exquisitely active with birds. It's a single long take, maybe an hour in length. The texture at the beginning of the recording is as delicate and lovely as a piece of fine Irish lace—an expansive sonic fabric that sucks me deep into the time and space of the original moment, as only sound can do.

A raven calls out intermittently, inscribing a horizontal path across the stereo space with a flight beginning in the left-hand side of the field and moving to the right. As it does, the illusion is suddenly broken by what sounds like a small private or military jet heading northbound, maybe twenty thousand feet above my mics. The noise reverberates in thundering waves, back and forth across the valley. It takes six or seven minutes to fully disappear. Meanwhile, during the flyover, the bird biophony quiets down to almost nothing. After ten more minutes the natural soundscape is just beginning to return to its pre-jet level of quality when the low-frequency *whomp-whomp-whomp* of a distant helicopter intrudes. The birds become quiet again. Really silent this time.

The late Gregory Bateson used to tell his graduate students a story about the venerated philosopher Alfred North Whitehead. Invited to join the Harvard faculty shortly after World War I, Whitehead accepted the position on the condition that he could bring along his great friend and collaborator Bertrand Russell, with whom he had coauthored the ambitious three-volume *Principia Mathematica*. Newly appointed faculty members were required to present a lecture on their subject of choice, and Russell chose to clarify Max Planck's quantum theory. It was a hot August night in 1919, and the auditorium near Harvard Yard was filled with eager faculty and, as Bateson told it, the bluest bloods in Boston. After laboring for ninety minutes without a break, a sweat-drenched Russell finally concluded his remarks and returned to his seat to polite applause. Whitehead, who had been sitting patiently on the dais, stood and walked slowly to the podium. When the applause died down, he intoned in his high-pitched English voice, "I'd like to thank Professor Russell for his brilliant exposition. And especially for leaving unobscured the vast darkness of the subject."

I tell this story because Russell's efforts parallel how I feel when trying to define noise. The turn-of-the-last-century wit

Ambrose Bierce once called it the "chief product and authenticating sign of civilization." Les Blomberg, of the venerable Noise Pollution Clearinghouse, defines noise as "aural litter" or "audible trash." The cause of most noise—from the viewpoint of the natural world, at least—is *anthrophony*. Altogether, biophony, geophony, and anthrophony make up the soundscapes of the world.

Anthrophony comprises four basic types of human-generated sound: electromechanical sound, physiological sound, controlled sound, and incidental sound. Electromechanical noises are produced by our means of transportation and the loud tools of various trades, including aircraft, pile drivers, snowmobiles, leaf blowers, automobile and truck sound systems, motorcycles, generators, cell phones, TVs, boom boxes, refrigerators, pencil sharpeners, dishwashers, air conditioners, microwave ovens, and many other complex technologies—such as the relentless clicking of the keyboard on which this book is being written or the faint continuous whisper of my laptop's cooling fan (although most current ones are inaudible beyond a few inches from the source). Physiological sounds—coughing, breathing, body sounds, sneezing, and talking, for example—tend to be much more subdued and localized. With a bit of mindfulness and consideration, we can manage our controlled sound, such as live or recorded music or theatrical performances, particularly when it comes in conflict with a sensitive biophony. Incidental sounds are made up of noises such as footsteps or clothes rustling and scratching; these, too, are controllable and localized.

Noise by itself attracts attention without delivering much useful information. It's wasted energy; if loud enough and in an enclosed space, it generates a small but measurable amount of heat. Hearing that claim in a physics class long ago, I subsequently imagined that, given what we endure in our cities, we might be able to create enough noise-related heat to wean us off fossil fuels, if we could only figure out how to rechannel it without a net loss.

If our goal is to communicate a clear unimpaired signal containing useful information — assuming, of course, that the source is providing an unambiguous message and the receiver is distortion-free — we must realize that we and other living organisms can accomplish this only if acoustic channels are unimpaired. This applies as much to the creature sounds in a biophony as to, say, communicating on a mobile phone via a cellular network. Good signal exchange means that the transmission is useful, pertinent, and relevant to the moment and that the recipient clearly gets the message. It is not corrupted by other acoustic, tactile, olfactory, or visual sources. This is referred to in the trade as a "clean" signal. In video parlance, *signal* refers to a perfectly clear series of images focusing on one or two subjects. In music, it usually represents clearly expressed thematic patterns of consonance or dissonance that evoke a wide range of emotional responses. Noise occurs when a clear signal is somehow compromised — usually by a number of competing and uncorrelated signals or distortion. A common expression in acoustics, the *signal-to-noise ratio* refers to a signal's power relative to the amount of background noise.

I think of noise as an acoustic event that clashes with expectation — loud heavy-metal music in an intimate restaurant is noise (or, for that matter, music in almost *any* restaurant). A straight-piping motorcycle gunning its way through the delicate landscape of Yosemite Valley shatters the numinous experience for both visitors and animals. When there are discontinuities between visual and aural content, aural and aural content, or visual and visual content, these breaks are usually received by us as various kinds of noise — in an extreme example, a contradiction such as a gentle classical guitar sound track set against a violent scene in a *Terminator* movie, unless the offset is meant as a joke. In the heart of many urban settings, acoustic noise can also be chaotic, disassociated sound, including that of car alarms, sirens, jackhammers, air brakes, downshifting diesel truck engines, and boom systems in cars.

I was not surprised to read that a sound-industry manufacturer's award was given in 2003 for the loudest documented sound system ever produced for the interior of an automobile. To my knowledge and as of this writing, few have matched or beaten the winning delivery technology, one designed to generate 130,000 watts of power driving nine fifteen-inch subwoofers, with a sound pressure level of 177+ dBA at a sustained intensity. That is more than twice as loud as a .357 Magnum pistol being shot off next to your ear, and a factor of seven louder than a Boeing 747 at full takeoff power — when you're standing ten yards from the jet. The NASA space shuttle launches typically registered between 160 and 180 dB on takeoff. Let's not forget that this car system was installed *inside* a Dodge Caravan.

Schafer tells us in *The Tuning of the World* that humans like to make noise to remind themselves that they are not alone (and to remind others, with whom they may have only a passing relationship, that they exist). The general presence of noise itself becomes really apparent when we introduce a microphone into the equation. A microphone, as an extension of our ears but very different in function, does not discriminate between useful sounds and noise. It will pick up *every* acoustic signal within its range and unique detection pattern. If you want to know how much noise there is in your environment, just plug a mic into a recorder and put on a set of headphones for a minute. Try this in a habitat that you consider to be "wild nature." After just a few seconds, the results will amaze you.

Sound in our human world is broken down into two general types: desirable and undesirable, or, in the field of bioacoustics, *information* versus *uncorrelated acoustic debris*. Although in the process of listening we often don't recognize noise—what the author Joachim-Ernst Berendt refers to in his book *The Third Ear* as "acoustic garbage"—it has detrimental effects on us. Unconsciously, our brains are hard at work filtering out undesirable sounds so that we can process the information that is beneficial. Broadly speaking, in most of our industrial societies, signal and noise are constantly competing for our acoustic or visual attention, and we spend a great deal of mental energy sorting out noise from the signals that more affably engage us.

We've all had the experience of talking with a companion in a noisy restaurant or on a crowded street. As we gaze at the source of the sound, we think we are hearing everything he or she is saying clearly. However, what we hear is largely filtered through *what we see*. Without that synchronous sight and sound, we'd probably get little useful information from the exchange. Our ears receive many sounds, but our brains do the heavy lifting, combining sounds with visual cues. Hard at work filtering out the background noise, it tricks us into thinking that the interference doesn't matter.

This signal processing (filtering) goes on whether or not we are conscious of it. Weimin Zheng, associate fellow in experimental neurology at the Neurosciences Institute in San Diego and one of the few researchers to consider the idea, reports that relative brain activity allotments...

are not a question that can be addressed directly, but can be inferred from behavioral observations at the system level. Even in a quiet environment, in order to understand the speech, attention has to be focused on the task. Attending a single task requires "actively" decreased performance in some regions of the brain and increased activities in others....In a noisy environment, greater effort (attention) is needed and often engaging other sensory systems, particularly the visual system for lip-reading. Thus, overall brain energy consumption will be increased....So, overall, brain activity will be greater in a noisy rather than in a quiet environment because of the engagement of other systems.

Donald Hodges, Covington distinguished professor of music education and director of the Music Research Institute at University of North Carolina, Greensboro, reminded me that loud noise was used to flush Manuel Noriega, military dictator of Panama, from his residence during the U.S. invasion in 1989, and that highly focused loud noise is employed by the military and police to break up unwanted gatherings of demonstrators.

Our auditory processing system is conditioned over time to know which signals are meaningful and which are not. Yet even as our attention is focused on what we see, our brains are working overtime to retrieve and process desired information, eventually causing a consequential effect such as the onset of weariness. In a 1998 Swedish noise study of fifty thousand state employees, twenty thousand of the respondents working in environments where the random background noise level was measured between 60 and 80 dBA—considered moderate (like an average residential city street) in the United States—commonly complained of fatigue and headaches, even after just a couple of hours of exposure.

In addition, researchers have shown that fatigue and stress are significant by-products — resulting from an increase in glucocorticoid enzyme levels that may escalate as much as 40 percent — of trying to separate noise from signal. It turns out that most of us find noise intrusive, repellent, or stressful — or all of the above.

Unwanted sound in our lives — sometimes referred to in the current literature as ISE or *irrelevant sound effect* — induces multiple kinds of physical and psychological reactions, many of them unhealthy, especially when the noise persists. And when noise obliterates the subtle sounds of natural soundscapes, we can detect reactions in a wide range of living organisms. For humans, the consequences of harmful noise — including nervous tension, fatigue, and irritation — can be found everywhere from our biggest cities to our offices to surviving tribal groups such as the Ba'Aka, who are drawn to the interior of their remaining forests, as far away from human industrial noise as they can, to mend.

Three separate studies by Anders Kjellberg, Per Muhr, and Björn Sköldström, and confirmed by other researchers more recently, found that even moderate noise in a workplace caused measurable exhaustion, blood pressure elevation, and negative attitudinal shifts after only a few days of exposure.

Beginning in the early 1980s, the relationship between exposure to urban noise and increased human stress levels has attracted a growing amount of research. One of the first landmark studies linking noise and stress took place in Strasbourg, France. Researchers invited three men and three women to sleep in a specially designed laboratory, where they were subjected to different sound and noise experiences each night over a period of several weeks. Wired to stress-level instrumentation that measured heart rate, finger-pulse amplitude, and pulse-wave velocity, each test subject was monitored throughout the night. For the first few nights, they experienced uninterrupted quiet. For the following two weeks, they were subjected to recorded traffic noise. All of the stress indicators dramatically increased when the traffic was introduced—even at relatively low levels. Upon waking, participants completed questionnaires. After two to seven nights of noise, the subjects reported that they were no longer aware of being disturbed. Each person had become used to it. However, the measured physiological stress levels were consistently as high as when the traffic sounds were first introduced. Despite the small size of this study and the fact that it was carried out nearly thirty years ago, it is still considered significant—while the minds of the subjects rationalized that there was no noise effect, their bodies told very different stories.

Noise has also long been understood to detract from a child's ability to concentrate and learn. In a recent article in *Noise and Health,* authors Maria Klatte, Thomas Lachmann, and Markus Meis show that there is a direct relationship between noise in a child's environment and his or her task performance. When a particular task requires high levels of concentration and unrelated distracting noise intrudes, a greater allocation of attention—often beyond the child's ability to engage—will measurably interfere with execution. And a 128-page World Health Organization E.U. study titled "Burden of Disease from Environmental Noise" released in March 2011 stated that, with children ages seven to nineteen, "Tasks affected are those involving central processing and language, such as reading comprehension, memory, and attention. Exposure [to noise such as that of auto traffic and aircraft] during critical periods of learning at school...impair[s] development and [has] a lifelong effect on educational attainment," sometimes affecting IQ by between five and ten points. After the noise sources were mitigated (e.g., the relocation of an airport farther from a school), the noted learning disabilities disappeared. The report went further, concluding that exposure to excessive noise not only impairs learning in young humans but can also—due to epidemiological level increases in blood pressure and release of stress hormones—lead to heart attacks, a negative environmental condition rated second only to air pollution.

In our industrialized world, there are times when mechanical noise is welcome and, in some cases, becomes "art." A well-placed noise cue crafted by a film or video sound designer that punctuates the narrative of a film for effect can be a creative use of noise. For others it could be the reassuring sound of a subway train approaching a station platform. It could be an oil well belching out percussive intervals of its diesel-powered drivetrain somewhere on the High Plains of Wyoming; the firing of a military cannon; or the deafening roar of a NASCAR event. People on the ground may not be so thrilled when pilots fly multiengine aircraft into their acoustic space, but the sound of synchronized engines—those that run at the same number of revolutions per minute and consequently generate equal pitch and power—is a steady beatless hum of the sweetest and most reassuring "music" the person at the flight controls can imagine.

Ocean and lakeside waves, the effects of wind, and the sound of streams contain elements of white noise. Analogous to white light, this class of sound is made up of an infinite number of audible frequencies that are distributed over the entire audio spectrum. Each frequency appears at random and, over time, has equal power. Naturally generated white noise provides a number of positive effects and is, more often than not, pleasant to our ears and relaxing to the psyche. The Wy-am once heard the natural geophonic white sound of Celilo Falls as a recognizable signal replete with profound practical and spiritual significance, just as the Nez Percé heard music on the wind in the reeds at Lake Wallowa. Yet, in settings where we have tried to harness white noise by reproducing it artificially, it often works to our disadvantage.

Whether conscious of the experience or not, most of us have visited offices where white noise has been integrated into the ambient design of the working spaces to mask conversation in nearby zones with open partitioning. With similar sales pitches to those used for marketing elevator or background music, slews of web advertisements claim that office white-noise installations are calming and relaxing, and are effective masking tools to keep one from hearing conversations in the next separated space. The intent is to increase productivity—the false premise being that any white noise sounds natural.

What was supposed to have a relaxing effect on employees, helping them to be more efficient, has not quite worked out that way. (In addition, white noise has been built into electronic bedside "sleep aids," with the assumption—and sales pitch—that it would help insomniacs sleep. It didn't.) Studies show that the synthetically created noise instead serves to tire employees and reduce efficiency and concentration. This is likely the result of the constancy of *manufactured* white noise. In the natural world, the sound of ocean waves, streams, and wind is dynamic—the intensity of the sound changes over time and contains inherent natural rhythms. White noise in the natural world is relaxing precisely because of those fluctuations: ocean waves produce cadenced patterns, streams and waterfalls have unique and subtle signatures that engage us in ways that tend to pacify. In office spaces where the sound level never varies, the white noise becomes another unconscious irritant, not unlike the fluorescent lights with which workers also have to contend.

Some industries deliberately manipulate their acoustic environments in order to trigger human stress levels. Until very recently — before a passing groundswell movement to quiet things down occurred at the end of the last century — it was an open secret that some restaurant architects and interior designers, for example, consciously planned certain eating establishments to be more or less stressful, with noise being the main ingredient. Anytime you walk into a restaurant that has hard, reverberant surfaces built into its architecture — walls, floors, and ceilings that reflect and amplify the slightest sound — you are choosing an environment likely designed to put you on edge. To complete the architectural intention, owners might add loud, intrusive, kick-ass music, or lots of TV monitors featuring sports programs, or both at the same time. While the noise coming from the venue may provide the momentary illusion of "action," the effect is a carefully calculated one; for those of us looking for more intimate settings in which to enjoy a quiet meal and another's company, the noise quickly triggers tension and fatigue responses that encourage quick patron turnover, resulting in higher profits for the restaurateur.

On the other hand, I know how relaxed my wife, Kat, and I feel in a quiet eating establishment with lots of sound-absorbent material factored into the design and minimal or no background music. It's remarkable how less likely we are to hurry out the door.

The *New York Times* discussed the problem of restaurant noise in a number of editorials in the mid-1980s — a time when the subject seemed to have more traction. For several years after, the paper reported noise levels as part of its restaurant reviews to give readers quieter options. Around the same period, the *San Francisco Chronicle* placed small bell icons in its restaurant reviews to identify establishments' noise levels. Many other newspaper and magazine food critics followed suit in their reviews but have since dropped all but the most oblique references. With recent attention focusing more on the star quality of the chef, food, decor, and clientele, noise levels in many restaurants are beginning to climb again, along with side effects. An article that appeared in *Scientific American* in the fall of 2010 stressed that high noise levels may even alter the taste of your food, making it seem more bland. The level readings at a new local restaurant my wife and I visited recently measured 94 dBA. And that was without music and at around six thirty in the evening, before the establishment had reached its capacity. We're unlikely to return.

One person's noise may be a meaningful sound to another—those who create noise have an investment in its origin, while others receiving it may not. I like to think of the sounds we give off as powerful additions to the visual cues we project—an extension of the clothes we wear, the cut of our hair, our body language—statements of the impressions we wish to convey and how, in turn, we experience each other.

The overwhelming sounds of industry—the true acoustic signatures of modernity—include soundscapes that many of us cherish, especially when we feel compelled to assert our presence. At the extreme, there is the story of James Watt, Ronald Reagan's secretary of the interior. According to R. Murray Schafer, Watt, in reference to the status of the Office of Noise Abatement and

Control (a department once within the fold of the EPA that he was determined to close down), observed that noise and power go hand in hand: the more noise we make as a country, the more powerful we appear to be. Think of boom cars calling attention to themselves as they cruise down the street and unmuffled motorcycles or muscle cars—their sounds conveying a certain bombast and arrogance ("Hey! Look at me!"). In another extreme example, after discussing his success shooting off cannons to frighten birds from airport runways, a biologist working at the U.S. Army's Aberdeen Proving Ground mentioned to a group at a soundscape science meeting in Washington, DC, that a colleague later remarked how she loved the noise. To her, cannons were the sound of freedom. The point, of course, is that it all depends on which side of the cannon one is standing.

Today, we humans seem compelled to bring our noise with us everywhere we go, creating soundscapes of random sources that some few enjoy and that a great many others—who have to endure the unwanted sounds that "spill" into their spaces—find annoying. We go to the lake, and we bring Jet Skis and motorboats; we go to the seashore, and we bring boom boxes; we go to the woods, and we bring dirt bikes, off-road vehicles, and chain saws; we go to the desert, and we bring dune buggies; we go to our national parks, and we bring straight-piping motorcycles, snowmobiles, and now firearms. There is the noise of machinery—toys we cannot seem to live without. There are the sounds of war. There is the noise of other people's music, and jets or private aircraft flying overhead nearly everywhere we live. No matter where we try to find relief from the din in our lives, noise intrudes.

Noise is a theme played out in our recreational activities. For example, on many July and August Sunday afternoons at Infineon Raceway, which is a forty-five-minute drive north of San

Francisco, a famous National Hot Rod Association drag-racing event takes place, drawing more than a hundred thousand fans to celebrate our fleeting supremacy represented by speed and noise. The track is eighteen miles south of our home. To reach us, the roar of the engines doesn't travel in a straight line—it must first traverse several ranges of inland coastal hills, valleys, protected wetlands, and a regional park. However, as each contest begins every five minutes or so, I can measure the sound coming from the track at troubling levels. The dragsters are so loud that I have recorded them well above the normal daytime ambient levels present at our property line—even when the wind is blowing in the opposite direction. R. Murray Schafer once said to me that if it wasn't for the noise, and speed was the only factor, attendance at drag races and U.S. Navy Blue Angels events would probably drop by more than 90 percent.

Sound levels in movie theater trailers with THX or Dolby Digital sound systems are now more than a factor of six greater than they were in the early 1990s—often beyond the safe levels of industrial noise mandated by OSHA and the Environmental Protection Agency, when it still had an active Noise Abatement Office. When I asked a member of the sound department at Skywalker Sound (part of the LucasFilm company) about the high level mixes for the promos, he responded on condition of anonymity: "It's all about marketing. High levels hold the audience's attention. Theatergoers have a hard time talking over a loud sound track. Otherwise the trailers would have no impact." Producers and sound designers are convinced that audiences want to be assaulted by the loud, low-frequency "punches" and sound effects that now define film trailers. They create a visceral sense of excitement and tension. To me, the relationship of film to sound appears to be inversely proportional—the less substance in the film, the quicker the distracting frame cuts and the louder and more frequent the sound effects. It's not 3-D glasses that should be supplied. When Kat and I go to the movies, we take earplugs.

Just when we've started seeing big strides in quieting down our environment, in part by introducing less noisy hybrid and electric automobiles, manufacturers have new concerns that the resulting quietude actually increases the danger to pedestrians and is thus a manufacturer's liability. In response, the Fisker Karma, a roughly $100,000 plug-in hybrid vehicle on sale in 2011, has added speakers to its front bumper to transmit a sound that is "a cross between a starship and a Formula 1 car"—a health trade-off in which the danger of not hearing an oncoming vehicle becomes more important than the psychological and physical stresses induced by the roar of a Formula 1, adding yet another layer of noise to our already anxious neighborhoods. Other manufacturers are considering similar options for their electric vehicles.

Even though it is generally thought of as an acoustic phenomenon, noise can also be visual, or a combination of both. For example, noise is introduced into the night skies by light pollution from cities—the light that spills up from streetlamps, billboards, buildings, and monuments—blocking out the heavens. Or consider a TV broadcast from any of several cable channels—a screen filled with disparate images and competing messages, further scrambled by an edgy, highly compressed, and modulated audio track, and nonstop mind-numbing aphorisms of unearned authority. All of these elements are designed to draw and hold our attention to screen images littered with multiple focus points. The combined "noise" from the audio and imagery is shrewdly calculated to keep us off balance. When we're off balance, we're uncomfortable.

When we feel a high enough level of discomfort and can't precisely identify the source, many of us express the accumulated frustration as anger, or more likely rage. Skew and repeat the substance of a distorted media message consistently enough, and the result is thought reform. It is a process that the psychologist Michael Langone refers to as the "systematic manipulation of psychological and social influences" through noise.

Our world is hardly ever quiet. Nevertheless, what happens when just one intrusive class of noise—jets and private aircraft—disappears from our lives? An eerie yet memorable effect of the security precautions put in place immediately after the disaster of September 11, 2001, was the stunning sense of tranquillity that descended over the country for a few days. Just prior to the 9/11 event, the Federal Aviation Administration (FAA) had changed inbound flight patterns from the northwest United States to San Francisco International Airport, so that descending commercial aircraft flew, at around seventeen thousand feet, right over our home in the Sonoma Valley. Our otherwise lovely spot (aka Jack London's *Valley of the Moon*) is also a private pilot training airspace for single-engine aircraft. Because air traffic was grounded for forty-eight hours after 9/11, no planes of any type were airborne. There was also a nearly complete absence of automobile traffic.

Emotionally drained, Kat and I sat quietly in our garden a day after the attacks. And with the anthrophony silenced, we listened to a late-summer natural soundscape that we had never before heard at that time of year. Goldfinches, juncos, bushtits, nuthatches, brown creepers, Anna's hummingbirds, house finches, towhees, and swallows were still faintly vocal—a transparent interweaving of voices we didn't know existed that late in the season. At one point, we turned to each other and remarked how guilty we felt for feeling mentally and physically refreshed by the absence of the aircraft—the "normal" signs of civilization and commerce. It's the astonishment city kids must feel when seeing the night sky during a blackout.

We were stunned by the previous day's events, but we welcomed the healing, relaxing ambience. Even more surprising was the number of e-mails and calls we got from as far away as Europe during and immediately after those dark days, commenting on the peacefulness that had swathed the world's airspaces for a moment in time. Every person who reached out was relieved and soothed by the serenity—amazed by the natural acoustic richness the moment revealed. We wondered aloud about the possibilities of our nation slowing down, perhaps for a National Day of Tranquillity, a time when we could take a moment to catch our collective breath and appreciate the sonic blessings in our own backyards.

Author Garret Keizer offered a thoughtful observation: terrorist attacks such as that of 9/11 posit a war between the noise signatures of different cultures. He suggests that the terrorists' motivations, in part, may have been based on a desire not to have the noise of Western culture bear down on them with such oppressive weight. He goes on to say: "I doubt we will ever be able to 'listen' to our enemies or cause them to listen to us until we can hear our own noise with their ears."

How can we deal with noise? Earplugs help when I have to endure a rock concert or a record mix. Yet, with something jammed in my ears, the quality of the entire soundscape is compromised—both signal and noise. So they help only when acoustic events are otherwise painful. When, in 1986, Bose introduced noise-canceling headphones—which use technology called active noise control (ANC)—they accomplished a tiny bit of what our brains do. These headphones continually sample noise from the surrounding environment and then introduce a mirror opposite (+1 and −1 = 0) of the audio waveform to cancel it, eliminating irritating background noise such as the sound of a jet engine. Now common, noise-canceling headphones cost anywhere from $30 to $350. But we can't rely on such technologies to quiet down the environments in which most of us choose to live.

One way we've managed the problem is to build ever quieter structures in which to find respite. Architecture has always influenced the ways in which sound is transmitted and controlled. Earlier, I discussed the medieval church structures that would attenuate sounds from the outside and enhance those from within. This aural architectural design philosophy has carried over into the present. Every aspect of large public-space design has been calculated to control, to one degree or another, the experience of the interior habitat, eliminating most outside sound, whether anthrophonic or biophonic in origin. Ironically, these structures may actually serve to amplify the noise levels on the street, making even more apparent the need for quiet interior spaces. With the knowledge and resources at hand to completely transform the spaces we build and inhabit, and with urban spaces becoming more densely packed and noise intense, there is every reason to create structures that completely eliminate the acoustic world outside and redefine inner spaces, conforming them to our most intricate requirements.

In a U.S. noise survey conducted a few years ago, it was estimated that the level of urban noise increased by approximately 12 percent across the United States from 1996 to 2005. More than one-third of Americans complained of noise, and over one in ten found it annoying. As established in previous studies, the noise problem has become so vexing that more than 40 percent claimed they wanted to change their place of residence. Meanwhile, European, North and South American, and many Asian communities experienced an exponential increase in human noise as the landscape was transformed to meet the needs of exploding populations. Now, the rate of escalation in urban soundscape intensity has accelerated to the point where cities can be difficult environments in which to spend any time in the open.

Recognizing the impact of noise on the quality of human and nonhuman life, the European Union has set the most stringent objectives on the noise automobiles can emit from a distance of ten meters (about thirty-three feet). Here's a short comparative rundown:

European Union = 74 dBA
Korea = 75 dBA
Australia = 77 dBA
Japan = 78 dBA
United States, Canada, Israel = 80 dBA

In the United States, the 80 dBA level is only a recommendation—not a mandate—and it's louder by a factor of two than the EU limit. With a segment of the U.S. populace already suspicious of government intervention and clearly supporting "noise-is-power" mantras, stricter, enforceable controls are unlikely to occur anytime soon.

To understand why noise regulation is ineffective in the United States today, we should refer again to the first years of the Reagan administration. When, in 1982, funding for the Office of Noise Abatement and Control (ONAC) was abruptly terminated, the department was shut down, giving the FAA exclusive control over aircraft noise. The Noise Control Act of 1972, under which ONAC was established, is still in force. It states: "It is the policy of the United States to promote an environment for all Americans free from noise that jeopardizes their health and welfare." However, since the funding for ONAC—the implementing department—was eliminated, the control of noise was remanded to the jurisdiction of the states, which have few resources available, very spotty records, and too many other fish to fry to address noise issues.

Each state interprets the subject of "noise" differently: most give deference to numerous special-interest groups and lobbyists who of course represent industries that make a lot of noise, including snowmobile, Jet Ski, motorcycle, and ATV manufacturers. The EPA, watchdog agencies, and activist groups have clamored for years to reinstate the ONAC, but so far to no avail.

The end result of all this noise is that, for most of us, hearing has become a blur. As the world's population continues adjusting from agrarian to industrial to software economies, the local folk know that their aural environment is being transformed: highways, railroads, and factories drastically alter the land and its soundscapes. We are on our way to an encompassing, global age of the machine and all the noise that it generates; noise now permeates our world's environments and masks more aesthetically resonant sounds—even though John Cage once referred to all sound as music. As Sasha Frere-Jones pointed out in a 2010 *New Yorker* music review: "To many people now, noise isn't necessarily an aggressive or alienating element; it sounds more like nature than nature does."

CHAPTER EIGHT

Noise and Biophony /
Oil and Water

It was a spring day at Mono Lake, California, a body of water located east of Yosemite in the Eastern Sierras and formed over 750,000 years ago. Because it lacks an outlet to the ocean, the water over time has become quite alkaline and salty — about two to three times the saline content of the sea. Ken Norris, then head of the Environmental Studies Department at the University of California, Santa Cruz, wasn't much interested in the lake. He wanted to know if there were any vocal organisms in the vernal pools that surround this stunning spot. An early supporter of the niche hypothesis, Norris encouraged me to take a hydrophone and have a listen. "I've got a hunch," he assured me.

A few hundred yards south of the road that cuts west to east tangent to the lake's north side off Highway 395, I found a shallow depression filled with about six inches of newly melted snow and ice. It was late March, and the weather was crisp, clear, and warm during the day — though still freezing at night. At first there was no wind and, except for a few California gulls, no other sound. Because the sandy and porous environment soaks up acoustic reflection, the High Desert tends to feel relatively quiet. But there is a sound that stands out. Great Basin spadefoot toads begin their synchronous performances around midafternoon, as the area falls under the shadow of the high mountains to the west, carefully injecting each iteration of their aggregated voices into the airspace around the edges of the water-filled depression.

I uncoiled the cable and carefully lowered the hydrophone into the pool, put on my earphones, and switched on the tape recorder—a well-established ritual sequence. Caught completely off guard, I heard my headset explode with a variety of small crunching sounds, high-pitched squeaks, pops, and scrapes—each one, I assumed, biological. After recording for a while, I took a small bucket and shovel I had brought along just in case and, sifting through the muddy water, discovered water boatmen, insect larvae, and tadpoles, each adding a face to the marine voices I had just captured. Eventually I plugged a microphone into one channel and a hydrophone into the other. With the hydrophone under the surface and the mic above water, I tried to see if the spadefoot toads transmitted their vocalizations simultaneously in and out of the marine habitat so vital to their existence. They do. It was an exhilarating experience to encounter this and to be one of the first to actually hear it. Norris's instincts were right again.

Great Basin spadefoot toads are wondrous critters. Once, when I was working as a field associate at the California Academy of Sciences, I walked into the renowned ornithologist Luis Baptista's lab for a meeting. I was early. "See this?" he asked excitedly, without a proper greeting. He pointed to a glass jar containing an object that looked like a small-size dolma—the Greek dish also known as stuffed grape leaves. "It's a carapace with a toad inside.

It's been sitting on my desk for five years without any food or water, and it's still alive."

"How is that possible?" I asked skeptically. "I didn't know you were into toads." Ignoring my comment—Baptista was into everything—he rose from his desk, picked up the jar, and walked with a quick, jaunty gait to the sink. He filled the bottom of the jar with about a quarter inch of water—just enough to partially dampen the carapace—and set it on the table. After our meeting we went to lunch. When we returned to the lab in a few hours, a spadefoot toad had emerged—alive—after five years in a jar.

When conditions are optimal, and the winter precipitation that has accumulated on the desert surface melts and moisture reaches the toads—which are buried under three feet of hardpan desert soil—they emerge with their spadelike feet from their wrappings and dig to the surface to breed, lay eggs, and mature. At the completion of their cycle, they burrow down a meter or so into the difficult terrain, where they remain encased in an almost impermeable membrane—sometimes for years—before surfacing to endure their brief breeding phase once again. (A spadefoot toad will have a life span of roughly eleven to thirteen years in the wild.) When they finally do appear, they congregate around the vernal ponds described earlier—to vocalize in well-calibrated choruses.

Historically, spadefoot-toad vocalizations have been thought to serve two main functions: attracting a mate and protecting territory. But we may have overlooked another important explanation that is tied to their survival: a synchronous chorus assuring a seamless protective acoustic texture. With synchronicity, when all the toads are vocalizing together, acoustically oriented predators such as foxes, coyotes, and owls must struggle to draw a bead on any one, because no individual becomes conspicuous. If the pulsating, rhythmic structure is lost, however, and individuals become noticeable when trying to recoup their place in the chorus, all hell can break loose. Avian raptor and canid opportunists are forever on call for such moments.

Chorusing is a function that can serve, among others, to thwart predation. Within the limited world of the species itself, the toads hear each voice as distinct. The vocal characteristics of spadefoot individuals are so unique that when heard by others in the resident group, they are able to compete for mates quite aggressively while at the same time protecting the integrity and survival of the group by lending their voices to the choir. Given our limited abilities to make fine acoustic distinctions, however, we're not easily able to hear the differences between individuals. Acting collectively, each vocal member within the crowd enjoys a degree of anonymity and protection.

Figure 10 demonstrates spadefoot-toad chorusing without any breaks in the sequence and no disruption from human-generated

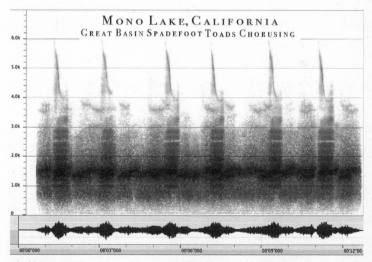

Figure 10. Synchronous Great Basin spadefoot toads (Spea intermontana) *chorusing.*

noise. It is a powerful story told through the aggregate voice of dozens of chorusing frogs in about ten seconds — the length of the audio clip from which this spectrogram was made.

Figure 11 illustrates the story line's denouement. In this ten-second clip, we see what happens when a military jet flies low over the terrain nearly four miles west of the site, its booming noise — measured at approximately 110 dBA at our monitoring location — masking the toad vocalizations. Most of the aircraft signature can be seen at the bottom of the page under 1 kHz. Note the breaks in the chorusing and how the toad group energy diminishes. Far less robust than the chorus in Figure 10, these "breaks" set up a momentary opportunity for predation to occur. In this instance, it took some time for the toads to reestablish their protective acoustic connection — from thirty to forty-five minutes after the noise faded — and under a bright moonlit sky, my wife and I watched from our nearby campsite as a pair of

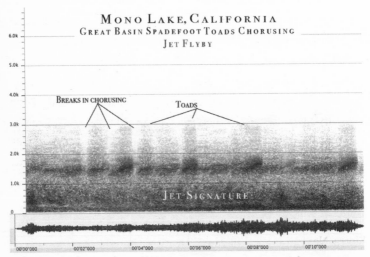

Figure 11. Spadefoot toad chorusing affected by military-jet overflight.

coyotes and a great horned owl swept in to pick off a few toads during their attempts to reestablish vocal synchronicity.

It's not just the sounds of a single species—those related to mating, territory, communication, or protection from predation—that are affected by noise. Human-generated noise affects entire biophonies. Midmorning, while I was recording in the Amazon in the early 1990s, a multiengine plane flew at two or three thousand feet directly over our research site. The engine roar was so loud that it completely masked the chorus of birds and insects. When we looked at the effect of the noise on the soundscape, we found that the interference caused many creatures to stop vocalizing and others to significantly alter their patterns. The momentary break in the integrity of the biophony left open the possibility that many creatures would become victims to opportunistic predators, such as hawks or resident mammals. Animal vocal behavior that morning had been critically disturbed just long enough for such events to occur.

Figure 12 represents a twelve-second sound clip illustrating the normal biophony of the diurnal transition between dawn and midmorning choruses. Notice the delicate biophonic patterns of insects, frogs, and birds. Figure 13, also twelve seconds, is taken from about two minutes later as part of the same recording sequence. It shows how the biophony broke up because of the plane flying overhead, its integrity shattered by the engine noise. It took a little more than five minutes for the jet noise to completely disappear—a result of the plane flying so low. If it had been at a higher altitude, the noise would likely have resonated for several minutes longer.

As in the Amazon, the effects of noise on the biophonies of the Sierra Nevada mountain range are beginning to be recognized. In the early 2000s, I, along with Stuart Gage from Michigan

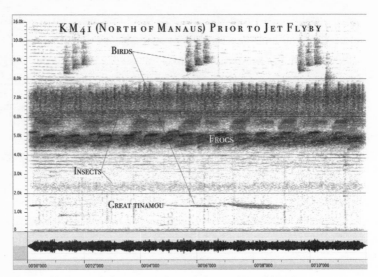

Figure 12. Amazon dawn-to-midmorning transitional biophony.

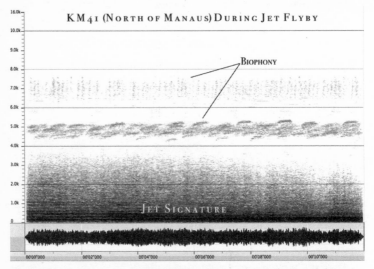

Figure 13. Same site as Figure 12 two minutes later, during multiengine jet flyover.

State University and a few other colleagues, received a commission to do a yearlong initial soundscape study in Sequoia and King's Canyon National Park — a large but not-as-well-known park as Yosemite and a few miles to its south. Our objective was to establish a baseline collection of soundscapes from four sites over each of the four seasons. During our third session, in late May, we had just set up our mic systems to measure the dynamics of a spring dawn chorus when a formation of F-18 military jets from the nearby Lemoore Naval Air Station flew overhead. Even though they were flying more than two miles above us, the low-frequency rumble at one end of the spectrum, combined with the high-speed screams of the aircraft hurtling by, caused the biophony to suddenly drop off. After the jet noise disappeared some six or seven minutes later, the area remained quiet — the dawn chorus not rebounding to the peak levels that we recorded when there was no aircraft noise.

David Graber, the chief scientist of the Pacific West Region of the National Park Service stationed at Sequoia and King's Canyon National Park, remarked to us that the mix of species, as well as the total number of birds, had been declining over the nearly two decades that he had been present. Since for several years the park had been affected by severe air pollution coming from the Central Valley to the north, by a period of drought, by a measurably warmer climate, and by a noticeable increase in noise from motor vehicles of all kinds and jet aircraft outbound to the east from the air base in nearby Visalia, he wasn't sure what combination of factors was causing observable changes in bird-species numbers and population declines overall. And while initially there was a decline in toad and frog populations, some of the species' numbers had appeared to stabilize. Having noticed the noise issue, Graber encouraged our study because it addressed, as a factor of our proposal, noise as a specific problem that could be examined in order to recommend improved policy guidelines.

During our Sequoia research program, we implemented new techniques and acoustic models with which we hoped to measure a wide range of conditions that affect the natural soundscape. These included all of Graber's concerns plus the issue of the habitat's landscape and biotic features (we were simultaneously working at four different types of sites within the park: oak forest, edge chaparral, riparian, and alpine). During these sessions, we began to confirm the loss that many of us had instinctively been feeling for some time. At every site I had recorded in the western United States and where I had returned over time to record again, patterns were beginning to emerge, such as shifts in the number of bird species and the density of their total numbers, as our work in Jackson Hole showed. Early indications from the data collected at Sequoia revealed that even distant noise-producing mechanisms interrupted the dawn chorus of many biomes within earshot—all at the same moment, many with cumulative impact. And although a lack of automated monitoring stations kept us from positively confirming this observation at the time, a shift in the biophonic mix of one site even appeared to have a similar bioacoustic effect on others nearby.

Little by little, data from the long-term audio collections we're building points to a noticeable overall decrease in creature density, diversity, and richness across many species in many environments, including some in Africa, Alaska, the Amazon Basin, Costa Rica, and the American West. However, we have yet to fully understand the operational mechanisms that determine the rates of recovery from noise intrusion (if the biophonies actually recover at all). As mentioned earlier, sometimes — if the biome is physically uncompromised and only intermittent anthrophony is an issue — revival of the natural soundscape from the effects of an event can take just minutes. On the other hand, depending on the relative impact of human intervention to the habitat, recovery can take much longer — nearly an hour, or a day, or even years. As many naturalists have observed, several species of birds, such as starlings, hawks, crows, sparrows, and robins, and some mammals, such as coyotes and even an occasional mountain lion, living in and around noisy urban environments seem to have habituated somewhat to the clatter we generate. There is no precise data on just how they have managed to acoustically accommodate to these surroundings. But, as their once-wild habitats are decreasing, mounting numbers of wild creatures have been observed finding new sites very close to or within range of human dwellings.

Noise wasn't much of a factor when I first ventured into the field in the 1960s. We were limited by the amount of time we could record with analog systems, so we needed to be selective. But even with so much to lug around and so little active recording time possible on-site, we didn't need to work so hard to find ideal spots — many were still viable — and the small sample sizes of our recordings made it less likely that we'd hear an interruption.

When much lighter and more portable digital audiotape (DAT) recorders came on the market in the late 1980s, granting us longer recording times, we began to capture more noise, partly because there *was* more noise but also because of the extended recording times themselves. It was becoming a noticeable and serious problem because it obscured the protomusical structures that made the biophonies particularly lovely to hear. Digital audio software for handling recorded sound was improving with each passing week, making it easier to handle and archive larger quantities of field recordings, so when we did manage to get clearly stated natural soundscapes, the recordings were more robust than ever.

Now, with solar-powered digital technologies containing no moving parts (only flash memory cards), not only are we tapeless but we no longer need to rely exclusively on hard drives on which to store data. We can place numerous recorders at given sites and record for hundreds of hours at a stretch with each unit—some packages weighing no more than a couple of pounds and providing quality recordings that well exceed those made just fifteen years ago with the best and most expensive gear. We hear it all: the good, and the bad.

The roots of our musical history can still be heard in the murmurs and sighs of a few remaining old-growth forests. At some very remote sites, the organized voices probably have shifted only moderately during the blip of geological time over which humans have existed. Yet the wealth of sonic information hidden within them is becoming more difficult to hear, because the biophonies are often masked. The impact of noise on my work has increased exponentially: taking into account the effect of habitat loss due to land development or resource extraction, I'm sorry to say that to record one noise-free hour of material now takes more than two hundred times as long as it did when I first began more than four decades ago. As the truly wild sites become fewer in number, the likely result is that human habitation or industry will always be close enough within range that anthrophony will almost never be completely absent. Based on many years of field experience and how much uninterrupted natural sound in a wild habitat I'm able to record in an hour, I'll make an educated guess that anthrophony can be heard in more than 80 to 90 percent of those biomes much of the time.

While noise diminishes our own experiences of the wild, creature behavior itself is likewise altered as a result of noise-induced stress. We know from observing wild animals held in captivity that they are greatly affected by their urban soundscape environments. (Captivity itself, of course, introduces its own behavioral stress issues.) In 1993, for example, a military jet buzzed Sweden's Frösö Zoo—about three hundred miles north of Stockholm—during a routine training flight. The tigers, lynx, and foxes panicked. The animals tore apart and ate twenty-three of their babies altogether, including five rare Siberian tiger cubs. Trying to protect their offspring from the onslaught of noise, the panicked animals resorted to infanticide.

Scott Creel, a professor at Montana State University, published a now-famous study on the effects of snowmobile noise on wolves and elk in Yellowstone, Isle Royale, and Voyageurs National Parks in 2002. Creel and colleagues measured the glucocorticoid enzyme levels in the feces of wolves and elk, which gave the researchers an indicator of the animals' stress responses. The secretion of glucocorticoids is a classic endocrine response to stress, and any measured increase in the levels found in many mammals correlates to escalated hypertension. The study concluded that the enzyme level found in the feces of both groups rose in direct proportion to the level of noise. When snowmobile noise was not present, the stress enzyme levels dropped back to normal. While it was clear that the noise induced stress, the authors also concluded that noise hadn't yet had an effect on the population dynamics of either group. (The study, incidentally, was partly funded by the timber industry in Michigan.)

When noise is introduced into a soundscape, disrupting the normal acoustic dynamics of a biome, animals tend to exhibit restless behavior. One of the first signs is that they either become silent or, depending on the noise, express fear through alarm calls.

Some animals are more obviously affected than others. In a spectrogram, the dropout of a number of insects often occurs. If the noise is intrusive and has a wide enough bandwidth, it will mask the voices of frogs and birds as well as mammals, and they, too, will stop vocalizing. In a rain forest, raptors, large wild cats, and other predators that rely on subtle changes in the soundscape need to adjust their behavior since it is more difficult for predators to hear their prey, and for prey, in turn, to hear the slight danger signs of potential attack. Noise in marine environments will cause fish to exhibit group aversion behavior, as many of us have witnessed when we tap the glass on the side of a large tank filled with several of the same schooling species. Simultaneously and instantly the school will veer in the opposite direction from the impulse noise. Noise may also weaken immune systems in mammals and fish—as is potentially the case with the elk and wolves exposed to snowmobile noise—and in the process compromise resistance to disease, the natural physiological result of high-stress hormone levels. And where the noise signal is loud enough, it may cause physical damage or death.

In the most severe cases, where the noise exceeds a level of tolerance, many species of whales and seals will beach themselves and die. Because sound introduced into marine environments can travel very long distances if unimpeded by landmasses, underwater mechanical or electronic noise can present special problems. This is apparent, for example, when assessing the impact of the excessive levels emitted by U.S. Navy Low Frequency Active Sonar (LFAS), which is thought to be a contributing factor to the deaths of Cuvier's beaked whales in both the Bahamas and the Mediterranean. Shortly after the sinking of the *Titanic* in 1912, researchers in the U.K. and Canada began experimenting with low-frequency ranging devices and developing a primitive class of oscillators and hydrophones that were used to detect submarines at the beginning of World War I. By World War II, mine and ship *sonar* (an acronym for Sound Navigation and Ranging) technology had vastly improved, with fairly accurate reception. As with bat echolocation, sub acousticians would send out a ranging signal that, when it bounced off a distant object, could help determine (by the returning difference signal) the object's distance and if it was static or moving. And, if moving, approximately in what direction and at what speed.

Breakthroughs in advanced naval ship design and construction during the Cold War made vessels much quieter and thus harder to identify; with those changes, more accurate detection equipment became necessary. By the 1980s, the U.S. Navy decided that the best alternative to the older models was the new LFAS. Without any environmental impact statement (EIS), the Navy bypassed the usual permitting required under the Endangered Species Act (ESA) and the National Environmental Policy Act (NEPA) and began testing. By 1996, after an increase in multiple whale beachings and public outrage, the Navy agreed to a review by a team that would evaluate the environmental response to the sound, in particular by marine mammals. Called the Scientific Research Program (SRP), the team consisted of both government and academic members. The output from the Navy's systems, the team determined, was reported to be in excess of 235 dB. At three hundred miles from the source, it still retains an intensity of 140 dB, potentially harmful and even lethal to many marine organisms within range. In 2003 a federal court judge in San Francisco mandated that the Navy reduce the system's use so that ocean wildlife would not be harmed.

In 2001 Ken Balcomb, a whale biologist and founder of the Center for Whale Research located in Friday Harbor, Washington, wrote an open letter to the LFAS program manager. In Balcomb's words:

When Cuvier's beaked whales are exposed to high intensity sonar at their airspace resonance frequency via LFAS or midrange sonar it can be painful and life threatening. Envision a football squeezed to the size of a ping-pong ball by air pressure alone. Now envision this ping-pong ball compressing and decompressing hundreds of times per second. Imagine this ping-pong ball located in your head, between your two ears. This is what the Cuvier's beaked whales experienced as a result of the Navy's sonar testing in the Bahamas in March 2000. Airspace resonance phenomena resulted in hemorrhaging which caused the stranding and deaths in the Bahamas.

The lethal impact of the LFAS signal—which can transmit extremely high levels of signal from twelve to sixty miles—affects beaked whales and other marine creatures such as dolphins, minke whales, killer whales, and fish.

But sonar is not the only anthrophonic source that affects marine life. While I was working on my doctorate, I was involved in a study done for the national parks in Glacier Bay, Alaska. We wanted to determine why, despite ample food resources, humpback whale populations in the bay were declining. Humpback whales were seen swimming away from the perceived danger of large tourist vessels that generated huge amounts of propeller and engine noise, and hiding in the acoustic shadows of island landmasses or large bodies of calved ice. The report concluded that uncontrolled loud vessel noise had been at least one of the major probable causes of the population decline. For several years the report wasn't made public because, according to Charles Jurasz, a biology teacher and naturalist from Juneau and the principal investigator of the study, the National Park Service was ordered to quash the findings by James Watt, then secretary of the interior. Given the negative impact it might have on tourist-vessel traffic in the bay, the park service complied with the order. Jurasz was never again allowed into Glacier Bay to confirm his data or to do a follow-up study. When I asked if he had tried, he told me that he had many times but was unable to obtain the necessary permit to continue his work. The rejection left him devastated. Nevertheless, Jurasz's groundbreaking humpback-whale bubble netting and identification efforts were recently honored by the National Oceanic and Atmospheric Administration.

Over the past few decades the noise emitted by commercial vessels in Glacier Bay has been somewhat mitigated with vessel engines, hulls, and propellers designed to generate less vibration. And recent reports show that the whale populations have returned to "near normal" numbers. Allison Banks and Chris Gabriele, National Park Service employees at Bartlett Cove in Glacier Bay, told me in June 2010 that the humpback whales are once again thriving.

In a recently published study on marine anthrophony, Hans Slabbekoorn of the Institute of Biology at Leiden University in the Netherlands demonstrated that loud industrial sounds of short exposure—like blasts and sonar pinging—can harm fish. Unlike marine mammals that receive and process sound and vocalize, many fish species have two organs that detect marine pressure waves, as mentioned earlier. One is the inner ear—they have no middle or outer ear—which can detect frequencies into the thousands of hertz. The other is the lateral line—a thin organ that runs in a straight, narrow line from the gill to the tail—which picks up low-frequency sound waves, usually those below 100 Hz.

Noises with longer exposures potentially impact larger areas and numerous species. Slabbekoorn noted that:

> Recent experimental evidence has unequivocally shown that sounds can modify mate choice decisions in fish. Female haplochromine cichlids provided with a choice between two males, matched in size and color, preferred to interact with the male associated with playback of conspecific sounds…[but] the sounds of passing boats were inferred to reduce detection distances by up to 100 times. Masking, leading to a reduction in detection distance, or the so-called active space, can lead to failure in mate attraction.

So, noise can affect sexual selection, breeding cycles, and population dynamics—but exactly to what extent remains unclear.

Several publications have resulted from current National Park Service noise studies. Among the recent studies in 2009 and 2011 are those by Jesse Barber, Kevin Crooks, and Kurt Fristrup, which examine the effects of noise on what is referred to as the "effective listening area," the territory over which animal vocal signals carry so that they can be heard and responded to. Each points out in different ways that even though minimal levels of noise were observed (such as a 3 dB increase from a wind farm, aircraft, or road traffic), the impact reduced the listening area (the ability of the study animals to receive their respective biophonic signals) by 30 percent. These studies are important because they go beyond the former tendency to concentrate obliquely on issues of noise vis-à-vis what humans are able to discern with the aid of technology or by real-time listening. In other words, previous focus concentrated on "audible noise" emanating mostly from aircraft without addressing the core questions of animal impact, causal behavior, and the effect on visitor experience. Instead, these new studies begin to address the ways in which anthrophony affects living organisms across all species lines and what specific classes of aircraft (or other) noises affect animal behavior and visitor experience. By finally embracing these fundamental issues, researchers have begun to examine evidence of cause and effect on a grander scale, taking seriously the idea that different species are affected by different types of noise, in different ways, at different times of day and night, and over the seasonal course of each year.

One late-fall holiday when I was a child, my parents took my sister and me to the snow-covered valleys of Yellowstone National Park. From where we stood, midway between the park entrance at West Yellowstone and Old Faithful, overlooking a wide valley, a complete absence of human noise engulfed us, even close to the road: a stillness punctuated by an extensive repertoire of ravens and the vocalizations of jays, magpies, horned larks, elk, and other four-legged creatures that were drawn to lower elevations by better prospects for protection and food. At moments, it was so still that we could locate organisms from the sounds of their breath, faintly detected over distance across the snowy fields. Even more subtle was the softer texture of space created by the hush of faraway streams and the slightest breezes diffusing through the upper reaches of the conifers. I dream of that enchanting moment still.

The last time I visited—February 2002, standing in the same spot where my parents had lingered beside the road to hear the winter over half a century ago—the magic was entirely gone, obliterated by engine noise and smog. More recently, the snowmobile issue has been moderated to some extent by restrictions on noise and speed, four-cycle technologies, and the number of vehicles allowed in the park at any one time. But nobody's completely happy. At one extreme—if you can call it an "extreme"—environmentalists don't want any snowmobile or straight-piping motorcycle noise in the parks. Snowmobilers don't like being confined to the park's speed restrictions and the necessity of traveling in convoys, thus having a government agency restricting their individual "freedoms." At least there is an option: there are two thousand miles of open, unrestricted national forest trails just outside the park boundaries in West Yellowstone. But for the promise of some tranquillity in the park itself, there is no such similar haven outside its protective borders for the rest of us and, without a long hike, relatively little within.

National parks are protected areas—it takes an act of Congress to establish one—yet anthrophony, such as snowmobile noise at Yellowstone, has been a problem at many nonurban U.S. national parks.

At Grand Canyon, noise from sightseeing flights and the whistling tourist steam train that travels along the rim intrudes into any awestruck reverie one might otherwise enjoy while standing above or hiking within the chasm. The pictures of the park really do convey only a tiny fraction of the experience.

And in Grand Teton National Park, a regional airport is situated midway in the valley that defines Jackson Hole. It's the only such airport located within national park boundaries. The Jackson tower releases as many as twenty flights an hour between six a.m. and eleven p.m., repeatedly annihilating the natural soundscape of one of the most beautiful spots in America. (The bulk of the flights are private; the airport in 2007 handled only about seven commercial flights each day.) In California's great Mojave Desert, dune buggies and dirt bikes fracture the natural quiet at many sites.

Still, there have been rays of hope. We are beginning to understand—albeit late in the game—that pristine natural soundscapes are reserves and resources as much as unimpeded sight lines and are just as critical to our enjoyment and awareness of the natural wild world. When sole federal authority for noise control fell under the aegis of the Federal Aviation Administration in 1982, the National Park Service was left struggling to deal with its noise issues. However, recognizing the crucial link between humanity and the soundscapes of the wild, a couple of activists within the NPS initiated a strong educational and administrative model to protect natural soundscapes as a valued resource.

The late Wes Henry and his colleague Bill Schmidt undertook this radical feat through a series of below-the-radar meetings and incremental steps beginning in the mid-1990s and concluding in 2001. For a short time within the NPS acoustic program, wild soundscapes were treated as a component of great value worth preserving for visitors and creatures alike. Henry, Schmidt, and a few others who later joined the program recognized that there were vast areas within the parks where soundscapes could still be enjoyed. Visitor reaction to the noise in the national parks convinced enough NPS and Interior Department employees that it was important to attempt to hear and treat soundscapes differently—as necessary to visitor enjoyment as the informed management of wild critter life and the habitats in which they thrive.

Efforts like these have had some positive results: snowmobiles have been moderately controlled and monitored in Yellowstone; tourist overflights in Rocky Mountain National Park have been pretty much eliminated; and flights over Grand Canyon have varying restrictions on a certain number of aircraft, areas, times, and conditions that the FAA and the NPS review and change from time to time, pretty much determined by the political climate in Washington at any given moment. Recently, tourist sightseeing aircraft noise in Grand Canyon has gotten much worse: as of this writing and according to the Grand Canyon Chapter of the Sierra Club, it is estimated that the daylight tourist overflight aircraft noise has increased to the point where 75 percent of visitors hear aircraft 100 percent of the time, and the remaining 25 percent hear it a minimum of 60 percent of the time in all but the most remote areas of the park. However, given the sweeping changes in priorities since 2000—when George W. Bush was elected president—and a current focus on other, more pressing matters, the ultimate fate of these policies remains uncertain, since the original directive under which they were implemented expired in 2004. Depending on the political climate of the moment, the resistance of many in government to environmental protections means that, at least in the near term, there is a high risk that activities such as the visitor soundscape program will not continue to be supported in the visionary ways they were originally intended.

In fact, I'm convinced that the concept of natural soundscapes represents a threat to some people. At one point, I was commissioned by Wes Henry to write the visitor soundscape activity plan for the program. Titled *Wild Soundscapes in the National Parks: An Educational Program Guide to Listening and Recording,* its agenda was, at first, administered under the "Natural Soundscape Program" moniker. The goal of the program was to preserve natural soundscapes within park boundaries as much for a more complete visitor experience as for wildlife protection, and its mandate extended within the parks and to some other Department of the Interior (DOI) areas. It gave large populations of folks accessibility to the sounds of the natural world many would not otherwise have been able to enjoy. But the name, Natural Soundscape Program, was changed in 2004 to the Natural Sounds Program — a neutered term evocative of nothing in particular — and the targeted visitor focus all but disappeared along with the title change.

On the surface, altering a name seems inconsequential enough. But the event did not come about without some powerful influence from outside the DOI, with the result that the change emasculated much of the insightful work that had preceded it.

Secretary of the Interior Gale Norton had been urged by Alaska representative Don Young, then chairman of the House Appropriations Committee, and his colleague Richard Pombo, the ex-representative from the 11th district of California, to alter the name. They felt that the term *soundscape* was too loaded (translation: "green," although the etymological roots of the word have no more political or social resonance than the words *landscape* or *seascape*).

Howie Thompson, a friend and part of the NPS soundscape program during the height of its development and subsequent discussions before he retired, recalled that because of the political pressure in early 2004 (a consequence of the Young-Pombo letter in November 2003), within a number of weeks of the new year, word had filtered down from Norton's office, apparently through Fran Mainella, then director of the National Park Service, advising the group that it would be wise to change the name to the Natural Sounds Program. Don Young, also chairman of the Committee on Transportation and Infrastructure—the group that oversaw the Department of the Interior—called the shots and spoke plainly about his contempt for restrictions on open public spaces and for those who tried to implement them. An impression of Young's passion can be found in a 2006 *Rolling Stone* article, where Young is quoted as saying that "environmentalists are a self-centered bunch of waffle-stomping, Harvard-graduating, intellectual idiots" who "are not Americans, never have been Americans, never will be Americans." During a debate on native Alaskans' right to sell the sex organs of endangered animals for the purpose of aphrodisiacs, he pulled out an eighteen-inch penis bone of a walrus and brandished it like a sword on the House floor.

When initiated by Wes Henry and Bill Schmidt, the NPS soundscape program was astute and two-pronged. One component concentrated on abating noise introduced by tourist helicopters, fixed-wing aircraft, and ground-level modes of transportation. The second dealt with protection of natural soundscapes for their own intrinsic value and involved comprehensive visitor programs and activities focused on the subject of soundscapes. This second component was a crucial step in making people aware of the importance of preserving them. During the Bush II administration, however—and according to Howie Thompson, fueled by the Young-Pombo warning letter to Norton—the visitor component of the Natural Soundscape Program was sidetracked, diminished, and, except for a small web presence still in place, minimally implemented. At the same time, federal funding resources directed to the national parks were reduced substantially, the underlying political idea at the time being that most operations within the system could be outsourced and privatized. Where the soundscape concept had been originally framed for visitors as an important resource, for several years that focus did not have the same sense of import within the agency. In the spring of 2011, there appeared to be a shift in direction when the NPS Natural Sounds Program office in Fort Collins issued an internal interpretative handbook titled *The Power of Sound,* designed, once again, to introduce the public to a natural soundscape overview.

The larger issue is that natural soundscapes are themselves one of the most fertile unexplored open sources of information we have. They contain secrets of our origins, our past, our cultural present, along with significant insights into our future — the increasing presence of our noise, the changes that are based on shifting climate or human evolution. But we need the sensibility, the education, the grace, the patience, and the curiosity to ferret out all these vital riddles. Bias- and agenda-free in the purest sense — with no way to frame them otherwise — biophonies contain the acoustic compass we need to guide us along the route of an ever-challenged planet. With ocean and atmospheric conditions warming, tides rising, and magnetic poles shifting, biophonies are adapting nearly everywhere as a result of interconnected impacts, many of which we simply do not fully understand yet. Some habitats contain whole new mixes of vocal organisms, while others have become seriously depleted or silent altogether.

When noise becomes part of our environment, we expend considerable amounts of energy to shut or filter it out. Yet, when we hear the soundscape organized in familiar patterns, it gets our attention—sometimes in very positive ways. I am reminded of my dad, who died more than a decade ago. Soon after he became afflicted with frontal lobe dementia in his late eighties, he was bedridden for nearly a year and could move only short distances on his own with the help of a walker or a nurse's aide. Yet, at his ninetieth birthday party, held at a restaurant with a small dance floor, we brought some easy dance music to play through the establishment's system. Seconds after it began, damn if he didn't get up off his chair, move to the middle of the dance floor, and, with his thirtysomething grandsons and several other genera- tions of relatives, *dance* unassisted and energetically for what must have been the better part of twenty or thirty minutes. Talk- ing, watching TV, and being read to did nothing to link him to the present; nothing in the nursing home where he had taken up residence could bring him to his feet. Only the organization of sound—that ancient link to a world long past—could do it.

In *Musicophilia,* Oliver Sacks refers to patients with numerous infirmities—from Parkinson's to brain tumors—who, when they detect a familiar rhythmic pulse or tune, seem to transform themselves, shaking off their states of inactivity and becoming one with the music, clapping, moving their bodies, singing, or actually dancing. Given this response to music, what, then, might be the effect of organized natural sound? Louis Sarno suggests that a partial answer can be found with the Ba'Aka: when they become psychically and physically diminished by the stress introduced through contact with modernity, the soundscapes of their traditional deep-forest homes—far from civilization— have the same effect on them as music did on my father.

CHAPTER NINE

The Coda of Hope

In early 1990, on our way to record at what is now called Parque Estadual do Rio Doce, a small protected biological island in the Minas Gerais region of Brazil, we had an overnight layover in Rio de Janeiro. Through a good friend, a colleague and I were invited to have dinner with Antônio Carlos Jobim, the composer of "The Girl from Ipanema," "Desafinado," and "One Note Samba" and a pioneer of the bossa nova musical style. When "Tom" (as he was known to all Brazilians) heard of our planned soundscape mission, he spent the entire evening and early-morning hours recounting the days of his childhood, when he and his friends played under the jungle canopy, performing music with the subtropical forest animals that once came right to the edge of Rio. To animate his stories, he imitated the calls and songs of the beloved birds, frogs, and mammals that he remembered — many now long gone — with an eloquence and ease that suggested the vocalizations were part of his native

201

language. His poignant imitation of a passerine — a finch — was so articulate that customers looked around to see if there was actually a bird in the restaurant.

"It's sad," he added, shaking his head slowly. "A couple of years ago I dedicated an album to these birds [*Passarim*]. Parque Estadual, where you're headed in the morning, is four hundred kilometers north of here. And it's a tiny remnant of what was one of the natural wonders of the world. It's what remains of the same forest where I used to play with my friends. Only, the jungle's edge used to be within walking distance of this restaurant. Last time I was there, the sounds were almost gone because the forest is split up into segments and completely surrounded by farms and development and its size is greatly reduced. Record it well. It's the last of what was once the great Mata Atlântica, the Atlantic Rain Forest."

It was close to sunrise when we finally returned to our hotel. With no time left for showers or a change of clothes, we were picked up early for the eight-hour transition from the hustle of central Rio de Janeiro to Rio Doce. Our campsite there was surrounded by huge deciduous trees over a hundred feet in height, especially the bottle-shaped barrigudas that sheltered us. On our first hike into the forest after we arrived, we found a rare group of golden lion tamarin monkeys high in the canopy, and captured high-pitched chatter perfectly forged. We were lucky. We never heard or saw them again.

Thousands of species that lived in this once magnificent forest are gone now. Many are extinct. Others that could migrate and required much larger unimpeded spaces moved elsewhere. By the time we arrived, less than 1 percent of the vibrant original forest habitat remained. The resident naturalist told us that it would be slow to recover even if more land was made available and returned from agriculture to a wild state, although some animals, such as the tamarin monkeys, were reintroduced with limited success. Many creatures, human and wild, that once established a precarious balance disappeared from this enchanted locale in just the last century. We could deeply sense the lack of density. A few rare woolly spider monkeys and some howler monkeys came near enough to record, but there was only light, sporadic birdsong. And there was nothing specific even from insects. The biophony sounded too thin—far less dense than we anticipated for a rain forest, even a dry one. It's as if a full pit orchestra and a cast of dozens for a Broadway show such as *Spider-Man* had been reduced to a trio. My colleague was ecstatic that we recorded the monkeys—but that feeling was tempered by the sadness we experienced when we saw the incredible devastation evident nearly everywhere we walked. Slash-and-burn deforestation feels to me like the loss of a beloved family member—the missing are never completely forgotten. No place we walked was far enough away for us to escape the ghosts of modern human impact.

While we are drowning out the intricate natural sounds of the biophony and geophony with human-generated noise, we are also altering—or destroying—the wild natural world itself. We're increasingly aware of that, of course, but with a global economy that progressively ignores the consequences of its own growth, it's helpful—and sobering at the same time—to see the diminishing extent of the wild as it's represented acoustically in my own archives.

In total, I've recorded the sounds of well over fifteen thousand species and collected more than forty-five hundred hours of natural ambience. Nearly 50 percent of the habitats I have in my library have become so seriously compromised—if not biophonically silent—that many of these once-rich natural soundscapes can now be heard only in this collection. It may not be the largest collection in total hours recorded—with solar-powered digital technologies and multiple systems in one venue, one can now collect thousands of hours of data in a single month. But my archive of focused and attended field recordings, emphasizing quality over quantity, holds the biggest and oldest collection of once-present biophonies from magical places, many of which we're unlikely to hear live again. Why the change? The most obvious reason, of course, is the loss of representative habitats. A second is the increase of human noise that tends to mask the subtle aural textures of the remaining environments. A direct result of those issues is a decrease in the density and diversity of key vocal creatures, both large and small, that make up typical natural soundscapes.

Scientists generally agree that we have had five previous mass extinctions over the course of life on our planet. The theme of a recent World Science Festival held in New York was the Sixth Extinction. The story of the Sixth Extinction is set in the era we live in—the Holocene, a period beginning a dozen or so millennia ago. To some, this era includes the whole of human agricultural civilization and begins with the earth's natural warming cycle following the last ice age—the time I wrote about in the opening pages of this book. At the beginning of the Holocene, the numbers and varieties of nonhuman animals were at a peak that we can barely imagine today. However, wherever humans migrated, great numbers of species were lost, usually beginning with the large mammals—the megafauna—and easy-to-capture ground-dwelling birds and their eggs. Now, according to one estimate made in the 1990s by the biologist Edward O. Wilson, approximately thirty thousand species per year are disappearing. In 2005 Wilson revised this prediction, saying that at the current rate of human disruption of the biosphere, half the life-forms on earth will have been lost by 2100.

Humans, populating Australia, New Zealand, smaller islands in the Pacific, the Caribbean, the Mediterranean, and the coast of Southern Africa, tapped into an abundance of animal and plant resources. No worldwide climactic or celestial event—such as an asteroid hitting the earth—triggered these great losses: it was our transformation of the environments we began to inhabit, combined with the invasive organisms that we introduced into our new habitats, including everything from microbes, to rats, to domestic cats, to other aggressive species, that have added to these effects.

Hawaii, for instance, may be a paradise for some. On the other hand, to others it is considered the extinction capital of the world. In a couple of centuries since the islands were populated by Europeans, fully half of the 140 bird species have disappeared. The Europeans, however, weren't entirely to blame. The plumage of many birds was prized first by Polynesian royalty and later by colonists from America. So the birds with pretty feathers didn't have much of a chance. Just one existing Polynesian cloak that was made entirely of avian feathers, dated to about six hundred years ago, required the killing of several thousand birds. But mollusks and some insects, such as a variety of moths, have also disappeared, their habitats utterly transformed by human intervention.

On the other side of the planet, off the eastern coast of Africa on the island of Madagascar, fifteen species of lemurs, an elephant bird (*Aepyornis*), a pygmy hippo, and giant tortoises have gone extinct—not to mention 90 percent of the lowland forests and an estimated half of the animals, including indigenous insects and birds. The forests no longer served as shelter for the creature life the Malagasy depended on, and an increasing cycle of loss became apparent not only from what was seen but from what was heard — and what wasn't. Just imagine the soundscapes we might be hearing now if not for those casualties.

If we compare what presently exists with what we believe was happening sixteen thousand years ago, the differences are distressing. It isn't only that species are dying off at alarming rates but, as Terry Glavin emphasizes in his book *The Sixth Extinction,* that we're also losing a legacy of music, languages, and ways of seeing, knowing, and living. It's a different world — and a different world won't sound as it did five or five hundred or five thousand years ago.

As the creatures go, so goes a vast storehouse of information that speaks to the roots of nearly every cultural facet of our existence. When I shared the World Science Festival stage at Columbia University with Richard Leakey in the fall of 2008, we spent several hours that evening recounting various perspectives on the Sixth Extinction. The largest species extinction rate is occurring among mammals. According to a *Scientific American* article printed that same year, a staggering one in four mammal species is threatened. With the exception of a few sites, frog populations are generally in decline worldwide. And birds, aside from sheer numerical drops, are beginning to show radical signs of territorial shifting at both ends of migratory routes and many places in between. Mostly, Leakey and I agreed that things are beginning to quiet down even in the most pristine habitats. Perhaps John Cage's "4'33"" was set as a cryptic expression of the natural world soundscape in anticipation of a coming event he neglected to share with us.

The combination of shrinking habitat and increasing human pandemonium has produced conditions under which the communication channels necessary for creature survival are being completely overloaded. At the same time, we are denying ourselves an experience of the wild natural world that is essential to our spiritual and psychological health—a source of rooted wisdom that we simply can't acquire from other aspects of our modern lives. The voices of the wild in their purest states, where no human noise is present, are splendid symphonies—ensembles to tap into and emulate. But echoing the sentiments of so many before him, the ecologist Bill McKibben once said: "What sets wilderness apart in the modern day is not that it's dangerous (it's almost certainly safer than any town or road) or that it's solitary (you can, so they say, be alone in a crowded room) or full of exotic animals (there are more at the zoo). It's that five miles out in the woods you can't buy anything." The resounding animal proto-orchestra—the concerto of the natural world that has inspired our own music—is diminishing in volume by the day. The fragile weave of natural sound is being torn apart by our seemingly boundless need to conquer the environment rather than to find a way to abide in consonance with it.

Given how hard it has become to locate the native orchestrations of our unaltered habitats, I find that exposing the fundamentals of our musical past and the origins of complex intraspecies connections—challenging already—has become even more difficult. Especially amazing to me are the radical acoustic changes that have taken place in just a bit more than half the course of my life—a geological nanosecond.

With the ebb and flow of "normal" climate cycles, most natural soundscapes can be expected to change gradually over a long span of time. But the rate is occurring much faster than any of us could have imagined. A Native American woman, ninety-one when I recorded her in 1971, was even aware of the shift in her lifetime. Part of that prescient account was told to me by Elizabeth Wilson, elder of the Nez Percé tribe, one fall day in that year. It's a narrative generated from a number of stories she told. And it is one that belongs to all of us. Incidentally, the flute melody heard at the beginning of this recording was from the same flute that Elizabeth's son, Angus, cut from the reeds, whittled, and played at the Lake Wallowa site mentioned at the beginning of chapter 2.

The way the medicine men went and got guiding spirit
Contact with animals or whatever it is,
They kept on dancing every winter.
They got strong and power came to them. Power came to
*   them.*
Everything was different.
It must have been in those times when everything was
*   different*
Clear air and wilderness, and they could get in touch with
*   animals like that.*
But I don't think they can now.
Everything gone — noise and all...
All right! Legend days will be over; humanity is coming soon.
No more legend days.
There will be no more
And they will be sad like I am,
Brokenhearted over my last child
Never to return again.
Death takes her.
And that's the way it's going to be;
I wander alone only in the higher mountains
And the heads of the streams all the way through.
I'm never down anywhere where it's civilized country.
I'm way up in the wilderness.

Years to come people will lose their only child
And they'll have the feeling just like I have; sad.
And that's why these days we are that way.
Sadness comes to us.

Later, in another recording, Elizabeth also made a remarkable comment about a melody revealed in the misty breath of a buffalo in winter-morning sunlight. "A kind of whistle and sigh," she said, her eyes looking off into the distance. "A whole song in a whistle and a sigh." She didn't elaborate. Yet these types of meaningful aphorisms were innate parts of every story she told.

Angus Wilson was reminiscing about the qualities of wind with his mother when I happened to catch their exchange on tape. "Up the Snake River, the wind blew in such a way that it sounded like a group of men and women off in the distance, all singing in a low soft voice at once," Angus recalled.

"It's a special wind that sounds like a whispered *timmmmm-mmm* as it blows through the dead snags. We used to hear it everywhere, but you only hear it now down in the valleys along the river where fire has swept through," his mother answered. "And even one snag will sound in the wind. But when there's a bunch altogether, they all sing out to us. It's a sad noise. I've heard that. It hits all the notes." Angus and Elizabeth mused how the wind taught the water to sing sad songs, an emotion expressed often. Then the water, lonely because it wanted to sing with spirits other than the wind, taught the insects, who in turn taught the frogs, who taught the birds and the bears and the squirrels. The Nez Percé learned their music and dances from the geophony and their animal guides — the sounds of the natural world always driving forces in their lives, until contact with "modern" humans altered the soundscape.

. . .

With so much of my collection of recorded sound coming from now-compromised or vanished habitats, the archive represents thousands of biophonies that no one will likely be able to hear again in their wild states. (When I began recording in 1968, fully 45 percent of our old-growth forests in the Lower 48 were still standing. By 2011 there were less than 2 percent of those forests remaining.) It is true that a habitat's acoustic properties change in time. But within relatively short periods (thousands of years, for example) it is reasonable to assume that, all things being more or less ecologically equal and untrammeled, habitats and soundscapes will remain within the limits of well-established ranges, adjusting only for natural changes in climate, weather events, or geological transformation.

At the end of the last ice age, natural soundscapes likely varied within the boundaries of a dynamic equilibrium in which the peaks of vocal species' density and diversity rose and fell with the twenty-four-hour cycles of weather and season—that is, animal sounds performed in more or less predictable ways, with the "normal" climate fluctuations of given spans of time, yet always adjusting for optimum transmission and reception within a body of multiple voices, just as they always have. Even in the late 1960s, when I first began recording, I could be relatively assured that when I returned to a favorite spot from year to year, the soundscape signature would be at least familiar. The biophony conveyed a thread of continuity, and there was variation only in the actual performance, not in the context or content. Then things began to change rapidly—mainly in the 1980s.

The soundscapes of newer biomes—those that endured transitions as a result of human activity — reflect various degrees of order and chaos. But to get a sense of how changes in a habitat might have evolved, we can only compare (because quality recording technologies are only about a half century old) what we think are relatively undisturbed old-growth habitats with those at different stages of growth or recovery. That is, while we can construct computer models that provide some sketchy information, we can't precisely evaluate the biophony of a biome that is currently changing against how it may have sounded a thousand — or a hundred or even fifty — years ago.

To get a feel for how a soundscape might evolve as a result of human activity, I've generated three successive spectrograms, related only insofar as they came from once healthy tropical or subtropical biomes. This is not meant to be a comparison of actual habitat types. It is only to show, in gross terms, the variations in structural biophonic density as a result of various degrees of human intervention and what we would expect to see if we had long-term before-and-after examples from the same site. Two of the following are from tropical and relatively similar habitats, and one is from a subtropical biome. The first, from Borneo (Figure 14), represents an old-growth habitat at dawn. Without going into creature-specific detail, we can look at the way in which all the sounds are clearly defined and how densely packed they are. The second (Figure 15), from Sumatra, represents a habitat that is stressed by some logging but that is also, from all visual appearances, in a stage of recovery. Note how there is some biophonic detail, but it is much less dense than in Figure 14. And the third (Figure 16), from Costa Rica, shows a habitat that was clear-cut in the 1990s and has not yet recovered. There is no density. Aside from a few insects, there is little discrimination to define any aspect of it.

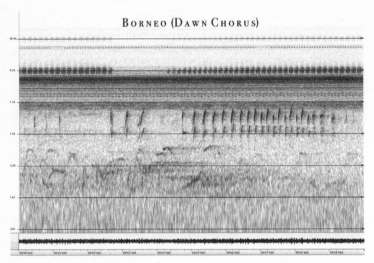

Figure 14. Borneo old growth.

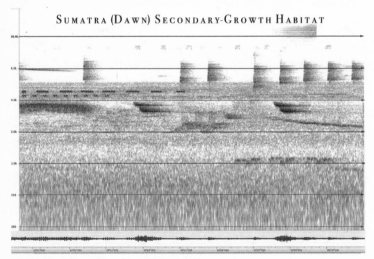

Figure 15. Sumatra secondary growth.

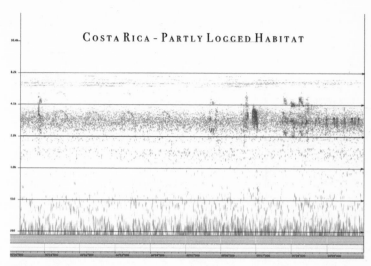

Figure 16. Costa Rica clear-cut to edge habitat.

The wild natural world—comprised of vast areas not managed by humans—rarely exists in much of any form now, except perhaps in a few isolated places such as the Alaskan wilderness, the far Canadian north, Siberia, and parts of the Antarctic. It certainly cannot be found now in Africa or Australia, or in the remaining millions of fenced and managed acres of nationally designated forest and parkland in the United States. That said, there are a few large private landholdings throughout the American West that have easements designed to protect both wildlife and wild vegetation—models introduced by nongovernmental organizations such as the Nature Conservancy and Conservation International—an idea that may have positive global implications.

If the U.S. national parks represent "America's best idea," as was suggested in the promos for the PBS television series about our national parks, then we have some serious thinking to do. The late-nineteenth-century-managed wild idea that makes up the flora and fauna in our park system was initially predicated on the plan to kick large Native American populations—human groups who lived in a quasi-dynamic balance with sustainable wildness—out of those areas so that federal lands could be developed initially as exotic playgrounds for wealthy white vacationers. In the last century, several federal and state government land-management agencies, particularly in Wyoming, Idaho, and Montana, mandated the elimination of key predator species— wolves, for instance—partly out of fear that visitors would become prey.

These managed environments, though treasured for their many unspoiled vistas, are hardly recipes for wildness. Wildness is not managed, and it's not marked with signage, or well-kept trails, or detailed maps, or gift shops selling mugs and T-shirts, or eager interpretive naturalists explaining the intimate habits of elk or grizzlies. As the author Jack Turner assures us, the wild exists when we find ourselves in places where we can walk steadily in one direction for a week without hitting a road or fence—as in the Arctic National Wildlife Refuge, for example—where we are one-on-one with and alert to the nonhuman creature and floral world in all its forms, and where we are made alive by the awareness of our solitude. Of course, that's difficult to do in the Lower 48, where 83 percent of the land area is located within two-thirds of a mile from a road.

In order to hear the wild biophonic world, we need to get to places free from human noise. I don't mean sites that are silent. If they were, we wouldn't hear anything at all. Few places are completely and naturally sound-free—and you don't want to spend too much time where they do exist. In most habitats—even inside a remote house, for example—there is some detectable level of ambient sound that provides us with a sense of orientation. It's an acoustic reference that many of us need in order to feel comfortable.

Almost no sentient creature can thrive in a completely silent environment. Silence implies sensory deprivation. Consider, for example, an anechoic chamber—usually a small room a few hundred square feet in size and designed to be dead silent with no reverberation. These highly controlled environments are typically used to test the noise characteristics of very high-end microphones and speaker systems. If you ever find yourself inside one, try to remain calm for more than a few minutes without experiencing the onset of a mental breakdown.

Once, while on assignment, I accidentally stumbled across a nearly anechoic location at the bottom of the Grand Canyon. It was the quietest place I've ever been in the natural world—a remote box canyon with high sandstone walls about a mile in from the river. I had hiked there and set up camp one afternoon. Resting quietly for a moment, I quickly realized that all I could hear was the blood coursing through my veins; a low-level pulsing thud at one end of the spectrum and a whine I had never heard before at the other, probably from a nascent case of tinnitus; and my own rustling as I scouted for a place to put my bedroll. For a moment, I thought I'd lost my hearing. When I checked a sound-level meter to test for ambient levels, its screen registered the lowest level it could read—bottoming out at 10 dBA—dead quiet. After a short period, I became so disoriented by the complete silence that I started to talk and sing to myself and throw rocks at the canyon walls just to hear some kind of sound other than the blood in my head and the growing internal din in my ears. I was being driven insane by the lack of any acoustic cues. It

215

didn't take long before I packed up my gear and moved back within the welcome earshot of the river, where the distant moving water provided an acoustic point of orientation.

Tranquillity, on the other hand, signifies something very different and is a fundamental condition healthy organisms need in order to feel physically and mentally vigorous. Speaking from experience, Chris Watson, formerly a musician and now a leading BBC natural world recordist, suggests that we crave locations and times where we can find this sense of tranquillity—a point of serenity much more subtle than what silence implies. It is that audible transition zone, an acoustic ecotone between measurable soundscape and dead quiet—one that affects our emotional brain and psychologically guides us to a sense of sheer peacefulness.

For a radio program he coproduced for BBC Four titled *A Small Slice of Tranquillity,* Watson spent some time investigating the nature of acoustic tranquillity, asking whether it's a state of mind or an actual place. Wanting to know how people thought about the concept, he visited a museum exhibit where the sounds of a pregnant woman's womb were represented, showing how a sixteen-week-old fetus might experience the sonic environment of heartbeats and pumping blood while immersed in amniotic fluid. Watson's further investigations, involving medical practitioners and psychologists, confirmed that there were certain sounds—such as breathing, footsteps, a heartbeat, birdsong, crickets, lapping waves, and flowing streams—that people described as tranquil. Researchers demonstrated that such sounds stimulate the limbic system in the brain, resulting in the release of endorphins and a feeling of serenity. Watson eventually concluded that tranquillity refers to a basic layer of sound—an elemental acoustic foundation—upon which we can rest our mental processes. The content of that base sound is akin to the impression of hearing the rhythmic patterns of rain on a roof. It's nearly always a muted but harmonically rich low level of ambience.

Since the Pleistocene, the human world has found within these special whispers a measure of quietude. As Watson points out, these are not soporifics but rather stimulating points of sonic light. They enable us to think clearly; there is a direct physical stimulus and a measurable clinical effect. In fact, the Council for the Protection of Rural England (CPRE), founded in 1926, devoted itself to these places, promoting a "sustainable future" for the English countryside. A "tranquil zone" was later defined by the CPRE as "anywhere that lies at least 4 km [about 2.5 miles] from a large power station, 3 km from a major motorway, major industrial area or large city, 2 km from other motorways, trunk roads or smaller towns, 1 km from busy local roads carrying more than 10,000 vehicles per day or the busiest main-line railways. It should also lie beyond the interference of civil and military aircraft." In addition, one of the criteria was the ability to turn 360 degrees and not have any visual interference from power lines or buildings.

In the 1960s there were still about forty places in the U.K. that one could visit and not hear any man-made noise, but with incessant development, the sites rapidly began to disappear. About five years into this century, the CPRE began to produce color-coded maps of tranquillity, which were used frequently by hikers, campers, cyclists, and those with their feet close to the ground. Now Watson is able to find and record only a couple of tranquil spots in the United Kingdom. He is dismayed at the price we pay as a society for the loss of tranquillity. He does tell, however, of one of his favorite uninhabited recording spots—in Northumberland, along the English-Scottish border—that until about four hundred years ago was heavily populated by thousands of testosterone-endowed humans. An area once settled by the Border Reivers (from which, because of their violent history, the word *bereaved* is derived), it is now all but abandoned — a place transformed back to its wild origins, soundscape and all. It's an open area with no inhabitants — a habitat where Watson can record for hours without ever hearing or seeing another human.

In *Last Child in the Woods: Saving Our Children from Nature-Deficit Disorder,* Richard Louv wrote: "Not that long ago, the sound track of a young person's days and nights was composed largely of the notes of nature. Most people were raised on the land, worked the land, and were often buried on the same land. The relationship was direct."

Though the landscape of my earliest years was in a state of transition from rural to urban, the sound track Louv speaks of — the soundscape burned into this child's brain seven decades ago — still resonates clearly. When we fine-tune our listening neurons early on, the skill and openness to the experience — like riding a bicycle or swimming — tend to stay with us, especially if we dust them off every now and then. While I was always mysteriously drawn to a sense of the wild, I did not have or make many opportunities to reconnect with it until I was nearly thirty years old. By then, my listening capabilities, although intact, were weakened from idleness and the peer and academic pressures that had led me from wild sound to the limits of more formalized music. I was further distracted by the presence and force of city soundscapes and the emerging music-industry technologies that were terribly seductive. With the synthesizer and my entry into the music world of Hollywood, I became part of a system — a rarefied circle of artists, studio musicians, and producers — in which everyone I knew was a willing captive. For a while, the money came in almost effortlessly. The ego got some solid affirmation. Yet the undercurrent of peaceful resonance from my early days was buried under a garbage pile of noise, only to be restored the moment I stepped outside into that Marin forest some forty years ago and switched on a recorder.

The ecologist Paul Shepard went so far as to speculate that the acoustic properties of primal landscapes might be encoded in our DNA. He imagined that possibility long before the genome had been mapped, and he believed that soundscapes, like all classes of sound, are received by us physically and would become, over time, innate. He, too, suggested that a live connection to the natural soundscapes of the world remains vital to our emotional, spiritual, and physical well-being. In this case, to emulate is to honor.

Vestiges of this genetic connection are buried deeply; over the course of our many discussions together, R. Murray Schafer has suggested that each of us is emotionally and physically drawn to a particular type of natural soundscape that surfaces at different times in our lives. Some of us are attracted to the sound of waves at ocean or lakeside beaches. Others tend toward riparian sites — streams flowing through wooded areas. Still others are beguiled by the subtle wind and the chatter of creature voices of the High Deserts or mountainous alpine regions of the world. And, to be sure, there are those who are lured to different types of music or to the web of metropolitan chaos, where lively "action" and purpose are signaled by noise. We each have within us what I refer to as *totem soundscapes,* which are expressed when we look in the mirror or turn to our mates to open a dialogue about a spot for a respite from our daily routines. Like the choices I made after my first day of recording in the woods, I tend to think that our limbic wild brains, otherwise pretty subdued, instinctively lead many of us to make some decisions in our lives—unconsciously, in a knee-jerk fashion—on the basis of sound.

As an eighteen-year-old, I never could have imagined the course my life would take. By now I have spent well more than half a lifetime recording the sounds of living organisms and natural habitats. For me, there is not a richer or more engaging endeavor. Nothing more exquisite. Nothing more healthful. Nothing more revealing about our relationship to wildness. Since each habitat expresses itself with a uniquely structured voice, I think of all of them as rich libraries of musical scores from which the entirety of "nature" performs for its own sake.

The natural world's collective voice represents the oldest and most beautiful music on the planet. But wild soundscapes aren't delivered in an instant—and if we're to hear them at all, they require careful attention and reverence.

Many people simply cannot stand being "in the country" (let alone in true wildness) and away from urban ambience. My wife, Kat, and I offer a vacation rental cottage on our property in Sonoma Wine Country, and a few years ago a young couple from New York City checked in for a restful late-summer weekend—an expectation most of our guests find thoroughly fulfilled. As I left the house at about six thirty the next morning—a spectacular warm and bright day—for a quiet run through the woods, I saw our guests, fully dressed, luggage piled at the bottom of the stairs, loading their car in the parking area and looking quite anxious. "What's wrong?" I asked, shocked to see them hustling to leave. "It's too quiet here," the female weighed in, a note of apprehension in her voice. "We couldn't sleep, and even with all the windows closed, all we could hear were those damned crickets. So we're checking out and going to San Francisco, where we've reserved a room downtown, right in the middle of everything." (Since that episode I've added to our collection of urban soundscape CDs, which are next to the guest bed, a series of recordings from New York, Chicago, Lisbon, Paris, and a couple of L.A. freeways.)

Many obstacles stand in the way of our engagement with the natural world. Walking a wooded trail near our house on the morning of the day I wrote this paragraph, I found the spring dawn chorus especially enchanting. Yet there was a spandex-clad thirtysomething woman on the path, cell phone hard to her ear, her distracted body language suggesting that she was completely oblivious to the world she was navigating and to the sound track performing for her. I felt bad about what she missed during that beautiful moment.

Though a number of studies, many funded by the gaming and high-tech industries, have indicated improvements in concentration and cognitive skills through engagement with the Internet and gamelike software, other more recent observations, such as those by the tech author Nicholas Carr, point to another conclusion—one that many of us have been sensing for some time. Indeed, stress and fatigue are measurable side effects of constant engagement with our technologies. In a *New York Times* article on the effects of technology and the counterproductiveness of its excesses, the journalist Matt Richtel described how the same distractions as those noted by Carr shatter our connections to the living world around us and even to members of our own families. Although the premise and conclusions of the article are debatable, data do suggest that our powers of concentration are seriously impaired precisely because of our drive for vast amounts of quickly delivered information, rendering us incapable of engagement with larger, more complex issues, while at the same time addicting us to such delivery systems and the levels of attention they demand.

During the past several decades, I've spent a lot of time with children in classes ranging from kindergarten through eighth grade, introducing them to the wonders of natural soundscapes. Early on, from the mid-1980s through most of the '90s, both the younger and older groups seemed able to concentrate intently and for long periods of time on listening for birds, frogs, and insects both outside their classrooms and inside, from the material I brought to play for them. But then things changed. According to a recent Henry J. Kaiser Family Foundation study, eight- to eighteen-year-olds spend a daily average of seven hours and thirty-eight minutes on iPhones, on smartphones, and texting. With such devotion to technology, the human one-on-one link disappears as the momentary social needs of young individuals — particularly those in the ten- to fourteen-year-old range — take precedence via the screens of handheld devices.

It is possible that the subject matter or the ways I was offering it didn't seem immediately relevant. But what is clear is that the noise of competing media has become more difficult to cut through, and I am sad to see it happen. Elements of the natural world are not usually engaged with or delivered as quickly. They are delivered in their own, very different extensions of time. To curb that disparity, perhaps we can find a way to harness these technologies — every smartphone is its own recording device — so that they reconnect young and old tech addicts with their natural roots.

In my exchanges with colleagues and writers who cover other aspects of the natural world, I am reminded of the question posed by the eighteenth-century philosopher George Berkeley: "If a tree falls in a forest and no one is around to hear it, does it make a sound?" It seems that Berkeley must have assumed the only acoustically sentient beings were human. This limited focus, centered on the human world, has remained — and maintained itself as a chasm between most of us and nature. The question is: Can we learn to reconnect to the wild through listening?

Except for music, I and individuals of forest-dwelling groups had no language in common when we met, so we didn't talk much. Still, my best teachers were those who lived more closely connected to the wild natural. It was during long silences in the Amazon and Africa that I paid careful attention and began to decipher the messages inherent in natural soundscapes — the same revelations that once had a presence in all our lives. Over time we have forgotten how to connect with and interpret the rich sonic accounts transmitted through a wild soundscape. As whole systems, their exclusion from our written histories and the literature of both the biological sciences and music testifies to the ways we've come to hear the world; it also reveals how we now accept and tolerate current acoustic environments as normal.

It is possible to learn to listen in a totally involved *active* rather than passive way. A keen awareness of the world of living sound is achieved by anyone willing to learn how to become a *careful* listener. Living sound surrounds us. Our awareness of it intensifies our connection to the biosphere. The more time I've spent in the field, the more devout I have become as a listener. Soundscapes, the primal natural ones in particular, nearly always give me important signs about events taking place within my surroundings. Older, less disturbed sites still retain a classic acoustic integrity in which the subtle indicators — slight changes in birdsong, shifts in insect intensity, frog choruses suddenly silent — tend to be much more informative than those of compromised habitats. With their counterpoint and solid rhythms, they are the Johann Sebastian Bachs of natural sound. I came to learn, in ancient forests, that we reject these signs at great risk.

As a recordist I am a wary voyeur—a cautious intruder—taking what I can for the moment within the limitations of what my equipment will allow. I'm careful not to disrupt nonhuman animal lives in their coveted dwellings. I used to think that what I captured on tape was "authentic." Now I know better, and I have become much more humble. The inherent meaning in soundscapes depends on the conditions of the environment from which they spring. When recorded and transferred to audio on a CD or iPod, for example, they become transformed and lose some—though not all—of their power. What you hear in your media performance center, sitting on a comfortable couch, encircled by an elaborate surround delivery system, is diminished when compared to what you would experience in real time in the natural world. It is there that the wind or rain on your skin, the smell of the forest floor, or the dry air of the desert combine with the stippled dawn or evening light, heightening the moment in ways that the playback of a recording can only begin to suggest. The very act of recording natural sound means to reach for an illusory momentary scrap, carefully selecting a time, place, and performance; like a great improvisational jazz recital, it is otherwise continuously variable because it is always selecting for and testing the limits of optimal acoustic expression. One day's biophony will not remain static or repeat ever again. It is this divine, highly selective mutability over the course of time that is the authentic biophonic manifestation of the wild.

Yet, to be sure, short excerpts of recorded soundscapes can be exquisite—listened to with minimum effort and maximum joy—and, as abstractions, are the one aspect of the wild natural world that you can capture at least fragments of. On playback, these recordings come closest of any known medium to a replication of the actual experience. With the soundscape, there is always some physical element left intact — an ethereal resurrection of a fleeting voice.

You'll hear creatures in almost any habitat on the planet, regardless of how wild it is or isn't. "Some sing low, some sing higher / Some sing out loud on the telephone wire." As I spend time actively listening, I discover totem natural sounds — sounds that are so exciting, they capture my attention and make me catch my breath. A mockingbird's vast repertoire startles even the most tone-deaf human. An injured beaver mourning its lost mate and offspring with a voice quite unlike any I'd heard before. An ant. An earthworm. A virus. Sometimes it's a frog soloist that stands out while appearing to be supported by the amphibian or insect voices of many other organisms.

Frequently the totem sounds I hear are made up of waves at the seashore. It could be the winter stream that runs full in the arroyo by our home during Northern California's winter storms. Today it's made up of the resolute calls and rapid hammering of a pair of pileated woodpeckers nesting just up the hill from my writing desk. These moments remind me why I began this odyssey in the first place. If I'm lucky, I'll hear them nearly every time I trudge off into the field, anticipating another great adventure.

Even though humans got a late start recording and listening to the natural soundscapes of the world, we are beginning to pay some attention. With insightful professionals such as Martyn Stewart, Chris Watson, Walter Tilgner, and Jean Roché spreading the word, and more recently a host of informed groups such as naturerecordists@yahoogroups.com, the Nature Sounds Society (www.naturesounds.org), and the World Listening Project (worldlistening@yahoogroups.com), access to great information is universal. The numbers of people sitting quietly in the forests around the globe with earphones on seem to be surging with each passing month. With easy-to-use technologies, these men, women, and youngsters are providing us with marvelous new insights with each gigabyte captured. And some of them will be transposing this material into new forms of musical expression we've never imagined. Given the extraordinary power of this approach, the ideas expressed through natural soundscapes are finally gaining traction in the larger community.

One thing is clear: Where biophonies and geophonies still exist unimpaired by human noise, we find places of awesome revitalization and inspiration. Each of us working in the field has uncovered a particle of truth that, when assembled as a whole and shared with the rest of the world community, begins to serve as a composite lens through which we may be able to finally confirm the incomparable value of our natural sonic resources. It is a life's effort that is deeply engaging and rewarding, both in an aesthetic sense and as a result of the sharpened sensitivity that natural-world expressions reveal. The work is physically and emotionally taxing, and often risky given the current difficulties of finding remote locations that remain tranquil and vital. Yet the sheer bliss and wonder that this endeavor bestows always outweighs the energy and the numerous hazards.

I'm often asked whether natural soundscapes could even be restored if we were not around to interfere. In addition to the now abandoned site in Northumberland, the example of Chernobyl, Ukraine, stands out. Humans completely disappeared from the site after the April 1986 nuclear power plant meltdown.

Postaccident, the abandoned environment around Chernobyl became immediately silent—so much so that the first scientists sent to monitor the venue were caught by surprise. But equally astounding to them was the gradual return of wildlife sound, beginning three years after the disaster. While it is true that no acoustic monitoring or soundscape recordings were made before or after Chernobyl was built and functioning, a few recordists have been paying particular attention to the aftermath. Peter Cusack is one of these. A British soundscape ecologist and musician, he traveled to Chernobyl to capture sound in the spring of 2006 and again in the summer of 2007. Cusack's work reveals a remarkably rich fusion of natural sound that is absent humans, a renaissance of part of the environmental structure that illustrates even more bandwidth discrimination than exists in some of the most pristine secondary-growth habitats in North America. The notes from his CD set titled *Sounds from Dangerous Places* summarize what even the most compromised and abandoned sites in the world would sound like without us. Of Chernobyl wildlife, Cusack writes:

In complete contrast to human life, nature at Chernobyl seems to be thriving. The evacuation of people has created an undisturbed haven and wildlife has taken full advantage. Animals and birds absent for many decades—wolves, moose, white-tailed eagles, black storks—have moved back and the Chernobyl exclusion zone is now one of Europe's prime wildlife sites. According to anecdote some species left the area immediately after the accident, but all returned within three years and have flourished since.

The wildlife numbers and variety means that the natural sounds of springtime are especially impressive. Birds are impossible to avoid and there is one singing somewhere on virtually every recording I made. For me the passionate species-rich dawn chorus that we heard every morning of our visit became one of Chernobyl's definitive sounds. Chernobyl is also famous for its frogs and nightingales; so nighttime concerts were equally spectacular.

Cusack told me:

The exclusion zone is now a prime site. However, I can't make a comparison with what was there before. I tried to interview one of the biologists there, but he didn't want to speak to me (don't know why). In fact, getting any real information from officials or scientists was extremely hard work.... Other outside researchers and regular visitors — academics or folklore specialists from Kiev — said they had noticed definite increases in variety and quantities of wildlife sound as well. My impression is that wildlife really has increased in the areas evacuated by humans. The soundscape reflects this.

There are other examples of natural voices in a world without us, places that have returned to a state that might have existed when we first appeared. From some of the remote monitoring systems we've set up in unoccupied or vacated places, and where the soil is still nutrient-rich enough to promote a return of vegetation, we find that the answer to the question about whether some soundscapes can be restored is a qualified yes. The world can be a very lively place when we aren't there to proclaim or assert our presence.

You'd think that desert habitats — dry, remote, thinly populated, and extremely fragile — would have a hard time returning

to the delicate balance they once knew before human intercession. Some of these, too, are showing us that if we leave them
alone long enough, they might return to a state of dynamic equilibrium. Often thought of as desolate places where nothing much
happens, deserts are actually thriving habitats. As we drive past
them at seventy miles per hour, what most of us see from the road
are flashes of occasional scrub, and cactus materializing from
mounds of sand or crusted soil. Our military shells and bombs
the desert. Miners dig it out and cast aside the tailings. There's a
whole recreational group that breaks what it considers to be dead
silence with dune buggies, dirt bikes, and ORVs, carelessly deci-
mating fragile wildlife in the process of asserting its existence.
Yet there are still deserts—even in the United States—that
remain as some of the world's more wild places.

When I lament that 50 percent of the sites I have recorded can
now only be heard in my archive, my wife—nudging me back to
the present—reminds me that 50 percent still remain. A few
sites within the transition zone of the Sonoran and Chihuahuan
Deserts make up some of the few locations in the Lower 48 that
are completely noise-free for extended periods of time. They
intersect beginning in northern Mexico and thrust into the United
States along the southern reaches of New Mexico, Arizona, and
California. While working on a Nature Conservancy site in the
New Mexican panhandle, Ruth Happel and I mapped out an area
of five square miles at Gray Ranch and recorded there in the
spring of 1992. This High Desert bioregion contains many different microzones characterized by distinctive biophonies. Those
still working on-site today report that the ranch is even more
vibrant, since cattle grazing has been minimized and a strict
conservation easement has been put in place. Not all of these
more open and dry areas contain the immediately obvious aural

territorial boundaries that we see clearly expressed in tropical regions. The density of living organisms is spread over a much wider territory; the biophony is far less rich. But it's still there.

After several hundred years of overgrazing, this habitat is now in the throes of a slow recovery, just beginning to return to a healthy state. Areas with aspen, juniper, oak, mesquite, cactus, manzanita, alder, hackberry, shrub, Indian ricegrass and saw grass, broom, sagebrush, arrowweed, and ocotillo have returned and contain a unique mix of vocal creatures. Invasive species — both plant and animal — are being replaced with those more natural to the environment. Populated with complex blends of cactus and rock wrens, common and Chihuahuan ravens, western meadowlarks, five species of sparrows, green-tailed towhees, blue grosbeaks, longspurs, loggerhead shrike, vermilion and ash-throated flycatchers, horned larks, western kingbirds, common poorwills, burrowing and great horned owls, ground doves, aplomado falcons, red-tailed hawks, scaled quails, katydids, crickets, coyotes, gray foxes, mountain lions, jackrabbits, squirrels, bats, mice, beetles, ants, termites, grasshoppers, Mormon crickets, toads and frogs of many types, geckos, tortoises, and snakes — each with an expressive voice of its own — it whispers to us now without cattle, sheep, dogs, planes, cars, trains, or trucks within hearing range. Who said there was nothing in the desert?

Another region that remains mostly intact is the Arctic National Wildlife Refuge — the site that the late Alaskan senator Ted Stevens and so many others had wanted to open up to oil drilling. In defense of his position, he tried to convince his colleagues that except for oil, nothing was there. During a 2005 tirade demanding that a remote and fragile site within the Arctic National Wildlife Refuge — known as the "10-02" — be opened up and leased for oil drilling, he passionately contended to members of the Sen-

ate chamber that the landscape was lifeless, holding up a featureless white poster board with no images, a clear symbol for him
that this was a resource to be tapped in order to benefit the dire
needs of consumers.

His arguments caused many to wonder, myself included. To
answer my own questions, in 2006 I led three bioacoustic teams
to record and film in the refuge. The region is a huge expanse in
the northeastern corner of Alaska. It's nearly the size of Maine,
and it has no roads, paths (except for game trails), signage, or gift
stores. Each of the three teams — headed by me (with Bob Moore
from Maine); Martyn Stewart, a BBC nature recordist; and
Kevin Colver, an ornithologist and medical doctor from Utah —
covered a different site to get an initial sense of the acoustic
dynamics of the refuge in contrasting biomes. One location, visited by Colver's team, was on the north shore of the Beaufort Sea,
almost at the Canadian border. Another was up the North Slope,
with Stewart presiding, at Sunset Pass. The third site, covered by
me and Moore, was located in the southern foothills of the Brooks
Range at Timber Lake, the westernmost extension of the boreal
forest that stretches from the Canadian Maritimes all the way
across Canada to the refuge. Over a period of ten days, we managed to record a total of about eighty hours of spectacular wildlife soundscapes that included more than seven dozen species of
birds, and we had sightings of bears, Arctic foxes, wolves, caribou, squirrels, and mice.

Like the soundscapes of desert habitats, Arctic vocal collec-
tives are sparse and subtle when contrasted with those of tropical
or subtropical rain forests, where the vegetation and climate support intensely rich diversity. The flora is not as dense or diverse,
and, where it does exist, the delicate tundra tussock spreads as far
as the eye can see. It is not easy to navigate. Even walking takes

some care and youthful skill. Food sources, for birds especially, are scattered widely. When the air clears from Siberian fires that occasionally foul the northern Alaskan sky in the spring and early summer, the smell of the tundra vegetation is numinous— it's fresh and herbally fragrant. Everywhere we hiked, we picked what Native Americans call tundra tea—otherwise known as *ayuk* or Labrador tea—and brewed it for a refreshing change in diet. Bird sound was extremely light and hard to capture because of the near-constant wind that blows in from Siberia and the Beaufort Sea to the north and west. Yet birds are present, and they are vocal. They have a lot to communicate and only a short season in which to do it. As in the desert, birds here spread themselves out over vast expanses.

Because there are no services over the 1.5 million acres of the designated landscape, human activity is minimal—except for hunters, summertime hikers, and river rafters. So for long periods of time there is little to interfere with wildlife and wildlife sound. While sitting around our campfire, we were told by our guide, the Fairbanks ecologist and poet Frank Keim: "I've sometimes hiked for weeks in the Brooks Range and never saw or heard another human being."

Introducing us to candle ice, Keim described how these formations break away from the leading edge of river ice when they melt. As they do so, they jingle like high-pitched glass wind chimes. The ice-melting soundscape portends other occurrences that Keim also asked us to consider. Holding up a fistful of pencil-shaped melting ice shards, he cautioned to no one in particular:

In the spring, whenever sunlight warms the ice, it travels down through the surface, first warming up motes of surface dust that absorb heat more quickly. Bits of dirt or dust penetrate the ice vertically, causing the ice to melt in pencil-thin shapes. At the base of the ice, there's an awful lot of algae, and the algae begin to bloom. With the blooming of the algae, the crustaceans — like copepods — eat the algae. The fish eat the crustaceans. The seals eat the fish. And then, of course, the polar bear and humans eat the seals. If this ice doesn't exist — and it's quickly disappearing because of global warming — if you don't have the ice, you don't have any of that.

Our time in the refuge reinforced for all of us a sense of what the natural world would be like with none or only a few of us around in a truly wild environment. On a more local scale, not twenty minutes from where my wife and I live in Northern California lies a low range of hills called the Mayacamas Mountains, which run north to south and divide the Napa and Sonoma Valleys. Near the top of the ridge, there is a state park that is both quiet and sonically active. It isn't old growth, which would be a bit much to expect in an active rural spot, but with thoughtful management over the past several decades, the area has returned to much of its original vegetation — oak chaparral, some alders, and Douglas fir — at an altitude of about twelve hundred feet. The dawn and evening choruses are resonant and lovely, although I'm sure they don't sound as they did a hundred or more years ago, when author Jack London roamed these same hills. In fact, the textures have changed even as I've been hiking, listening, and recording there over the course of nearly two decades. The obvious changes mostly have to do with the climate and possibly the subtle effects of newly recognized shifts in the earth's magnetic field. Rainfall amounts have changed — precipitation varies much more widely over the course of the year — and the winter seasons are weeks shorter. Birds reach the peak of their dawn chorusing between eleven and twenty days earlier, on average, than when I first began to visit this site in 1994.

Otherwise, the park, a 2,700 acre site with miles of trails, is pretty quiet. Early in the morning, with little aircraft traffic and almost no visitors, there are few interruptions. At first light, one can expect to record for half an hour or more without hearing a single plane or motorized vehicle — a remarkable feat in our time and in this part of the country. That's because the airspace on either side of the park is framed by plane traffic either inbound from the north to San Francisco International Airport or outbound from the south to northwestern parts of the country or Europe (over the North Pole route), and the planes are usually out of acoustic range of the park's airspace.

In more youthful moments and younger days, I would feel a deep yearning to "get out of town" and travel to exotic places to experience real, wild sound. Then I realized that right in my own backyard are locations that have hardly ever been approached with a microphone. I'm willing to bet that there are many more of these unusually active biological islands than we think. Most professional recordists I know have favorite local spots that they like to visit but are reluctant to speak of for fear of having them overrun by those of us looking for places to listen and record.

To get to überexotic places to hear the remaining intact, majestic animal orchestras, you're going to have to take a bit of a hike, I'm afraid. It'll be worth it, though — something akin to catching a glimpse of an ivory-billed woodpecker, or a truly dark starlit sky. The problem is that even in remaining old-growth stands in temperate regions, the numbers and kinds of seasonal and migrating birds, frogs, and insects have changed, due in part to the fact that key aspects of their normal habitats both inside and outside the old forests have been altered. Changes include the introduction of exotic and invasive species of insects such as Africanized bees, the yellow crazy ant, fire ants, and the Argentine ant; mammals such as rabbits in Australia, possums in New Zealand, and the mongoose in Hawaii; and aggressive birds, mollusks, fish, and even frogs—some, but not all, brought in to mitigate other problems that we felt needed attention.

Typical of these remaining major sites is the Dzanga-Sangha rain forest in the southwestern part of the Central African Republic—home to the Ba'Aka described earlier. It, too, is changing because of heavy logging pressure from countries in Europe and Asia. But at the time when Louis Sarno's recordings were first made, the African soundscape was likely much as it had been fifteen or twenty thousand years ago. The music of the forest that Sarno described when he first arrived in the mid-1980s was "older than the pyramids, unchanged over time with all its emotional content, intricacy, and all of the permutations worth chasing after." Sarno, more than anyone, exemplifies the idea that there is a numinous and practical connection between the sounds of an unaltered landscape and the evolution of human music, dance, and even, probably, language. He has witnessed firsthand, over the course of almost three decades, the transformative processes that turn soundscape into human musical performance. Because he is on-site, living in the forest with his new family, Sarno is now observing the impact modern civilization is having on those who once got every sonic inspiration from the vocal organisms that surrounded them.

But it is not too late. Sites in the far reaches of Alaska, the pampas of Argentina and Uruguay, Canada (Ontario, parts of British Columbia, and the Northwest Territories), the floodplains of Brazil's Pantanal, protected regions of Papua New Guinea, and even sections of northern Minnesota and the Adirondacks are still rich with natural sound. To the extent that we travel lightly, conscientiously, and with respect, some of these locations still remain as sonic monuments—places within the otherwise clamorous labyrinth we've chosen to live in that vibrate with wisdom, spirituality, healing, and musical inspiration.

At the conclusion of my public talks, I'm invariably asked what we can do to help preserve our remaining natural environments. It's easy: leave them alone and stop the inveterate consumption of useless products that none of us need. Whenever we decide to go into the wild, we should go quietly and leave things as we find them. We must disabuse ourselves of the notion that any of us can improve on the natural world by our presence or by what we manage to create. It evolved naturally, selectively, and adaptively over the great sweep of time, through all kinds of trial and error. Bending the natural world to our will and purpose is done at a level of self-inflicted violence that has wide-reaching implications we cannot necessarily see or hear.

In the end, before the forest echoes die, we may want to step back for a moment and listen very carefully to the chorus of the natural world, where rivers of sound flow from crickets, the tiniest frog, whirring insects, wrens, condors, cheetahs, wolves—and us. The whisper of every leaf and creature implores us to love and care for the fragile tapestry of the biophony, which—after all—was the first music our species heard. Those messages told us that we weren't separate but rather essential parts of a single fragile biological system, voices in an orchestra of many, with no more important cause than the celebration of life itself.

Acknowledgments

For support and/or inspiration, special thanks to: Phil Aaberg, David Abram, Animal Welfare Institute, Skip Ambrose, Jelle Atema, Frank Awbrey, Joseph and Addie Axelrod, Phil Bailey, Ken Balcomb, Christina and Carroll Ballard, Luis Baptista, Gregory Bateson, Paul Beaver, Terry Bell, Wendell Berry, Doug and Cheryl Breitbart, Anne and Alexander Buck, John Cage, Calgary Zoo, California Academy of Sciences, Jack Campisi, Laurence Campling, Joel Chadabe, Leila Chamma, Cleveland Metroparks Zoo, Kevin Colver, Community Foundation, Mike Cumberland, Jim Cummings, Peter Cusack, Lauren Dewey-Platt, Jannie Dresser, Bob Drewes, Dan Dugan, Loren Eiseley, Evan C. Evans III, Gina Farr, Wolfgang Fasser, Kurt Fristrup, Stuart Gage, Google, Patricia Gray, Herman Gygi, John Hanke, Mike Hanke, Gerry Haslam, Don Hodges, Wes Henry, Al and Michal Hillmann, Bob and Olivia Hillmann, Jack Hines, Institute for Music and Brain Science, Antônio Carlos Jobim, Charles Jurasz, Roger Kaye (U.S.

Fish and Wildlife Service, Alaska), Sam Keen, Frank Keim, Garret Keizer, Andy Keller, Sherry and Dan Krause, David Kuhn, Linda and Jim Kuhns, Casey Langfelder, Aldo Leopold, Lobitos Creek Ranch (Steve Michelson), Rick Luttmann, Madrone Audubon Society, Malcolm Margolin, George Marsh, Sir George Martin, Doug and Kathy McConnell, Chuna McIntyre, Bill McKibben, Craig Miller, Nick Miller, Stephen Mitchell, Robert Moog, Bob Moore, Rebecca Moore, Farley Mowat, Murie Center (Steve Duerr), NASA (James Hansen), National Park Service, Nature Sounds Society, Nick Nichols, Ken Norris, Kevin O'Farrell, Mary Oliver, Pauline Oliveros, Loran Olsen, Bob Orban, Tim and Meara O'Reilly, Kevin Padian, Aniruddh Patel, Bryan Pijanowski, Ken Plotkin, Doug Quin, Richard Ranft, Jeff Rice, Mark and Sarah Roos, David Rothenberg, R. Murray Schafer, Bill Schmidt, Alan Shabel, Florence and Paul Shepard, Skywalker Sound, Smithsonian Institution, Derek Solomon, Stanford University (CCRMA and the library), Wallace Stegner, Christopher Struck, Howie Thompson, Mark Tramo, Karen Treviño, Rudy Trubitt, Jack Turner, U.S. Fish and Wildlife Service, University of Utah (Marriott Library), Van Dyke Parks, Casey Walker, Lilla and Andy Weinberger, Hans-Ulrich Werner, Terry Tempest Williams, E. O. Wilson, Sam Wong, and Aaron Ximm.

I owe a huge debt of gratitude to the pioneers and leaders in the field, such as Ludwig Koch, Jean Roché, Walter Tilgner, Lang Elliott, Louis Sarno, Steven Feld, Fred Trumbull, Roger Payne, Katy Payne, Chris Clark, Martyn Stewart, Chris Watson, Ruth Happel, Rob Danielson, David Monacchi, and Volker Widmann, to name a few of the outstanding ones. And then the major film field recordists and media sound designers, such as Randy Thom, Ren Klyce, Andy Wiskes, Gary Rydstrom, Walter Murch, Joe Harrington, and Ben Burtt, all of whom understand that sound, abstracted from its original context, is simply an illusion in which every choice is an edit, every edit a work of art, and each subsequent creation an ode and homage to places of great splendor—real and imagined. It's a world where some produce magic while others choose to think of their work as unmitigated within an abyss of delusion.

Gillian MacKenzie, my superb agent, lit the fire. John Parsley, my editor, stoked it with insight and his finely tuned combo of eye and ear for proper voice and structure. Jeff Galas put the lyrics in order. Karen Landry, copyeditor, perfected the entire narrative. Kat Krause, my dear, tolerant wife, waited ever patiently while I sat each day for nearly two years figuring out how to shape a single thought into a story.

And to Seaweed, who, when she sensed moments of desperation during the process, would jump into my lap and purr in a voice of quiet inspiration—the sound of all animal life, if one's ears are sufficiently attuned. Or maybe she was just plain hungry.

Notes

Chapter 1: Sound as My Mentor

A note about the recording of Muir Woods: The original field recordings done for *In a Wild Sanctuary* were of quite poor quality. Although originally I was going to include my own recording, the tape hiss on the sample I saved was completely unacceptable. Remember, it was my very first attempt to capture natural soundscapes in the "wild." Instead of that example, I've used a terrific audio clip from the archive of Dan Dugan, field recordist, audio electronics designer, and current board member of the Nature Sounds Society (http://www.naturesounds.org), who has done extensive work at that site over the past several years and who has really captured the acoustic moment of the place as I remembered it.

Citadels of Mystery, Takoma Records, 1975, was the first album to use a guitar synthesizer and to include a Western composition of material with lyrics in the Quechua language.

Impressed by the sounds of the waters off the coastal environments of Normandy and Brittany, Claude Debussy was so passionately inspired by the acoustic seascapes that he wove those feelings indelibly into his signature piece, *La Mer.*

The information on Walter Murch, Academy Award–winning sound designer for *Apocalypse Now* and also sound designer for *The Conversation, The Rain People,* and *The Godfather,* is from a recorded interview in Bolinas, California, on February 17, 2010.

With regard to the relative sound levels between the Grateful Dead and snapping shrimp, the loudest concert currently on record was measured on July 15, 2009, at a KISS show presented at the Cisco Ottawa Bluesfest in Ottawa, Canada. It was there that a level of 136 dB was measured by City of Ottawa By-Law officers at the sound tent during the actual live performance, making it the world's loudest show played by any band.

Just prior to the time Schafer first used it, the term *soundscape*— introduced to describe a general notion of sound within a cityscape— had been mentioned briefly in a paper by Michael Southworth titled "The Sonic Environment of Cities," *Environment and Behavior* 1, no. 1 (June 1969): 49–70. Southworth never expanded on the concept. Schafer is credited as the first to give the word its more inclusive definition and to use it as a term of art within the field of acoustics.

In order to consider the brilliant structural components of a piece of audiotape, imagine millions of tiny microscopic particles of metal, each aligned randomly in relation to the others. When the magnet head of the recorder transmits an analog of signal, the fragments reposition themselves in a way that, when developed in a certain type of solution, creates an image on the tape that kind of looks like a bar code. That "bar code," when drawn across a playback head on an analog recorder, "reads" as sound.

The incomplete sense of the acoustic world that we get from sound fragmentation is sufficient but for the one major shortcoming revealed in a quote from an article about birdsong published in an anthology entitled *The Origins of Music* (2000), edited by Nils L. Wallin, Björn Merker, and Steven Brown: "Song has two main functions: repelling rivals and attracting mates." Although this is considered to be a major reference, not one of the twenty-six articles in the anthology speculated on the connection between an individual bird's song and the complex acoustic structure of the soundscape in which the bird sings. This seminal connection is crucial to our understanding not only of birdsong but of all animals' sounds and their influence on the origins of human rhythm and music.

Chapter 2: Voices from the Land

Of the many ancient water and sound myths, one folktale I love comes from the Kawésqar, a tribal group—of which less than two dozen native speakers remain—that lives in southern Chile on Wellington Island.

A tale is told about a young man in the past that, a day in which his father was off hunting nutria [a large rodent] and birds, left in search of a taboo nutria, and killed it. He did so when his father and mother were not there, since they left long before he killed the nutria: this is what the story tells.

But then the story tells that a heavy wind rose, and a violent storm began. And the rain came down till water covered all of the earth.

The young man who killed the nutria remained alive, and ran to save his life, and, how the story tells, he ran to the top of a hill. He remained in the top of the hill, and waited for the flood to retreat. The flood always retreats quickly, doesn't it?

So the flood retreated, and when he saw he could do it, he went down the hill. When he saw that his brother and mother and father were drowned and hanged from a tree, he went down off the hill, as the story tells.

So he saw that everybody was drowned; and he also saw animals, whales and dolphins scattered throughout the woods, as the flood retreated. So the young man of the past went away. Along the way he met a girl, and the two of them began to build a boat.

They had nothing to build the boat with; so they decided to cover the boat with grass, and they remained there till morning came, this is what the story tells.

When the cold came, the young man had a vision: he dreamed of a *coipo* [another Chilean term for *nutria*], he said he saw the rodent in his dream. He also said he dreamed of food, and that he ate in his dream, it was a kind of vision of the future.

And while he was eating in his sleep, he woke up, and said to himself:

Why was I dreaming of this *coipo?* I killed the *coipo,* and ate it while I was sleeping; but how, if I have no fire?

Then he fell asleep again, and then he woke up: then he woke up his woman, too, who had become his wife, how the story tells. And he said to his wife:

Look, go and get a big wooden stick, I dreamt that a *coipo* was coming, so I send you to fetch the stick to kill him, and we will eat it.

So he felt asleep again, and everything he dreamt, appeared. So the earth was full of animals, their songs, and things again, this is what the story tells.

Chapter 3: The Organized Sound of Life Itself

Bloat is the term used to describe a group of hippos.

In the realm of acoustic imaging, I had the opportunity to work as an occasional intern with the late Dr. Thomas Poulter, who, in the latter part of the '60s, worked for the Stanford Research Institute in California designing echo ranging experiments with sea lions. In one experiment, he placed two different kinds of same-size disks — made of wood, plastic, and/or metal — at a distance of twenty-five yards to test if, by echolocation, the subject animals could distinguish between them. In most cases they did — with remarkable accuracy.

With regard to the Pitjantjatjara and sonic GPS, while recording in a riverine rain forest north of Daintree in northeast Australia in 1989,

I was introduced to the late Simon Fjell, an ecologist who worked in the field of sustainable agriculture. After dinner in our forest lodgings beside a river, he recounted some of his experiences with the Pitjantjatjara, a nomadic Central Australian aboriginal tribe:

One group member, for example, will often describe a distant meeting place to another almost completely by acoustic clues. They speak in great detail, mind you, of what would appear to us an immense habitat of flat, dry, featureless landscapes, where we would find almost nothing to distinguish one location from another. Parts of Australia are filled with open spaces like these, and it isn't as if there are obvious geological features there — to the Pitjantjatjara, it is the combined acoustic effect of small local plants and animals that serves as a guide. Sound is one of the most important features they isolate as part of their holographic map, the three-dimensional map of the world as it manifests in their minds.

As members of the Pitjantjatjara travel either alone or in small groups from semiarid to arid country, they identify the species of animals that range through the biomes [distinct habitats] they traverse. They have also learned that the syntax, timbre, frequency, and duration of those animals' vocalizations have evolved to match subtle geographic and climactic variations in their habitats. These vocal differences serve as beacons to them as they travel through the desert.

(The quote above comes from Fjell's description. A recorded session originally published in Notes from the Wild, *Ellipsis Arts, 1996, by the author.)*

Rainsticks from the Amazon Basin region are typically four- or five-foot-long hollowed-out bamboo cylinders about three to four inches in diameter. Tiny holes are bored along the length of the shaft, and either thorns or metal tines are inserted into the holes so that they protrude throughout the inside of the column. Then, small seeds or glass beads are added to the inside of the shaft, and the tube is sealed off at both ends. When the stick is rotated or shaken, or when either end is raised off a horizontal plane, the seeds hit the tines and the resulting effect sounds like drops of rain.

Chapter 4: Biophony: The Proto-Orchestra

While capturing those first field recordings in Kenya in the early 1980s, I was not yet completely separated from the idea that individual animal recordings, based on a species-specific model, were more relevant. My limited field task was reinforced by requests coming from the California Academy of Science's birds and mammals department, with which I was then associated. Recording with a wider scope and objective was not an easy step to take for a couple of reasons: One was because there was almost no support or precedent, so I could not call on others to tap into their experience. The other was that the equipment needed to record in stereo outside a very controlled interior environment (such as a traditional recording studio) was not readily available, making improvisation with available technologies the key to any success. Wind and humidity were the biggest impediments. The learning curve was precipitous.

The first time I heard a hyrax it scared the hell out of me, its ratcheting voice filtered by my exhausted brain as some kind of warning growl. Except that it's a completely friendly, cute, and furry animal about the size of a small domestic cat. Anatomically and genetically, it's remotely related to an elephant.

As the nighttime Kenyan soundscapes began to reveal themselves as structured acoustic fabrics, my lingering doubts about what I was hearing began to disappear; buttressed by the spectrogram images that I later printed out, the soundscapes showed enough detail to infer that frog and insect choruses occupied several distinct frequency niches. When the birds and mammals vocalized, their characteristic expressions fit neatly within the free slots not taken by insects. Additional free slots were filled by the bat and hyrax, while distant hyenas and elephants found still other niches.

Ken Norris, then head of the Environmental Studies Department at the University of California, Santa Cruz, had distinguished himself as having discovered the mechanism through which dolphins and other toothed whales perform echolocation. He was a singular supporter of niche hypothesis and immediately saw the connection once it was shown. Other biologists, such as Luis Baptista, E. O. Wilson, and several entomologists who were at first skeptical finally began to accept the relevance of acoustic partitioning and the roles it plays in the field of bioacoustics.

The other great ape species include orangutans, bonobos, and chimpanzees.

Ruth Happel currently lives and works in North Carolina, raising a daughter with her husband and working as a naturalist and wildlife videographer and photographer.

The field of soundscape ecology, being so new, has few noted or published observations related specifically to the subject of *how* animals learn to partition their voices. From my recordings and time in the field in minimally altered old-growth habitats, I have found that the spectrograms from soundscapes captured at those sites demonstrate clearly partitioned patterns — far more than those from stressed or secondary-growth biomes, whose patterns either tend toward entropy or are nonexistent. So I would make an educated guess that the signals evolve in concert with one another to accommodate the characteristics of each creature's unique voice.

Chapter 5: First Notes

Ross Lee Finney, head of composition at the School of Music at the University of Michigan when I applied in the mid-'50s, used that exact expression ("the guitar is not a musical instrument") when I went for my interview one fall day. The other music institutions (Juilliard and Eastman, in particular) dismissed the guitar in much the same terms. At the time, the guitar was not on the list of acceptable musical instruments within the Academy in the United States.

The early May 1963 Weavers reunion concert at Carnegie Hall

featured Pete Seeger, Ronnie Gilbert, Lee Hays, Fred Hellerman, Erik Darling, Frank Hamilton, and me. Bill Lee, the father of film director Spike Lee, played bass.

The "control of sound" idea was and is controversial only for the reason that every person, musician, and researcher has a different idea of music's components.

A young child at a piano keyboard can randomly choose and hit a particular key, thus controlling a sound (amplitude and pitch). But there is not necessarily structure, nor is the key chosen necessarily intentional.

Curt Olson, a soundscape recordist and naturalist living in Minnesota, told me the details of this beaver-dam-encounter story and provided a recording. He gave his permission to use both.

The Joel Selvin conversation is from January 23, 2011. Used with permission.

In one "orchestra" scenario—almost following an evolutionary course—the insects lay the foundation. The frequencies of whirring wings and rates of stridulation are generally fixed by the particular species, but they will subtly shift as a result of constantly adjusting for external forces such as temperature, sunlight, and weather. Once those positions are taken in the ensemble of the audio spectrum, the amphibians and reptiles enter to claim sound-free niches. Then birds enter the chorus, followed by mammals. Eventually each voice finds an open channel or time to perform. If nonhuman creatures depend on their voices to survive, then they will each need a niche in which to be heard unimpeded.

Oka! Amerikee is also a 2010 film partly based on Louis Sarno's life, produced and directed by Lavinia Currier.

Chapter 6: Different Croaks for Different Folks

Girolamo Savonarola, the dictatorial Florentine friar who ruled between 1494 and 1498, when he was finally executed, tried to ban the output of all forms of art that he considered morally corrupt.

Chuna McIntyre's recordings can be heard on the title *Drums*

Across the Tundra, available at http://www.wildsanctuary.mobi/buy/
index.php?route=product/category&path=39.

As we came to define our sense of order in the world with regard to
nature, it became logical to deconstruct the whole into parts that contrast sharply with a more holistic natural reality. Thus, the rational
extension became "it" (nature) and us.

AmbiSonic sound fields work best when playback is transmitted
through anywhere from three to more than a hundred fifty speakers
in a given space. It is one of the few systems that truly provides a
three-dimensional spherical illusion of space on playback.

"All God's Critters Got a Place in the Choir," copyright 1979, was
written by Bill Staines. There's a wonderful recording of the tune
by Tommy Makem and the Clancy Brothers at http://www.youtube
.com/watch?v=NcG1JNpazN4&feature=related. Lyrics used with
permission.

Chapter 7: The Fog of Noise

The Yellowstone recordings include a horned lark, black-capped
chickadee, cedar waxwing, tree sparrow, rosy finch, house sparrow,
song sparrow, Steller's jay, raven, magpie, and northern flicker.

When sound is present—particularly in a closed space—as the
air molecules generated from the source are excited into motion, they
tend to warm the environment slightly.

In automobiles or motorcycles, *straight-piping* is a modification in
which the catalytic converter and muffler are removed in an effort to
increase performance, with the subsequent result of greatly increased
noise, the latter often being the goal in itself.

In addition to *acoustic debris,* many English words and phrases
describe noise. No single definition has emerged victorious, and they
each represent pretty much the same phenomenon. Among them,
acoustic garbage, unwanted sound, and *useless acoustic information.*

Weimin Zheng's quote is from personal correspondence, February
3, 2011. Used with permission.

Even in our recreational activities, the powerful material world that symbolizes the relentless American dream of prosperity and freedom may be at the very heart of our noise problem. As a nation, we have been historically preoccupied with the machinery that drives our sense of might.

The World Health Organization report "Burden of Disease from Environmental Noise" concludes as a guideline that the annual average nighttime exposure to outside noise should not exceed 40 dB. Before my wife and I got rid of our twenty-year-old refrigerator, it registered a noise level of 55 dBA one yard away from the appliance.

Chapter 8: Noise and Biophony / Oil and Water

Before the spring of 1984, my first trip to Mono Lake, no one to my knowledge had experimented with the effect of species' vocalizations taking place half submerged in a marine environment. To do that, we had to record in two media—water and air—simultaneously. We subsequently and in short order captured recordings of alligators and hippos doing much the same thing. The sounds, because of the media in which they are transmitted, are very different from one another. One can only wonder if they carry multiple streams of information.

As far as recovery from human intervention, depending on the impact, raptors (Swainson's hawks, for instance) have been known to abandon their nests when disturbed, never to return to the same spot, while other species are not affected in the least and have learned to thrive even in the most heavily populated urban areas. Even though my wife and I live in a relatively quiet rural spot, it is still quite noisy—way too noisy to record natural sound, for example. Traffic noise from a highway 1.5 miles away, constant private and commercial aircraft overhead at all hours of the day, and our human presence do nothing to deter a pair of house finches from nesting only a few feet above us in the rafters just outside our door. Each spring and summer, they breed several clutches of offspring.

The relatively slow pace of bioacoustic research has largely been the result of four factors: disinterest on the part of traditional institutions still favoring older models, the lack of funding necessary to acquire technologies or software needed to conduct the studies and evaluate huge amounts of data, a lack of trained personnel, and finally—except with regard to indoor spaces (as addressed in books such as *The Soundscape of Modernity* by Emily Thompson)—a lack of collective cultural will to probe too deeply into the realm of natural acoustic environments. That climate is changing, with new studies and publications coming from Michigan State University's Envirosonics program, and a similar investigative program firmly in place at Purdue University under the aegis of Bryan Pijanowski.

Our recording choices at the time were based on the limits of our technologies and levels of funding: a seven-inch reel of tape on an early portable stereo recorder would last a total of about twenty-two minutes if we were recording for optimum quality. Each tape reel weighed nearly a pound, and it was expensive. So for every hour of recording, we needed about three pounds of tape and 20 percent of a fresh battery supply, for a total outlay of roughly forty dollars. The tape machine itself weighed twenty-five pounds when loaded with the twelve D-cell batteries needed to power it. With just the equipment alone—and for just about eight hours of recording time—our backpacks began at a minimum weight of around fifty pounds. These days, with ultralight trail packs, equipment, etc., weighing about twenty pounds altogether, we are able to hike into the field with clothes, food, water, sleeping bags, a tent, *and* recording equipment, with enough technology and supplies to record comfortably for a week or more.

Along the same lines as Ken Balcomb's work, a summary of the impacts of marine anthrophony can be found in "Lethal Sounds," NRDC report, October 6, 2008, http://www.nrdc.org/wildlife/marine/sonar.asp.

Information from Allison Banks and Chris Gabriele was gleaned from personal correspondence, June 29, 2010. Used with permission.

To establish "effective listening areas," research models need to take into account a wider range of factors. For example, the sound signatures of single- or twin-engine private fix-winged aircraft, different types of helicopters, motorcycles, etc., as they are affected by a range of atmospheric conditions. Each signature will have a different effect not only on wildlife but on the human experience as well.

I obtained a copy of the Don Young and Richard Pombo letter to Gale Norton, secretary of the Department of the Interior, November 21, 2003, from the National Park Service in Boulder, Colorado. At one point, Young, together with Senator Ted Stevens, had tried, with taxpayer money, to fund a $400 million bridge to a tiny community of fifty residents, funded through congressional earmarks. It was the famous "Bridge to Nowhere."

The following description of the content of Young and Pombo's letter gives a sense of the hostility that existed with regard to noise regulation, even within our protected areas. Basically, attempting to undermine the program that had been implemented in the late '90s and early 2000s, the legislators, who by the way served on key congressional committees that funded the NPS, expressed concerns about how noise controls would be implemented by first targeting the term *soundscape* and then expressing skepticism that one could quantify the effects of human noise either on animal behavior or on visitors—questioning the kinds of studies that had been previously done or that were already in the planning stages. The letter, which did not address the significant efforts to incorporate soundscape monitoring and visitor activity models into the NPS programs, appeared to be a clear attempt to put the brakes on further soundscape activity development. Young and Pombo also asserted that the natural soundscapes had never been sufficiently described and were, in any event, "radical" (in the political sense) concepts. In a final thrust, the document raised questions about how natural soundscapes (if, in fact, there were such phenomena) could be affected by human noise; whether the public had ever been invited to comment on noise, the program, and park ideals (they had indeed); and whether or not the program administrators really believed that visitors would be affected by the noise of aircraft overflights.

A full statement of the original scope of the park service soundscape program can be found in "Director's Order #47: Soundscape Preservation and Noise Management," National Park Service, 2000, at http://www.nps.gov/policy/DOrders/DOrder47.html.

Chapter 9: The Coda of Hope

The example of how a soundscape might evolve as a result of human activity would likely be more powerful if we had before-and-after spectrograms from the same site. But with the field of bioacoustics and soundscape analysis being only thirty years old, we don't have sufficient recorded data from the same sites to do actual comparisons yet. However, from the few locations where we do have before-and-after data, we would anticipate something similar to the result described earlier at Lincoln Meadow, California, in chapter 3.

Our inattention to the importance of listening to and capturing natural soundscapes until very recently has meant a tremendous loss of informative biophonic data that might have been useful to aspects of resource management, a more comprehensive understanding of the complex role each voice plays within the entire sonic mix, a knowledge of the bioacoustic affects of global warming on density and diversity, and an appreciation of how soundscapes inform our mental, physical, and cultural lives.

Extended examples of the Arctic National Wildlife Refuge soundscapes can be obtained at http://www.wildsanctuary.mobi/buy/index .php?route=product/product&keyword=voice&product_id=74.

Bibliography

Books

Abram, David. *The Spell of the Sensuous.* New York: Pantheon, 1996.

Bateson, Gregory. *Mind and Nature.* New York: Hampton Press, 2002.

Beaver, Paul, and Bernie Krause. *The Nonesuch Guide to Electronic Music.* New York: Nonesuch Records, 1967.

Bell, Paul et al. *Environmental Psychology.* 5th ed. London: Psychology Press, 2005.

Berendt, Joachim-Ernst. *The Third Ear.* New York: Henry Holt, 1988.

Bible. 1 Kings 5:15; Romans 8:7.

Bierce, Ambrose. *The Devil's Dictionary.* Mineola, NY: Dover Publications, 1958.

Carr, Nicholas. *The Shallows: What the Internet Is Doing to Our Brains.* New York: W. W. Norton, 2010.

Cokinos, Christopher. *Hope Is the Thing with Feathers: A Personal Chronicle of Vanished Birds*. New York: Warner Books, 2000.

Dowie, Mark. *Conservation Refugees: The Hundred-Year Conflict Between Global Conservation and Native Peoples*. Cambridge, MA: MIT Press, 2009.

Eiseley, Loren. *The Unexpected Universe*. Boston: Harcourt Brace, 1969.

Glavin, Terry. *The Sixth Extinction: Journeys Among the Lost and Left Behind*. New York: Thomas Dunne Books, 2007.

Keizer, Garret. *The Unwanted Sound of Everything We Want: A Book About Noise*. New York: PublicAffairs, 2010.

Krause, Bernie. *Wild Soundscapes: Discovering the Voice of the Natural World*. Berkeley, CA: Wilderness Press, 2002.

Langone, Michael D. *Recovery from Cults: Help for Victims of Psychological and Spiritual Abuse*. New York: W. W. Norton, 1995.

Leopold, Aldo. *A Sand County Almanac*. 1949. Reprint, New York: Oxford University Press, 2001.

Louv, Richard. *Last Child in the Woods*. Chapel Hill, NC: Algonquin Books of Chapel Hill, 2008.

Mathieu, W. A. *The Listening Book*. Boston: Shambhala Publications, 1991.

McKibben, Bill. *The Age of Missing Information*. New York: Random House, 2006.

Mithen, Steven. *The Singing Neanderthals*. Cambridge, MA: Harvard University Press, 2006.

Muir, John. *The Mountains of California*. 1894. Reprint, Whitefish, MT: Kessinger Publishing, 2010.

Perlin, John. *A Forest Journey: The Role of Wood in the Development of Civilization*. Cambridge, MA: Harvard University Press, 1991.

Piaget, Jean. *The Language and Thought of the Child*. London: Kegan Paul, Trench, Trübner, 1926.

Pinker, Steven. *How the Mind Works*. New York: W. W. Norton, 1997.

————. *The Language Instinct*. New York: William Morrow, 1994.

Proust, Marcel. *Swann's Way*. New York: Penguin, 2004.

Robbins, Martha M., Pascale Sicotte, and Kelly J. Stewart. *Mountain Gorillas: Three Decades of Research at Karisoke*. Cambridge, U.K.: Cambridge University Press, 2001.

Sacks, Oliver. *Musicophilia*. New York: Vintage Books, 2008.

Sarno, Louis. *Bayaka: The Extraordinary Music of the Babenzélé Pygmies*. Roslyn, NY: Ellipsis Arts, 1996.

Shepard, Paul. *The Others: How Animals Made Us Human*. Washington, DC: Island Press, 1996.

Small, Christopher. *Musicking*. Hanover, NH: Wesleyan University Press, 1998.

Thompson, Emily. *The Soundscape of Modernity: Architectural Acoustics and the Culture of Listening in America, 1900–1933*. Cambridge, MA: MIT Press, 2002.

Truax, Barry, ed. *Handbook for Acoustic Ecology,* series ed. R. Murray Schafer. Vancouver: ARC Publications, 1978.

van Gulik, Robert. *The Gibbon in China: An Essay in Chinese Animal Lore*. Leiden, Netherlands: E. J. Brill, 1967.

Wallin, Nils, Björn Merker, and Steven Brown, eds. *The Origins of Music*. Cambridge, MA: MIT Press, 2001.

Wallon, Henri. *De l'Acte à la Pensée*. Paris: Flammarion, 1942.

Weisman, Alan. *The World Without Us*. New York: Thomas Dunne Books, 2007.

Williams, Terry Tempest. *Finding Beauty in a Broken World*. New York: Pantheon Books, 2008.

Wilson, Edward O. *The Future of Life*. New York: Alfred A. Knopf, 2005.

Periodicals

Andrews, Mark A. W. "How Does Background Noise Affect Our Concentration?" *Scientific American,* January 4, 2010.

Balcomb, Kenneth. "Letter to J. S. Johnson, SURTASS LFA Sonar OEIS/EIS Program Manager," February 23, 2001. Published with permission.

Barber, Jesse R., Kevin R. Crooks, and Kurt M. Fristrup. "Animal Listening Area and Alerting Distance Reduced Substantially By Moderate Human Noise." *Trends In Ecology and Evolution* (forthcoming).

———. "The Costs of Chronic Noise Exposure for Terrestrial Organisms." *Trends in Ecology and Evolution* 25, no. 3 (2009).

Beal, Timothy. "In the Beginning(s): Appreciating the Complexity of the Bible." Huffington Post, February 15, 2011.

Benzon, William L. "Synch, Song, and Society." *Human Nature Review* 5 (2005).

Burros, Marian. "De Gustibus; Restaurant Noise: Does It Spoil a Good Meal?" *New York Times,* October 29, 1983.

Conard, Nicholas J., Maria Malina, and Susanne C. Münzel. "New Flutes Document the Earliest Musical Tradition in Southwestern Germany." *Nature,* June 26, 2009. doi:10.1038/nature08169.

Creel, Scott et al. "Snowmobile Activity and Glucocorticoid Stress Responses in Wild Wolves and Elk." *Conservation Biology,* 2002.

Crocker, Malcolm J., ed. "Surface Transportation Noise." *Encyclopedia of Acoustics,* 1997.

Dickinson, Tim. "The 10 Worst Congressmen." *Rolling Stone,* October 17, 2006.

Foote, Andrew D. et al. "Killer Whales Are Capable of Vocal Learning." *Biology Letters.* doi:10.1098/rebl.2006.0525, http://www.orcanetwork.org/nathist/vocallearnbiolett.pdf.

Frere-Jones, Sasha. "Noise Control." *The New Yorker,* May 24, 2010.

Fritschi, Lin et al. "Burden of Disease from Environmental Noise: Quantification of Healthy Life Years Lost in Europe." World Health Organization publication, March 2011.

Gabriele, Christine M., and Tracy E. Hart. "Population Characteristics of Humpback Whales in Glacier Bay and Adjacent Waters: 2000." National Park Service report.

Gage, Stuart, and Bernie Krause. "Testing Biophony as an Indicator of Habitat Fitness and Dynamics." National Park Service report, February 2002.

Graham, Sarah. "Satellites Spy Changes to Earth's Magnetic Field." *Scientific American,* April 11, 2002, http://www.scientificamerican.com/article.cfm?id=satellites-spy-changes-to.

Hinerfeld, Daniel, and Andrew Wetzler. "Federal Court Restricts Global Deployment of Navy Sonar." Media Center, NRDC, August 26, 2003, http://www.nrdc.org/media/pressreleases/030826.asp.

Intagliata, Christopher. "Restaurant Noise Can Alter Food Taste." *Scientific American,* October 18, 2010.

Ising, H., and B. Kruppa. "Health Effects Caused by Noise: Evidence in the Literature from the Past 25 Years." *Noise and Health,* 2004.

Jones, Douglas, and Rama Ratnam. "Blind Location and Separation of Callers in a Natural Chorus Using a Microphone Array." *Journal of the Acoustical Society of America* 126, no. 2 (August 2009).

Jurasz, Charles M., and V. P. Palmer. "Distribution and Characteristic Responses of Humpback Whales *(Megaptera novaeangliae)* in Glacier Bay National Monument, Alaska, 1973–1979." National Park Service report, Anchorage, Alaska.

Keim, Brandon. "Baby Got Beat: Music May Be Inborn." Wired.com, January 26, 2009, http://www.wired.com/wiredscience/2009/01/babybeats.

Kjellberg, Anders, Per Muhr, and Björn Sköldström. "Fatigue After Work in Noise—An Epidemiological Survey and Three Quasi-experimental Field Studies." *Noise and Health* 1, no. 1 (1998).

Klatte, Maria, Thomas Lachmann, and Markus Meis. "Effects of Noise and Reverberation on Speech Perception and Listening

Comprehension of Children and Adults in a Classroom-like Setting." *Noise and Health* 12, no. 49 (2010).

Krause, Bernie. "Bioacoustics, Habitat Ambience in Ecological Balance." *Whole Earth Review,* winter 1987.

———. "Loss of Natural Soundscape: Global Implications of Its Effect on Humans and Other Creatures." Speech presented before San Francisco World Affairs Council and NPR, January 31, 2000.

Mâche, François-Bernard. "The Necessity of and Problems with a Universal Musicology," *The Origins of Music,* ed. Nils L. Wallin et al. Cambridge, MA: MIT Press, 2000.

Marean, Curtis W. et al. "Early Human Use of Marine Resources and Pigment in South Africa During the Middle Pleistocene." *Nature* 449, October 18, 2007.

Marler, Peter. "Animal Communication Signals." *Science* 157, no. 3790 (August 1967).

———. "Origins of Music and Speech: Insights from Animals." *The Origins of Music,* ed. Nils L. Wallin et al. Cambridge, MA: MIT Press, 2000.

McLean, Sheela. "Work of Pioneering Whale Researcher Provides Longest Record on Humpbacks." NOAA newsletter, May 14, 2007.

Merker, Björn H., Guy S. Madison, and Patricia Eckerdal. "On the Role and Origin of Isochrony in Human Rhythmic Entrainment." Elsevier, ScienceDirect, www.sciencedirect .com.

Mitani, John, and Peter Marler. "A Phonological Analysis of Male Gibbon Singing Behaviour." *Behaviour,* 1989.

Motavalli, Jim. "Hybrid Cars May Include Fake Vroom for Safety." *New York Times,* October 14, 2009.

Napoletano, Brian. "Biophysical and Politico-Economic Determinants of Biodiversity Trends." PhD diss., Purdue University, 2011 (forthcoming).

Patel, Aniruddh D. et al. "Experimental Evidence for Synchronization to a Musical Beat in a Non-Human Animal." *Current Biology* 19 (May 26, 2009).

Philipp, Robin. "Aesthetic Quality of the Built and Natural Environment: Why Does It Matter?" *Green Cities: Blue Cities of Europe,* eds. Walter Pasini and Franco Rusticali. Rimini, Italy: WHO Collaborating Centre for Tourist Health and Travel Medicine, 2001.

Raloff, Janet. "Noise and Stress in Humans." *Science News* 121 (June 5, 1982).

Richtel, Matt. "Hooked on Gadgets, and Paying a Mental Price." *New York Times,* June 6, 2010.

Rideout, Victoria J., Ulla G. Foehr, and Donald F. Roberts. "Generation M^2: Media in the Lives of 8- to 18-Year-Olds," January 2010, http://www.kff.org/entmedia/upload/8010.pdf.

Ritters, Kurt H., and James D. Wickham. "How Far to the Nearest Road?" *Frontiers in Ecology and the Environment* 1 (2003).

Sietsema, Tom. "No Appetite for Noise." *Washington Post Magazine,* April 5, 2008.

Slabbekoorn, Hans. "A Noisy Spring: The Impact of Globally Rising Underwater Sound Levels on Fish." *Trends in Ecology and Evolution,* 2010 (forthcoming).

Suter, Alice H. "Noise and Its Effects." Administrative Conference of the United States, November 1991, http://www.nonoise.org/library/suter/suter.htm. Accessed October 10, 2006.

ter Hofstede, Hannah M., and Holger Goerlitz. "*Barbastella barbastellus:* 'Whispering' bat Echolocation Tricks Moths." *Science Codex,* August 19, 2010, http://www.sciencecodex.com/barbastella_barbastellus_whispering_bat_echolocation_tricks_moths.

United Nations Environment Programme (UNEP). " 'Garden of Eden' in Southern Iraq Likely to Disappear Completely in Five Years Unless Urgent Action Taken," March 22, 2003, http://www.grid.unep.ch/activities/sustainable/tigris/2003_march.php.

Verzijden, Machteld N. et al. "Sounds of Male Lake Victoria Cichlids Vary Within and Between Species and Affect Female Mate Preferences." *Behavioral Ecology* 21 (2010).

White, Tim et al. "Macrovertebrate Paleontology and the Pliocene Habitat of *Ardipithecus ramidus*." *Science* 326 (2009).

Audio

Beaver, Paul, and Bernie Krause. *All Good Men*. Warner Brothers Records, 1973.

————. *Into a Wild Sanctuary*. Warner Brothers Records, 1970.

————. *The Nonesuch Guide to Electronic Music*. Nonesuch Records, 1968.

Dugan, Dan. Muir Woods recording.

Krause, Bernie. World soundscape collection, http://www.wildsanctuary.mobi/buy/index.php?route=product/category&path=36.

Monacchi, David. "Nightingale" excerpt, http://www.earthear.com/ecoacoustic.html.

Olson, Curt. Wounded beaver recording.

Parker, Ted III. Common potoo and musician wren recordings.

Sarno, Louis. *Bayaka: The Extraordinary Music of the Babenzélé Pygmies*. Ellipsis Arts, 1996.

Schafer, R. Murray. *Once on a Windy Night*, www.patria.org/arcana.

————. "Winter Diary." Angewandte Musik [B] Musik Für Radio: Das Studio Akustische Kunst Des WDR, RCA Red Seal, Catalog # 74321 73522 2, 2001, Track 11.

Wilson, Elizabeth. *Nez Percé Stories*, Wild Sanctuary, 1991, http://www.wildsanctuary.mobi/buy/index.php?route=product/product&path=39&product_id=93.

Main Bioacoustic Websites and Chat Groups

British Library of Wildlife Sounds: http://www.bl.uk/reshelp/findhelprestype/sound/wildsounds/wildlife.html

Macaulay Library (Cornell University): http://www.birds.cornell
.edu/page.aspx?pid=1676
Michigan State University Envirosonics program: http://www
.cevl.msu.edu/envirosonics
naturerecording@yahoogroups.com
naturerecordists@yahoogroups.com
Purdue University Department of Forestry and Natural Resources:
http://www.ag.purdue.edu/fnr/Pages/default.aspx
Wild Sanctuary: http://www.wildsanctuary.com
World Forum for Acoustic Ecology: http://wfae.proscenia.net/
World Listening Project: worldlistening@yahoogroups.com

Index